Winning *in the* Workplace

Winning *in the* Workplace

Uncovering and Managing the Relationships
Responsible for Career Success

ONAJITE AKEMU

RESOURCE *Publications* • Eugene, Oregon

WINNING IN THE WORKPLACE
Uncovering and Managing the Relationships Responsible for Career Success

Copyright © 2022 Onajite Akemu. All rights reserved. Except for brief quotations in critical publications or reviews, no part of this book may be reproduced in any manner without prior written permission from the publisher. Write: Permissions, Wipf and Stock Publishers, 199 W. 8th Ave., Suite 3, Eugene, OR 97401.

Resource Publications
An Imprint of Wipf and Stock Publishers
199 W. 8th Ave., Suite 3
Eugene, OR 97401

www.wipfandstock.com

PAPERBACK ISBN: 978-1-6667-9500-4
HARDCOVER ISBN: 978-1-6667-9503-5
EBOOK ISBN: 978-1-6667-9504-2

APRIL 8, 2022 8:52 AM

Unless otherwise indicated, Scripture quotations are taken from the Holy Bible, New International Version®, niv®, © 1973, 1978, 1984, 2011 by Biblica, Inc.® Used by permission. All rights reserved worldwide. Scripture quotations marked (KJV) are taken from the King James Version of the Holy Bible. Scripture quotations marked (NKJV) are taken from the New King James Version®. Copyright © 1982 by Thomas Nelson. Used by permission. All rights reserved. Scripture quotations marked (NLT) are taken from the Holy Bible, New Living Translation, copyright © 1996, 2004, 2015 by Tyndale House Foundation. Used by permission of Tyndale House Publishers, Inc., Carol Stream, Illinois 60188. All rights reserved. Scripture quotations marked (MSG) are taken from THE MESSAGE, copyright © 1993, 2002, 2018 by Eugene H. Peterson. Used by permission of NavPress. All rights reserved. Represented by Tyndale House Publishers, Inc. Scripture quotations marked (TLB) are from The Living Bible copyright © 1971 by Tyndale House Foundation. Used by permission of Tyndale House Publishers Inc., Carol Stream, Illinois 60188. All rights reserved. Scripture quotations taken from the Amplified® Bible (AMP), Copyright © 2015 by The Lockman Foundation Used by permission.www.Lockman.org"

As always ... To Grace—always there for me.
To Eden—my one and only daughter.
To Efe and Mofe—you guys give me a reason to press forward.

For, in the end, it is impossible to have a great life unless it is a meaningful life. And it is very difficult to have a meaningful life without meaningful work.

—Jim Collins

Contents

List of Tables | ix

Preface | xi

Acknowledgments | xv

First Word: Career 101 | 1

Section 1	**Managing 'Up': Managing Your Relationships With People Who Have Power Over Your Career** | 17
Chapter 1	Sheep Among Wolves: (Displaying Strategic Behavior in the Workplace) | 19
Chapter 2	Power Play: Understanding How Power Works in Organizations | 32
Chapter 3	Managing Your Boss | 47
Chapter 4	Managing a Difficult Boss | 56
Chapter 5	Managing Career Transitions (1) | 68
Chapter 6	Managing Career Transitions (2) | 82
Chapter 7	Managing Career Transitions (3) | 98
Chapter 8	Problems and Pitfalls of Managing 'Up' | 106
Section 2	**Managing 'Across'** | 113
Chapter 9	Social Networks 101 (Why Who You Know is Crucial to Workplace Success.) | 115
Chapter 10	Managing Your Personal Network | 125

Chapter 11	How Mentoring Can Advance Your Career	132
Chapter 12	Give and Take: Understanding Reciprocal Behavior in the Workplace	143
Chapter 13	How Insensitivity to Others Can Negatively Impact Your Career	152
Chapter 14	Pitfalls and Problems of |Managing 'Across'	158
SECTION 3	**Managing 'Down': Managing Your Relationships With Subordinates and Associates**	**170**
Chapter 15	Carrot or Stick: What's Your Default Leadership Style?	172
Chapter 16	Getting Results Through Others	180
Chapter 17	Pitfalls & Problems of Managing 'Down'	202
SECTION 4	**Managing Yourself**	**213**
Chapter 18	Personal Effectiveness 101	215
Chapter 19	Personal Effectiveness 102	227
Chapter 20	Principles of Personal Development	241

Last Word: Untangling the Roles of Chance, Time, and Skill in Career Success | 254

Bibliography | 269

List of Tables

Chapter 16. Table 1 (3 Kinds of Jobs: Jobs that 'Buy My Hand', 'Buy My Mind' or Tap into My Heart)

Chapter 17. Table 2 (Comparing 'Command and Control' Methods with Methods for Managing Knowledge Workers)

Preface

For, in the end, it is impossible to have a great life unless it is a meaningful life. And it is very difficult to have a meaningful life without meaningful work.

—JIM COLLINS

CAREERS ARE MORE THAN just the practical or "bare bones" vehicles through which we obtain the economic resources needed for life and livelihood. They are, as the above words of management writer Jim Collins imply, also the vehicles through which we can experience fulfillment and find meaning in our lives. That careers can provide for *both* material and psychosocial needs is one reason someone like me (the unusual combination of Bible teacher and management consultant) is deeply interested in the subject. Indeed, I have long mulled writing a book on careers and workplace success, but the last straw that broke the proverbial camel's back occurred as I read Stanford professor Jeffrey Pfeffer's excellent book, *Leadership BS: Fixing Workplaces and Careers One Truth at a Time*. In that book, the eminent professor said that,

> "In the fall of 2013, the world celebrated the five-hundred-year anniversary, more or less, of the appearance of Machiavelli's *The Prince*. One commentary on this important and still-relevant work noted:
>
> Machiavelli teaches that in a world where so many are not good, you must learn to be able to not be good. The virtues taught in our secular and religious schools are incompatible with the virtues one must practice to safeguard those same institutions..."

"*The virtues taught in our ... religious schools are incompatible with the virtues one must practice ...*" Professor Pfeffer makes a startling claim; the

PREFACE

biblical leadership principles that he—and most other such well informed persons—are acquainted with are grossly inadequate to helping leaders lead and succeed in the real world! That is, if you work in an organization—the context in which most modern careers occur—and dutifully follow biblical principles, you're unlikely to go far! That line of thinking left me scratching my head. While it's apparent that following the biblical principles *currently* being taught about workplace success—principles which emphasize *only* virtue—can put one at a disadvantage in the real world; the little-appreciated truth is that the *whole counsel* of Scripture (which gives equal weight to being virtuous *and* being *strategic*) certainly can help people experience career success.

In part, this book seeks to challenge Professor Pfeffer's claim—and correct the popular misconception—that biblical principles aren't adequate for persons who want to rise to the highest rungs of their organizations or, who want to "safeguard those same institutions." As an aside, one might even ask; why is someone as eminent as Professor Pfeffer so poorly informed about the whole counsel of Scripture? Or, more to the point, why do so many persons think that biblical principles are inadequate to the practice of leadership in the *real world*? A probable answer is this: it's because most people are only acquainted with . . .

JESUS ON LEADERSHIP 101 (BEING VIRTUOUS)

By saying,

> "You know that the rulers of the Gentiles lord it over them, and their high officials exercise authority over them. Not so with you. Instead, whoever wants to become great among you must be your servant, and whoever wants to be first must be your slave," (Matt 20:25-27, NIV)

Jesus introduces us to servant leadership, the *normative* or aspirational dimension of leadership—what should be the norm and how our leadership can, by serving others, help further both their interests and the interests of the organization. This dimension of leadership encourages leaders to be virtuous and to do good. But, and this is crucial, most people—like the proverbial workman whose only tool is a hammer, and who thinks every problem is a nail—think that this dimension is applicable to *every* leadership situation. Predictably, they get their fingers burnt—after

Preface

which they become converts of Machiavelli! These leaders—Professor Pfeffer inclusive—need to learn about . . .

JESUS ON LEADERSHIP 102 (BEING STRATEGIC)

By saying,

> "Look, I am sending you as wolves among sheep. Therefore be shrewd as snakes an innocent as doves," (Matt 10:16-17, NIV)

Jesus introduces the *descriptive* dimension of leadership—a dimension that describes the brutal reality of the current circumstances in which we live and work, and the naked truth about the use (and abuse) of power in organizations. Since, snakes normally don't expose themselves (preferring to hide in the grass and other suitable cover) and, since no snake has ever come face to face with a human and thought "I am meeting a friend," Jesus' words mean that people who want to rise to the highest echelons of organizational leadership must internalize an uncomfortable truth—success in an organizational setting demands that you know how to protect yourself ("shrewd as snakes") without being harmful to others ("innocent as doves"). In effect, this little-appreciated dimension of leadership requires that you be strategic in your dealings with people—especially those with power over your career. To be clear, the normative and descriptive dimensions of biblical leadership aren't in conflict—they are simply two sides of the same coin. The one—without being polyannaish—describes current realities, while the other attempts to transform those same realities. But, and this is important, when it comes to dealing with people with power over your career—a key to workplace success—the model that's appropriate is the descriptive.

Notwithstanding, this book is more than mere 'apologetics-lite' or cursory defense of the Gospel. It does something even more important; it, as the subtitle suggests, identifies the four 'relationships' that are mission-critical to workplace success and shows readers how, by correctly managing those 'relationships', they can make career progress. Those mission-critical relationships are,

1. Relationships with bosses and people with power over your career (Managing 'Up'),
2. Relationships with people at your own level (Managing 'Across'),

Preface

3. Relationships with people at levels lower than yours (Managing 'Down") and,
4. Relationships with 'yourself' (Managing Yourself).

Whatever your definition of workplace success, one thing is clear: most career failures or derailments have their roots in a less-than-effective management of one or more of those four mission-critical 'relationships'. And, if a teacher's job is to take the mystery out of a subject, then I will consider my work done if this book clears some of the fog surrounding the subject of career success and workplace progress—and, in some way—furthers your own career!

ONAJITE AKEMU,
Abuja, Nigeria.
01/31/2022

Acknowledgments

IF EVERY CHILD IS the product of a set of parents then, this book must be the product of many 'parents'! The first 'parents' of this book are the members of the Big House of Faith platform—a 250-man strong online community of former pastors of the Living Faith Church. Over the last few months, these wonderful men and women have served as both sounding board and proving ground for many of the ideas set forth in this book. To the members of BHFM, our shared experiences, our current fellowship, and our ongoing relationships have been of great intellectual benefit to me. On a more personal note, another important 'parent' of this book is my brother Dr. Onajomo Akemu (lately, a management teacher at Nazarbayev University). The latter's willingness to engage me in plenty of intellectual fencing has over the long haul sharpened my ability to think critically, and to birth and land ideas—abilities essential to the writing of books. Interestingly, "Akpekilodo" (my brother's alias) often mended fences with me after most episodes of intellectual fencing by recommending or sending me management literature!

First Word

Career 101: What is a Career? + 2 Types of Careers + 2 Types of Career Success + 3 Phases of a Career + What Exactly Does it Take to Taste Career Success?

CAREER 101

BECAUSE CAREERS ARE ESSENTIALLY work or employment relationships, one can best understand them in the context of work and work-roles. I define work as that activity which produces goods and services that are of some economic benefit to another person—a "consumer"—who may be an employer or a market. That is, work's value, like beauty, is in the eye of its beholder or 'consumer'. Interestingly, the words of the writer of Proverbs corroborate this line of thinking,

> "Finish your outdoor work and get your fields ready; after that, build your house." (Prov 24:27, NIV)

By linking " . . . your . . . work," to the construction of your house (" . . . build your house"), the writer of Proverbs cuts to the chase and shows us an under-appreciated truth: work is that activity which can generate the financial resources you need to build a house! In effect, work is an *economic* activity that produces goods and services that another person (a "consumer") is willing to pay for. This biblical perspective sharply differentiates work from hobbies, pastimes or play—the latter three being, by division, activities that are not driven by economic or financial considerations. Since careers are essentially work relationships, and since, as we've seen, work is an economic activity, one can then say that *a career is work-related activity that is economic in nature and focus*—even if the worker works for a nonprofit!

That said, *a career can also be defined as a series of transitions from one work-role to another within an organization or occupation*—like a person who begins work in production, moving through engineering, and ending up at corporate headquarters. For professionals and technical specialists, these transitions may involve starting out as a junior lawyer, moving on to jobs with increased responsibilities for serving key clients, and finally ending up as partner in a law firm. While it's true that a very small group of persons—founders, entrepreneurs, craftsmen, etc—often do basically the same jobs all their lives, the fact is that majority of workers experience some kind of work-role transition in their careers. Because the heart of this definition of careers is the *progression* in work-roles which happens over time, *career progress* is said to occur when each succeeding work-role is more well-paying, more prestigious, more weighted with responsibility, and/or better fulfills a person's need for meaning, flexibility, autonomy, etc. In other words, people who don't experience "positive" career transitions tend to end up feeling like their career is going nowhere—a line of thinking that leads smack dab to the concept of "dead end" jobs (jobs that offer little, limited or even no transitions). Dead end jobs, e.g., when a person is "kicked upstairs," tend to produce plenty of frustration and negative emotional energy precisely because they lead nowhere and offer precious little in the form of future transitions.

Crucially also, the nature of the relationship a worker has with her "consumer" determines the type of career she is in. In this light, there are two broad types of careers. . .

1. Organizational or hierarchy-based careers and,
2. Market-based careers.

Organizational or Hierarchy-based-based Careers (OCs)

These are the classic "careers"—the thing that comes to mind when most people think about work careers. Here the "consumer" is an organization or other such social group which employs the worker. OCs often come with formal employment contracts and require that you retire after a set period of time. The words of the writer of Ecclesiastes best describe these careers,

First Word

"If you see the poor oppressed in a district, and justice and rights denied, do not be surprised at such things; for one official is eyed by a higher one, and over them both are others higher still." (Eccl 5:8, NIV)

"*. . . for one official is eyed by a higher one, and over them both are others higher still.*" These words show the operations of a classical hierarchy—each lower office or position is under the control or supervision of a higher one—with vertical divisions of labor. People who work for organizations and corporations—where there's some degree of hierarchy and where you climb up the proverbial corporate ladder—are engaged in hierarchy-based careers.

The words of the Psalmist throw more light on the nature of organizational careers (OCs),

"For promotion cometh neither from the east, nor from the west, nor from the south. But God is the judge: he putteth down one, and setteth up another." (Ps 75:6–7, KJV)

Much reflection on these amazing words has helped me see the following truths . . .

In Organizational Careers, Progress is Measured by How High You Climb Up the Corporate Ladder

By juxtaposing the word "promotion" with the phrase " . . . *he putteth down one, and setteth up another,*" the Psalmist shows us that, not only are we dealing with a hierarchically structured organization, but also that promotion is going up, not down, the hierarchy. Here, career progress is measured by advancement up the proverbial corporate ladder—what MIT professor Edgar Schein refers to as the logic of advancement.

In Organizational Careers, Progress Comes Easiest to Persons Who Cultivate Healthy Relationships with Bosses

"Promotion cometh not from the east . . . God is *the judge* . . . " Just like God is the ultimate judge of promotions in the universe—the person who decides who gets promoted, demoted or passed over—so organizations have persons with authority to 'judge' or decide who gets to be promoted. And, this is crucial, your relationship with those "judges"—in colloquial terms, your ability to "accept the hierarchy"—hugely influences whether you experience progress or stagnation. Researchers Dan Cowler and Karen Legg, in *Handbook of Career Theory*, drive this point home, saying,

> "In bureaucratic organizations, an individual's progress depends crucially on the evaluation of his or her superiors. Hence managing a career or—in everyday language—"having a career at all" involves the development of a "high profile" and "targeting" it at those with the authority to "ease one's way up the ladder."

These words help us see that "managing up"—managing your relationships with the people in power—is crucial to success in OCs (more on this in Chapter 1).

In Organizational Careers, the Higher You Go, the Less the Number of Spaces Available

"Promotion cometh not from the east . . . *God putteth down one, and setteth up another.*" These words also reveal an uncomfortable truth about organizational careers—the higher you go, the less the number of spaces available! Come to think of it, although a company may have two or three executive vice-presidents, it can have only one president at any point in time—making the career transition from executive vice-president to president a zero sum game in which one person's gain is another's loss. This structurally induced scarcity tends to create a competitive tournament mentality in organizations.

Organizational Careers are the Most Prevalent Type of Career in Modern Societies

Modern society is essentially a society of organizations. Just look around and you'll easily notice that there's an organization set up to provide almost every kind of need or service you desire. Need security services? Call the Police. Need health-care for your sick relative? Call the hospital. Need some food delivered to you quickly? Call the pizza company. The Police, the hospital, and the pizza company are all organizations. Indeed, many professionals like doctors and lawyers who hitherto plied their trades in small one-person firms now have to work for medium-sized or large law firms and hospital groups. Even entrepreneurs, who famously dislike working for organizations, often end up creating organizations! Just ask entrepreneurs Steve Jobs, Larry Page, and Jeff Bezos, who separately created the giant organizations Apple, Google, and Amazon. It's precisely because modern society, unlike ancient or medieval society, is a society of organizations that organizational careers are the most prevalent kind of careers today. Therefore, much of this book is dedicated to OCs.

Market-based Careers (MCs)

These are "employment" relationships that are basically nonhierarchical because they require that the worker interact with a "market." Most self-employed persons—professionals, craftspersons, consultants etc—are in this category. Since the market doesn't really "know" you, there's no formal employment requirement. Crucially, you don't normally have to "retire" from this kind of career. MCs can be further subdivided into Professional Careers and Entrepreneurial Careers . . .

Professional Careers

Professionals are persons—craftsmen, doctors, architects etc—who perform jobs based on complex knowledge and skills. For this reason, and because they value their independence, professionals prefer to work in places where merit, not hierarchy, is the primary yardstick for determining who gets ahead. In his excellent book, *Career Dynamics: Matching Individual And Organizational Needs*, MIT professor Edgar Schein, has this to say about this group of workers,

> " . . . major growth, as in craft work, is increasing skill in the area of competence but not much hierarchical rise. Success for people in this group is determined more by feedback that they are expert in their areas and by increasingly challenging work in those areas rather than promotion or monetary rewards per se, though these are obviously important as well."

" . . . *increasing skill in the area of competence, but not much hierarchical rise.*" Those words show that the logic of reputation and skill—a desire to be take on challenging work and to be recognized as an expert—is what colors the definition of success for people involved in professional careers. The writer of Proverbs makes the same point, saying,

"Do you see a man diligent and skillful in his business? He will stand before kings; he will not stand before obscure men." (Prov 22:29, AMP)

These words mean that,

Skill and Reputation are the Drivers and Measures of Success in Professional Careers

"Do you see a man . . . skillful in his business?" In the beginning—when we first see this skilled worker—he may be serving obscure audiences; but with the passage of time and the growth of his reputation, he ends up at the top, serving kings. The keys to career success for this worker are basically his proficiency and his reputation. As those two factors grow, so does his career.

Professional Careers are Distinguished by Clearer Connections Between Work and the Person Who Does the Work

A professional's (craftsman's) work is easily traceable to him. Come to think of it, if I call a plumber to repair the faucets in my bathroom and the pipes are still blocked after he finishes work then, to all intents and purposes, that plumber is probably incompetent. Why? Because the work a plumber does is directly traceable to him—a thing which makes it easy to differentiate between skilled and not-so-skilled plumbers. It's this ease of attribution that allows a professional's reputation to grow with time. In contrast, because of the multiple individual inputs required to get bureaucratic work done in organizations, it's a little harder to pinpoint who exactly is responsible for work done in an organizational context. Which is why the popular adage "The cream always rises to the top," best applies to professional careers. Notwithstanding, because modern society is basically a society of organizations, most professional careers today tend to take place in the context of organizations. Indeed, many technical professionals and specialists (engineers, lawyers, and doctors) often work for organizations or large professional firms. To a large extent, career success for this group of persons will be determined by a mix of the logic of reputation and skill, and the logic of advancement.

First Word

Entrepreneurial Careers

Entrepreneurial careers encompass the unique work that a relatively small proportion of persons do. Since these careers majorly entail the creation, growth, and sustenance of organized forms of providing goods and services, workplace progress is measured by how far and how fast the organization grows or expands. To paraphrase Professor Schein "Success in entrepreneurial careers is driven by the logic of enlargement." The words of the writer of First Chronicles bear this out,

> "Jabez was more honorable than his brothers. His mother had named him Jabez, saying, "I gave birth to him in pain." Jabez cried out to the God of Israel, "Oh, that you would bless me and enlarge my territory! Let your hand be with me, and keep me from harm so that I will be free from pain." And God granted his request." (1Chr 4:9–10, NIV)

The Logic of Enlargement is the Driver and Measure of Success in Entrepreneurial Careers

By saying *"Jabez was more honorable than his brothers,"* the writer of First Chronicles helps us see that Jabez was already relatively successful. But, by going into say *"... Jabez cried out to ... God, "Oh, that you would bless me and enlarge my territory,"* he shows us a much overlooked truth: Jabez was probably an agribusinessman who was hungry to bring more land under cultivation! Jabez's attitude mirrors that of the classic entrepreneur—hungry to see the establishment, growth, and spread of his business or organization. While people like Bill Gates—with his drive to create and grow Microsoft—exemplify the entrepreneur in her early stages, entrepreneurs who work for already established companies may be driven, not by the desire to start their own enterprises, but by a desire to, like Jabez, expand their organizations.

Although I have, as much possible, sought to place these career types in clear cut categories, in real life, these demarcations are not so clear cut, and most careers will be located somewhere on a continuum between rigid organizational careers and less rigid market-based careers.

3 PHASES OF A CAREER

Careers are like journeys. Indeed the word "career" is derived from the Latin *carraria*, meaning a road or carriageway—a concept that evokes pictures of deliberate movement, direction, stops, detours, and destination—things which, in turn, evoke images of the different phases of a journey. At the beginning of this chapter, I said that a career can roughly be defined as a series of transitions from one work-role to another. I gave the example of a young person beginning a career in, say engineering, moving on to production, before ending up at corporate headquarters, and finally proceeding to retirement—implying that every career is made up of different phases or stages. Leadership expert John Maxwell buttresses the point, saying,

> "When leaders are *early in their journey*, they don't possess much influence of their own. I think it's natural for young talented leaders to work hard and get less credit and recognition than they deserve for their efforts; and it's natural for *older established leaders* to receive more credit than they deserve for theirs. Young leaders aren't that bad, and old leaders aren't that good!" (Emphases mine)

"*... early in their journey ... older established leaders ...*" Dr. Maxwell's words are broadly applicable to most kinds of careers. Indeed, most work careers can be divided into early-, middle-, and late-career phases. Moving successfully from one phase to another (and avoiding "plateauing" or stagnation)—which is what career progress is all about—requires that you pay plenty of attention to learning. Therefore, in the descriptions of career phases which follow, I have included short paragraphs on learning ...

Early Career:

The words of the writer of Ecclesiastes best exemplify this stage,

> "Whatever your hand finds to do, do it with all your might, for in the grave, where you are going, there is neither working nor planning nor knowledge nor wisdom." (Eccl 9:10, NIV)

The phrase "*Whatsoever your hands find to do, do it,*" is most applicable to a young person—a novice—seeking work; who has to take whatever turns up. That phrase paints a picture of a person in an explorative or early career phase. Here the individual is exploring different aspects of work and seeking to discover her area of major contribution. By working eagerly at whatever comes her way, the novice gains insight into her own strengths and weaknesses, learns to work with others (especially bosses), and comes to better understand the culture of her organization. The significant challenges in this career phase revolve around winning respect and becoming accepted by other members of the organization or profession. In his book, *Career Dynamics*, Edgar Schein pithily describes this phase, saying,

> "The key process during the preentry period of growth and exploration is the obtaining of valid information about oneself and occupations and the making of valid choices which optimize one's chances of both using one's talents and achieving success and satisfaction."

Learning in Early-Career

Most of the learning occurs as we listen to, and watch, others who are ahead of us. This is essentially a stage of dependence. At this stage, the worker is a novice who receives more than she gives.

Mid Career

The words of the writer of Proverbs best describe this phase,

> "Do you see a man skilled in his work? He will serve before kings; he will not serve before obscure men." (Prov 22:29, NIV)

The phrase *"skilled in his work,"* is a dead giveaway. This worker, because he is skilled and proficient, is no novice and is definitely not in the early stages his career. This workman is in midcareer—an independent master craftsman who can work alone and/or for himself This is the exploitative phase of a person's career, a time when she begins to *"serve before kings,"* and receive her greatest rewards and recognition.

Learning in MidCareer

Most of the learning in midcareer comes via personal reflection (and personal insight) on our own experiences. This is essentially a stage of independence. At this stage, using the language of crafts, the worker is a master craftsman. Again, the real nature of this career stage is writ large in the words of the writer of Proverbs,

> "I walked by the field of a lazy person, the vineyard of one lacking sense. I saw that it was overgrown with thorns. It was covered with weeds, and its walls were broken down. Then, as I looked and thought about it, I learned this lesson:" (Prov 24:30-32, NLT)

Independence—the ability to work without supervision—is the hallmark of a master craftsman. By saying *"I walked by the field of the lazy man . . . Then, as I looked and thought about it, I learned this lesson,"* the writer of Proverbs shows us that this workman could, without recourse to others, learn and make discoveries. It is this ability to work independently that differentiates the midcareer phase from the early-career one.

Late-Career Phase

The words of the Psalmist offer a poignant description of this phase,

> "O God, you have taught me from my earliest childhood, and I have constantly told others about the wonderful things you do. Now that I am old and gray . . . Let me proclaim your power to this new generation . . . " (Ps 71:17-18, NLT)

" *. . . Now that I am old and gray . . .* " These words point clearly to an older person. Crucially, by going on to say " *. . . Now that I am old and gray . . . Let me proclaim your power to this new generation,"* the Psalmist shows us what's uppermost on this older worker's mind—mentoring and developing younger workers. Therefore, we can say that the late-career phase is a generative phase—a phase concerned with developing and mentoring younger workers.

Learning in Late-Career

Late-career is the stage of interdependence, a time when learning depends on the worker's access to the works and thinking of other master craftsman. Indeed, failure to access the works of other leading contributors can lead to 'plateauing'. The words of the writer of Daniel drive this point home,

> "During the first year of his reign, *I, Daniel, was studying the writings of the prophets. I learned* from the word of the LORD, as recorded by

First Word

Jeremiah the prophet, that Jerusalem must lie desolate for seventy years." (Dan 9:2, NLT)

These amazing words show that Daniel—an old, experienced, and well-educated prophet—needed to access the writings of Jeremiah the prophet (and other prophets) before he could understand God's plan! Learning and growth in late-career require that you become a member of a wider community of master craftsmen.

2 TYPES OF CAREER SUCCESS

When it comes to defining career success, it does seem like everyone you meet has a very private definition—much like the proverbial story of the blind men of Hindostan who, coming upon an elephant, proceeded to describe that pachyderm entirely from their individual points of view! Although some would admit that they are experiencing career success only when they climb the corporate ladder, others insist that career progress occurs only when they take on a series of increasingly challenging jobs. For a small minority, holding jobs with plenty of 'flex time' for family is the hallmark of workplace progress. Notwithstanding, the question still remains; what exactly is career success, and how does a person know she's making progress at work? We cannot begin to answer these questions without first understanding...

The Story of Work

Work. Job. Employment. Career. It is nigh impossible to talk about workplace success without mentioning these terms. Crucially also, those terms mean pretty much the same to many simply because they all offer an economic lifeline—a means of earning money to pay the bills. This way of looking at careers is what psychologists refer to as the instrumental perspective of work The writer of Second Thessalonians, in his warning to the Christians of Thessalonica (who, because they thought that Jesus' Second Coming was imminent or already passed, refused to work) corroborates this perspective, saying,

> "For even when we were with you, we gave you this rule: "*If a man will not work, he shall not eat.*" (2 Thess 3:10, NIV) (Emphasis mine)

These very practical words help us see that,

Work is First a Tool for Earning the Financial Resources Needed for Life and Livelihood

By linking "eating" to working, these hard-hitting words show us the clear connection between work and earning the financial resources needed for life and livelihood. In this sense, work is merely an instrument or means for obtaining the economic resources you need to live. Although this instrumental view of work is popular and taken for granted, it is only part of the story of work. How do I mean? Listen to the writer of Ecclesiastes as he shows us another—often underappreciated—side of the story of work . . .

> "A man can do nothing better than to eat and drink and find satisfaction in his own work. This . . . is from the hand of God." (Eccl 2:24, NIV)

Work is Also a Source of Meaning and Satisfaction

No doubt about it, these words of the writer of Ecclesiastes mean that whenever you find work that provides for you financially, while also—simultaneously—giving you psychological satisfaction, then you can rest assured that you have received a gift from God! More to the point, the pungent phrase " . . . *find satisfaction in his own work*," shows us the other side of the story of work—work is a source of satisfaction, enjoyment, fulfillment, and meaning—what I refer to as the psychological perspective of work. Management writer Jim Collins, in his bestselling book, *Good to Great: Why Some Companies Make the Leap . . . And Others Don't*, drives the point home, saying "For, in the end, it is impossible to have a great life unless it is a meaningful life. And it is very difficult to have a meaningful life without meaningful work." His words help us see that our work (jobs, employment, and careers) can also give meaning to our lives. Work supplies meaning by meeting a person's need for challenge, autonomy, and identity. Work that safely stretches and challenges you, can also help you grow and make a personal contribution—things that enhance your identity and self-esteem.

First Word

The Instrumental and Psychological Perspectives are Two Ways of Defining Career Success

After all is said and done, the story of work is this: work is more than just a tool for obtaining the economic resources needed for life and livelihood. It is also what helps give meaning to the lives we live—a reason for the rootlessness and lack of meaning that dogs the lives of the unemployed and the members of the "leisure class" (people who, for any reason, don't have to work). Whatever your definition of workplace success is, it's likely to be rooted in, or derived from, either the instrumental view (that sees work as a tool for obtaining economic benefits) or the psychological view (that sees work as a provider of meaning). For example, people who measure career success by how high they climb up the proverbial corporate ladder or by how much they earn, are defining workplace progress from an instrumental perspective. Those who think they have succeeded only when they are challenged by their jobs are defining workplace progress from the psychological perspective. Others, who measure career success by their becoming part of the 'inner circle'—the small group of persons who run the show in any organization—are also defining workplace progress from the psychological perspective. Notwithstanding, the fact that career success, like beauty, is in the eye of the beholder, means that individual definitions of workplace progress are often colored by a mixture of these two perspectives.

That these two perspectives color much of the popular thinking on career success was brought home powerfully to me as I read the following words of social scientists Brooklyn Derr and André Laurent in the *Handbook of Career Theory*,

> "... there are five different internal career success maps: getting ahead (upward mobility), getting secure (company loyalty and sense of belonging), getting free (autonomy), getting high (excitement of the work itself) and getting balanced (finding an equilibrium between personal and professional life)."

"... *getting ahead ... getting secure ... getting free ... getting high ... getting balanced ...*" These five ways of defining career success, in one way or another, probably encapsulate what career success means for most people. If you see success as climbing the corporate ladder, then "getting ahead" best applies to you. If you equate career success with becoming part of the small number of persons who run the show in your company, then "getting secure" probably describes you etc. Notice carefully that while "getting ahead" correlates with the instrumental view of work, all the other four measures of career progress—"getting secure," "getting free," "getting high," and "getting balanced" are majorly associated with the psychological perspective of work. In other words, there are really only two ways of looking at career success—the instrumental perspective (which is achievement oriented), and the psychological perspective (which associates success with emotional and psychological milestones).

The Instrumental and Psychological Perspectives are Different Ways of Keeping Score

If you measure how far you have come in your career by the size of your salary, by how high you have risen up the corporate ladder, or by how much your income is greater than the incomes of your peers—then you're majorly driven by the instrumental view of work. Because your measures of career progress are more easily seen by outsiders, they are *external* hallmarks of success. In contrast, if career success for you is majorly about freedom, autonomy, challenging work, flex time etc, then you are driven by the psychological perspective. Because the way you keep score is harder for outsiders to see, one can say that the psychological perspective offers *internal* hallmarks of success. Both hallmarks—internal and external—are like a person's right and left hands; equally valuable and necessary for balanced living. People who overly emphasize one hallmark over the other tend to experience some degree of imbalance. For example, undue emphasis on external hallmarks (the instrumental perspective) is like succeeding in the 'rat race' or climbing the proverbial career ladder only to find that it means nothing to you, or that success has come at the expense of your health or important relationships with your spouse or children. Career success comes from balancing both internal and external hallmarks. All this brings us to the million-dollar question . . .

WHAT EXACTLY DOES IT TAKE TO SUCCEED AT WORK?

What exactly does it take to win in the workplace, to succeed in a career, and make a mark in a vocation or calling? As I read social scientist Gene Dalton's article in the *Handbook of Career Theory,* I stumbled on the following words,

First Word

"Working in organizations often involves learning to deal more effectively with materials, information, customers, colleagues, and organizational processes. It involves the management of oneself and one's time capably enough that others entrust you to work independently to carry off a project, operate sophisticated equipment, handle a territory, or make a loan."

"*...learning to deal more effectively with...customers, colleagues, and organizational processes. It involves the management of oneself...*" These words brought me to the proverbial 'Aha' moment; helping me see that career success in organizations—or, for that matter, in any other context—requires the careful management of four types of relationships...

- Relationships with People with Power Over Your Career: "*...learning to deal more effectively with...organizational processes..*" The term "organizational processes," is a code phrase for the hierarchical power relationships existing in every organization. Therefore, one key to career success is managing "up," managing the often delicate relationships with people who have power over your career.

- Relationships with Colleagues and Customers: "*Working...involves learning to deal more effectively with...customers, colleagues...*" There it is in black and white: the people who make the most career progress are those who best manage their relationships with customers and colleagues—what I call managing "across." Clearly, because customers play a more decisive and direct role in the success of independent professionals, craftsmen, and entrepreneurs, the aforementioned trio must accord greater weight to managing their relationships with customers.

- Relationships with Subordinates: "Working . . . involves learning to deal more effectively with . . . *organizational processes* . . . " Like I said before, implicit in the term "organizational processes," is the presence of hierarchical relationships. And, this is crucial, hierarchical relationships also imply that there will be subordinates to handle. Therefore, career success comes easiest to persons who are best able to manage "down"—to manage their relationships with people 'below' them in the hierarchy.

- The Relationship with Yourself : "Working . . . involves . . . the *management of oneself* . . . " The final relationship that must be managed if you hope to taste workplace success is the relationship with 'yourself', what is referred to as managing yourself.

Although most persons naturally find it easier to manage one or two of the four mission-critical relationships enumerated above, the truth is that sustainable career success comes easiest to persons who take the time and make the effort to learn how to manage *all* four types of relationships. And the aim of this book is to help you do just that.

This book is divided into four broad sections—with each successive section addressing the four 'relationships' mission-critical to workplace success—Managing 'Up', Managing 'Across', Managing 'Down', and Managing Yourself. Each section begins with a 'Preamble' or introduction to the subject matter, followed by a series of chapters dealing with the principles and practices associated with the same subject matter. The final chapter of each section (except Section 4) addresses the pitfalls and problems associated with the subject matter already discussed in the same section. For example, Section 1 opens with a 'Preamble' introducing Managing 'Up', followed by a series of chapters unveiling the principles and practices of Managing 'Up', and closes with a chapter dedicated to the pitfalls and problems associated with Managing 'Up'. Drawing from the now-famous words of the Preacher—". . . time and chance happens to them all"—I close the book with a "Last Word" that attempts to untangle the roles of time, skill, and chance in career success.

SECTION 1

Managing 'Up'
Managing Your Relationships With People Who Have Power Over Your Career

PREAMBLE

" . . . upward mobility within a hierarchical system implies acceptance of the hierarchy." —STEVEN LUKES

WHAT DOES IT TAKE to climb the proverbial corporate ladder and to, as it were, manage 'up'? What qualities must a person possess or display if she wants to taste the grapes of success in the context of an organizational workplace? These questions have exercised the minds of practitioners and scholars down the ages; and many will immediately answer "Competence and professional smarts." But this top-of-mind answer merely reveals the biases that underpin our thinking. We tend to give undue weight to factors most under our own control (e.g., our professional competence), and less weight to factors least under our control—the role of bosses and colleagues within the organizations in which we work, the role of chance etc. That that kind of thinking is wide off the mark isn't hard to see. Just take a look around you, and you'll immediately notice the many professionally competent persons who seem not to do so well in the hierarchical relationships which define careers in organizations. It does seem that professional competence is necessary but not sufficient for success in organizational careers.

As I read political scientist Steven Lukes's practical and hard-hitting book, *Power: A Radical View*, I came across the following words " . . . upward

Section 1 | Managing 'Up'

mobility within a hierarchical system implies acceptance of the hierarchy." For a person in search of the holy grail for career success in organizations, those words were a firelighter. Taking poetic licence, I paraphrase Dr. Lukes's insightful words thus " . . . upward mobility [promotion and career success] within a hierarchical system [organization], demands acceptance [an understanding] of how hierarchies operate." In simple terms, promotion in organizations comes easiest to people who best understand and accept how hierarchies operate. And the uncomfortable truth about how hierarchies operate is this: hierarchies are instruments for enforcing conformity! This is why the people who rise to the top—the classic "organization men and women"—tend to think alike, have the same values as, and tend to "fit" with, the leaders of the groups where they work. Organizations achieve this kind of conformity by weeding out nonconformists—people who don't 'fit'—through the processes of selection, promotion, posting etc. People who, wittingly or unwittingly, choose to not conform are not only not managing 'up', they're also openly communicating that they don't "accept the hierarchy." This section deals with all the issues involved in "accepting the hierarchy"—the crux of managing 'up'.

Chapter 1

Sheep Among Wolves
(Displaying Strategic Behavior in the Workplace)

As we saw from the 'Preamble', career success comes easiest to people who "accept the hierarchy." But there's a specific dimension of "accepting the hierarchy" or conformity that's especially crucial to workplace success. Stanford professor Jeffrey Pfeffer, in his illuminating book, *Power: Why Some Have it, And Others Don't*, shows us this dimension, saying,

> "People give up their power in other ways, too. *They don't behave strategically toward people with power over them, such as their boss, and instead let their true feelings show.* As a very skilled news reporter told me, he expressed his resentment toward his distant bosses who mostly spent their time managing up and did not provide the support to the news-gathering field operations that he and his colleagues wanted. But as a result, he was just perceived negatively and had even less influence." (Emphasis mine)

" . . . *They don't behave strategically toward people with power over them . . .* " These words show that, unbeknown to many, there's a power that people in the middle or bottom of of a hierarchy have, something that can help them win the silent battle to conform or "accept the hierarchy"—it's the ability to display strategic behavior in their dealings with bosses; to keep their real emotions and feelings under wraps, especially when those feelings are in opposition to those of the people in power. The worker who openly expressed his resentment to his bosses was being anything less than strategic. And he paid dearly for it! Imagine my astonishment when I saw that same principle writ large in the words of Jesus,

> "Stay alert. This is hazardous work I'm assigning you. You're going to be like sheep running through a wolf pack, so don't call attention to yourselves. Be as cunning as a snake, inoffensive as a dove. "Don't be naive. Some people will impugn your motives, others will smear your reputation—just because you believe in me. Don't be upset when they haul you before the civil authorities . . . " (Matt 10:16–18, MSG)

Much reflection on these amazing words has helped me see the following truths,

Being Strategic is Key to Dealing With People Who Have Power Over Your Career!

Jesus makes a startling and "uncharacteristic" statement in this passage. How? Imagine telling his disciples to *"Be cunning as a snake!"* In popular culture, snakes are a metaphor for all that's crafty, wily, and artful—the epitome of strategic behavior. Surely that kind of serpentine behavior should be the last thing a 'good' teacher like Jesus would demand from his disciples! The question becomes, why did Jesus demand serpentine behavior from his disciples? The answer to that weighty question is revealed, as usual, by taking a closer look at the context in which Jesus spoke,

> " . . . *Don't be upset when they haul you before the civil authorities."*

There it is in black and white: Jesus was preparing his disciples to deal with civil authorities—with people with power over them (people who had power to imprison or kill them). Rightly divided, Jesus' words mean that, when it comes to dealing with people with power over you—power over your career, finances etc—you need to be strategic. Most Christians, seeing only the part where Jesus said " . . . *be . . . inoffensive as a dove,"* are full of virtue and goodness when relating with people with power over their personal finances or careers. All well and good, except that, by neglecting the words " . . . *be . . . cunning as a snake,"* they forget that snakes habitually avoid exposing themselves to danger. Come to think of it, the first thing most snakes do on seeing a human—a creature with the power to kill them—is run and hide! All this means that,

Managing 'Up' Begins with Being Strategic—with Never Showing Your True Feelings to Your Boss, Especially when those Feelings can Land You in Hot Water!

Accepting the reality of hierarchies begins with accepting the uncomfortable truth that in an organization not everyone is equal, and that there are people (higher-ups) who have power over your career. Dealing with this cadre of persons means that you ought to apply some serpentine wisdom. You ordinarily shouldn't reveal your true emotions or feelings, especially when those feelings are at odds with theirs. That being strategic is a way to not getting hurt when dealing with people with power over you is writ large in the story of a man called Shimei; a story to which we now turn . . .

The Case of Shimei the Unstrategic!

Shimei (a man from the Israelite tribe of Benjamin) who unnecessarily revealed his true feelings about David the king, is the poster boy for how not to behave in organizations and hierarchical relationships. Listen as the writer of Second Samuel narrates Shimei's unfortunate story . . .

> "As David and his party passed Bahurim, a man came out of the village cursing them. It was Shimei son of Gera, a member of Saul's family. He threw stones at the king and the king's officers and all the mighty warriors who surrounded them. "Get out of here, you murderer, you scoundrel!" he shouted at David. The LORD is paying you back for murdering Saul and his family. You stole his throne, and now the LORD has given it to your son Absalom. At last you will taste some of your own medicine, you murderer!'" (2Sam 16:5–8, NLT)

A 'Subordinate' Opens Up and Let's his 'Boss' Know his True Feelings!

" . . . Get out of here, you murderer, you scoundrel!" As a member of Saul's family, a family that lost power when David became king, Shimei sure had an axe to grind! In this passage, we see an embattled King David, on the run from an insurrection led by, of all people, his own son Absalom. In the middle of all this comes a frustrated Shimei—a man with a chip on his shoulder. Shimei literally lets David have it—hurling stones and unleashing a tirade of insults—behavior that's not only shocking, but also inappropriate.

Section 1 | Managing 'Up'

Showing great restraint, David reins in the armed men accompanying him; men who, unsurprisingly, want to kill Shimei for insulting their principal. Although David, after putting down Absalom's rebellion, appeared to "forgive" Shimei and even swore not to execute him (2Samuel 19:23), the breach had occurred and David—the person in power—did not forget the incident. How do I know that? Listen to the writer of First Kings as he narrates the sequel to this eye-opening event,

> "As the time of King David's death approached, he gave this charge to his son Solomon: "And remember Shimei son of Gera, the man from Bahurim in Benjamin. He cursed me with a terrible curse as I was fleeing to Mahanaim. When he came down to meet me at the Jordan River, *I swore by the LORD that I would not kill him. But that oath does not make him innocent. You are a wise man, and you will know how to arrange a bloody death for him.*" (1Kgs 2:1,8–9, NLT) (Emphasis mine)

A 'Boss' Clobbers his 'Subordinate'!

"...*I [David] swore...that I would not kill him [Shimei]...You [Solomon] are a wise man, and will know how to arrange a bloody death for him.*" Those grim words say it all: David, at the end of his life, gave marching orders to his son and successor Solomon to execute Shimei for the tirade of insults many years back! As most Bible students know, Solomon cunningly had Shimei executed sometime later (1Kings 2:42–46)—a bloody denouement for an unwise 'subordinate'. From the point of view of managing 'up', all this means that,

The Best Subordinates Rarely Display their True Emotions Before their Bosses!

Shimei the son of Gera was safe and secure until he gave up his own power by openly expressing his true feelings—his abhorrence of King David—to, of all people, David! If Shimei had kept his mouth shut, his head would never have been endangered. While your head may never be endangered if you vigorously express your true emotions to your boss (especially when those emotions are in conflict with your boss's feelings)—or to people who'd likely tell your boss your words—the truth is that your career may be endangered. Managing 'up' means that you never give up your own power—the ability to keep your true feelings under wraps. It also means that you increasingly display another quality that can help a sheep survive among wolves—that you become healthily distrustful and quit being naive. And it is to the subject of a healthy distrust that we now turn our attention . . .

SHEEP AMONG WOLVES (2) . . . DEVELOPING A HEALTHY DISTRUST OF PEOPLE WITH POWER OVER YOUR CAREER

In 1976, a tsunami hit Nigeria's federal civil service as a new military government, disregarding the implicit promise of lifelong employment which went with jobs in the public service, engaged in a wholesale retrenchment of civil servants. That unprecedented exercise left many ostensibly hardworking and trusting federal employees shellshocked, and many more penniless and without careers. In retrospect, that landmark event called to mind the words of Stanford professor Jeffrey Pfeffer who, in his book, *Leadership BS: Fixing Workplaces and Careers One Truth at a Time*, said that

> "The advantages of not trusting too much, of harboring a good degree of skepticism and distrust in most situations and interactions, seem obvious for the gullible individuals who lose money and careers when their trust is violated."

In the light of Professor Pfeffer's words, it does seem that the only thing those hapless federal employees did wrong was to trust their employer too much! It also seems that cultivating a healthy distrust of the people with power over your career is one way to manage 'up'. Again, Jesus' oft-ignored words drive the point home . . .

> "Look, I am sending you out as sheep among wolves. Be as wary as snakes and harmless as doves . . . For you will be handed over to the courts . . . And you must stand trial before governors and kings . . . " (Matt 10:16–18, NLT)

To better understand this passage, one must zoom in on the words "wary," and "wolves." The Cambridge dictionary defines "wary" as "not completely trusting or certain about something or someone." In effect, Jesus is saying that,

Section 1 | Managing 'Up'

Cultivating a Healthy Distrust of People with Power Over Your Career is at the Heart of Managing 'Up'!

By saying "*. . . Be wary as snakes,*" Jesus means that we should, like snakes in the wild, be healthily distrustful and aware of the damage that others can inflict on us. The question becomes: in what kind of relationships, and with which kind of persons, are we to remain wary? Because Jesus also said "Look, I am sending you out as sheep among wolves," the answers to that question are best revealed by a detailed study of the word "wolves." To know who these 'wolves' are, listen carefully to the writer of Zephaniah,

> "Its [Israel's] leaders are like roaring lions hunting for their victims—out for everything they can get. Its judges are like ravenous wolves at evening time, who by dawn have left no trace of their prey." (Zeph 3:3, NLT)

"*Its* [Israel's] *judges* [leaders] *are like ravenous wolves . . .* " These illuminating words show that the term "wolves" refers symbolically to leaders; to persons who control organizational resources, albeit those who are in it for themselves. Therefore we can say that,

A Healthy Distrust is Necessary in 'Unequal' Employer-Employee Relationships

"*Look, I am sending you out as sheep among wolves. [Therefore] Be wary as snakes . . .* " Since, in the natural, snakes are essentially distrustful (no snake meets a human and thinks "I am meeting a friend!"), Jesus' words mean that when dealing with people with power over us (wolves have power over sheep), we need to be healthily distrustful. In short, you need to be distrustful when power (over your career, personal finances etc) lies in the hands of others. The most 'unequal' relationships tend to occur in the boss-subordinate context of organizations, and that's where many miss it—tending to unreservedly trust the good intentions of bosses (even when those bosses wear cassocks, skull caps or collars!) and leave themselves exposed. But the truth is this: your financial future is not your boss's responsibility; your financial future is your responsibility. Whatever, career success within a hierarchical context requires that you remain wary, maintain a healthy distrust, and not be naive—things so important that they cannot be overemphasized. Since many workers have overlooked this principle to their own hurt, I take a deep dive into the topic in . . .

The Case of Bathsheba the Naive

If custom permits historians to add terms like "the Great," and "the Terrible" (describing character and achievement) to the names of kings, queens and other eminent persons in history—e.g., Peter the Great, Ivan the Terrible, and Tarquin the Proud—then, taking poetic licence, one might speak of Bathsheba the Naive! Why? Because if there's one person in the Bible record who never had a leadership 'bone' in her body—who was completely naive and open to manipulation—it must be Bathsheba, wife of King David and mother of Solomon. The writer of First Kings show us just why this is so, saying,

> "Then Nathan the prophet went to Bathsheba, Solomon's mother, and asked her, "Do you not realize that Haggith's son, Adonijah, has made himself king and that our lord David doesn't even know about it? If you want to save your own life and the life of your son Solomon, follow my counsel. Go at once to King David and say to him, 'My lord, didn't you promise me that my son Solomon would be the next king and would sit upon your throne? Then why has Adonijah become king?'" (1Kgs 1:11–13, NLT)

Bathsheba Dodges a Bullet!

The story is the stuff of many a Sunday school class: David the king is old, weak, and about to die—exposing a gaping power vacuum in the government. A wily Adonijah, David's eldest living son, steps into the vacuum and declares himself king (1Kings 1:1,5). The problem with all this is that Adonijah's supporters do not include Bathsheba and her son Solomon—a clear danger for Bathsheba in the context of ancient Israel. But a naive Bathsheba doesn't even see the danger until Nathan the prophet says to her "Do you not realize that Haggith's son, Adonijah, has made himself king, and our lord David doesn't even know about it?" If you want to save your life and the life of your son Solomon, follow my counsel . . . " It was this warning that jolted Bathsheba and made her go in to speak with King David. The rest, as they say, is history—David appointed Bathsheba's son Solomon as his successor. Bathsheba had dodged the bullet! If Adonijah had taken power, he would have had her executed because her son was his rival for power in the dog-eat-dog situation that existed in the palace.

One would think that this near-death experience would always color Bathsheba's subsequent dealings with Adonijah. But a naive Bathsheba was never going to learn how to protect herself from power at its subtlest form—manipulation. Sometime after that first unsuccessful power grab, the 'wolf' (Adonijah) approaches the 'sheep' (Bathsheba) and requests the latter to ask a small favor on his behalf from her son King Solomon. Listen as the writer of First Kings narrates the incident,

> "One day Adonijah, whose mother was Haggith came to see Bathsheba, Solomon's mother. "Have you come to make trouble?" she asked him. "No," he said, "I come in peace. In fact, I have a favor to ask of you. What is it?" she asked. He replied, "As you know, the kingdom was mine; everyone expected me to be the next king. But the tables were turned, and everything went to my brother instead; for that is the way the LORD wanted it. So now I have just one favor to ask of you. Please don't turn me down. What is it?" she asked. He replied, "Speak to King Solomon on my behalf, for I know he will do anything you request. Ask him to give me Abishag, the girl from Shunem, as my wife." "All right," Bathsheba replied. "I will speak to the king for you." So Bathsheba went to King Solomon to speak on Adonijah's behalf . . . and she sat at his right hand. "I have one small request to make of you," she said. "I hope you won't turn me down. What is it, my mother?" he asked. "You know I won't refuse you." "Then let your brother Adonijah marry Abishag, the girl from Shunem," she replied "How can you possibly ask me to give Abishag to Adonijah?" Solomon demanded. "You might as well be asking me to give him the kingdom! You know that he is my older brother, and that he has Abiathar the priest and Joab son of Zeruiah on his side."'" (1 Kgs 2:13–22, NLT)

As any reasonably competent Bible student knows, Solomon—a dyed in the wool student of power—immediately saw through Adonijah's treasonous schemes and had him executed. Indeed, Adonijah's request for Abishag's hand in marriage helped Solomon "see" Adonijah's co-conspirators—Joab the army commander and Abiathar the priest—and put the former to death. This shows that, not only was Bathsheba naive, but also that . . .

Naivety is Reduced When You Deal with People According to their Histories With You and With Others

Bathsheba's naivety gets the silver cup! I mean, how do you explain the fact that she totally forgot her history with Adonijah—a man who, in his attempt to become king, had posed a clear threat to her and Solomon? Indeed, how do you explain her forgetting the warning she'd received from Nathan about Adonijah's intentions to kill her and her son Solomon? If, as philosopher John Locke famously stated "The actions of men are the best interpreters of their thoughts," then leaders overcome naivety when they always keep in mind their history with individuals or groups, and use that history to interpret the actions of those same persons today. But, and this is crucial, there's something better than a person's history with you, it's that person's history with others! Simply taking the time to find out how that person has behaved toward others like you can give you the wisdom you need to handle him.

Anyone who desires upward mobility within a hierarchy must agree that people who have to be rescued again and again from 'danger' by others (like Bathsheba was rescued by Nathan, and then by Solomon) are unlikely to rise to the highest echelons of organizational leadership. And the reason isn't far-fetched; it's because they have not internalized this uncomfortable truth—success in an organizational setting demands more than just mastery of technical skills; it also demands that you know how to protect yourself without being harmful to others.

SHEEP AMONG WOLVES (3) . . . NAVIGATING CULTURE'S MINEFIELD

The Cambridge Dictionary defines the word "minefield" as "a situation or subject that is very complicated and full of hidden problems and dangers." When applied to the area of an organization's culture—the widely shared, deeply held and, more often than not, unwritten rules that guide the behavior of individuals in a group—that definition is spot on. In simple terms, the culture of a group (in colloquial terms, "the way we do things around here") is a minefield that employees, associates and subordinates must master if they want to get promoted. Social psychologist Geert Hofstede, in his landmark co-authored book, *Cultures and Organizations: Software of the Mind,* exposes the connection between culture and career success, saying,

Section 1 | Managing 'Up'

"Culture is always a collective phenomenon, because it is at least partly shared with people who *live* or *lived* within the same social environment, which is where it was learned. *Culture consists of the unwritten rules of the social game.* It is the collective programming of the mind that distinguishes the members of one group or category of people from others. Culture is learned, not innate." (Emphases mine)

If you replace the highlighted words "live," and "lived," with the words "work," and "worked," that insightful paragraph is imbued with new meaning, helping us see that,

1. Culture is majorly a body of *unwritten* rules guiding the social game in a group: simply put, culture—like the rules of games like basketball, football etc—determines which actions are acceptable and, by division, what actions are not acceptable in a particular organization. The difference between an organization's cultural "rules" and the rules of say, a game like basketball, is that the latter are written and known even by outsiders, while the former are often unwritten and known only by insiders.

2. Every organization has a distinct culture: " . . . *It* [culture] *is the collective programming of the mind that distinguishes the members of one group . . . of people from others.*" In essence, the culture of Company A where I currently work is often very different from Company B where you now work.

"So, how," you might ask, "do #1 and #2 determine or influence a person's career success?" Here's how; since it's only things that are acceptable in a company that get rewarded (things that aren't acceptable are punished or discouraged), not being conversant with a company's culture means that I would probably not rise to the highest rungs of the corporate ladder there. For example, if I leave Company A (where I currently work) and move over to Company B (with a culture distinct from that of Company A), I would probably have to learn and master the culture of Company B before I can hope to succeed there. All of this means that the most culturally savvy workers are the ones likely to be promoted. To put it bluntly—and unbeknown to many—being culturally savvy is also a precondition for workplace success in organizations!

The writer of First Kings, in his narrative of the leadership of King Solomon of ancient Israel, helps us see how cultural smarts helped the young king detect and put down an incipient coup d'etat. Although, unlike

Solomon, your life may never be at risk if you aren't culturally savvy, the truth is that your career may be derailed if you lack cultural smarts.

King Solomon's Minefield

Solomon, son and successor to King David, began his leadership journey as a complete neophyte. In the vicious power struggle that occurred as old King David became increasingly enfeebled and unable to govern, Solomon was nowhere to be found. Indeed, when Nathan the prophet and Bathsheba attempted to convince an enfeebled King David to appoint Solomon as his successor, the latter wasn't even part of the picture! (1 Kings 1:11–13) Fast forward a few years, and we see a more mature and culturally savvy King Solomon. The latter showed himself a masterful student of power—a sheep who could successfully work among wolves—by quickly sniffing out a rival's plot to overthrow him. The writer of First Kings narrates the whole incident, saying,

> "Then let your brother Adonijah marry Abishag, the girl from Shunem," she replied. "How can you possibly ask me to give Abishag to Adonijah?" Solomon demanded. "You might as well be asking me to give him the kingdom! You know that he is my older brother, and that he has Abiathar the priest and Joab son of Zeruiah on his side." Then King Solomon swore solemnly by the LORD: "May God strike me dead if Adonijah has not sealed his fate with this request." (1 Kgs 2:21–23, NLT)

Much reflection on this passage has helped me see that when you're culturally savvy . . .

'Little' Things Can Have 'Big' Consequences!

The story can provide material for a bestselling thriller. Adonijah, who had lost out in a power struggle with Solomon, craftily approaches a naive Bathsheba. He asks the latter to make a "small" request on his behalf to her son, King Solomon. And what was the request? Adonijah wanted King Solomon to grant him permission to marry a Shunnamite woman named Abishag. To an outsider, Solomon's explosive and violent response ("How can you possibly ask me to give Abishag to Adonijah? . . . You might as well be asking me to give him the kingdom! . . . May God strike me dead if Adonijah has not sealed his fate with this request.") was totally out of proportion to Adonijah's small and innocuous request. That seemingly innocuous request led to a cascade of events—the uncovering of an attempted coup d'etat, the execution of Adonijah and a co-conspirator, and the banishment of yet another co-conspirator.

The question becomes: why was a 'small' thing like asking for a woman's hand in marriage such a big deal to Solomon? The editors of *The Life Application Bible,* have this to say about the matter,

> "This was not a case of thwarted love; Adonijah had more in mind than his supposed love for Abishag. Although she was still a virgin, Abishag was considered part of David's harem. Adonijah wanted Abishag because possessing the king's harem was equivalent to claiming the throne. Absalom had done the same thing in his rebellion against David (2Sam.16:20–23). Solomon well understood what Adonijah was trying to do."

"Adonijah wanted Abishag because possessing the king's harem was equivalent to claiming the throne . . . " Those words say it all. Abishag was no ordinary woman. She was a woman who had provided care for King David just before he passed on. In the culture of the Near East, Abishag was a wife, part of David's harem. And, this is also crucial, in the culture of the Near East, the only person who could inherit the old king's harem was the new king. By seeking Abishag's hand in marriage, Adonijah was actually laying claim to the throne. A culturally naive Bathsheba didn't see all this, but a culturally savvy King Solomon saw it (*"Solomon understood well what Adonijah was trying to do."*)—and moved quickly to out the plotters. For people who work within the context of organizations, all this means that,

Success in Organizational Careers Requires You to Be Culturally Savvy

As the case of Bathsheba and Adonijah above reveals, *culture is a sense-making tool that helps you make sense of the often difficult-to-understand environments in which you operate. It can, like Solomon's unusual insight into the real meaning of Adonijah's request, help you appreciate the true import and significance of the actions of others, and imbue otherwise ordinary events with new and special meaning.* Solomon survived the plotting of Adonijah only because he was well acquainted with the cultural nuances and symbolisms of the Near East. Adonijah, to his own hurt, didn't think Solomon knew that much about the culture of Israel. By helping you make sense of the environment, culture also helps you better understand the power dynamics of the group—and detect the landmines which often lie buried in the social interactions which necessarily occur in work groups. If you work in any kind of organization, you need to spend time studying the culture so that you can understand the nonverbal and unwritten communications that are constantly taking place; communications which signal who or what group of persons has power and, by division, who doesn't have power (I take a deep dive into the subject of power in organizations in Chapter 2). Learn to look at who is sitting where, who's sitting next to who, and who's not standing next to who—these and many other such 'small' things are the cultural symbolisms that communicate the thinking and feelings of people within that particular organization or group.

Wrap Around

Organizations are instruments for enforcing behavioral conformity. And the key word in that statement is "enforcing"—a word that hints at the presence of an "enforcer" or person in the hierarchy with power to punish or reward. The persons who best understand this concept of organizations, hierarchy, enforcement, and conformity are the ones who, in the words of political scientist Steven Lukes "accept the hierarchy," and are also the ones most likely to experience upward progression and promotion. Accepting the uncomfortable realities of hierarchies begins with being strategic in your behavior with people with power over your career; it continues with maintaining a healthy distrust of those same persons, and berths ship when you become increasingly culturally savvy. Those three factors—to the chagrin of the many who put professional smarts right, front, and center—are the first, second, and third rungs of the proverbial corporate ladder. Miss them, and your career will probably go south—no matter how talented you are!

Chapter 2

Power Play

Understanding How Power Works in Organizations

WHAT EXACTLY IS POWER?

"Too many people are profoundly—and willfully—illiterate [about] power: what it is, what forms it takes, who has it, who doesn't, why that is, how it is exercised."—Eric Liu

If Chapter 1 dealt with "Managing Your Relationships With People Who Have Power Over Your Career," this chapter takes a deep and specific dive into the subject of power itself; what power is, how to get and wield it, how to know who has it, etc—important topics for people who want to experience any form of workplace success. Unfortunately, Harvard professor Rosabeth Moss Kanter's now-famous words "Power is America's last dirty word. It is easier to talk about money—and much easier to talk about sex—than it is to talk about power," best encapsulate the attitude of most Christians toward power. Although many preachers regularly rail against sexual infidelity and financial malfeasance, almost everyone seems to give power a wide berth—making it a taboo subject. This unwillingness or inability to address the subject is not only responsible for the ambivalence of many Christians to issues concerning power, but may also be the reason why some Christians see power as inherently evil and consider anyone who desires it as having an evil agenda!. But, just take a look around you, and you will see plenty of hierarchies—organizations or groups with relatively few persons at the top who have decision rights (power) over the lives and conduct of many at the bottom or middle. Indeed, because hierarchies are the way most of society's institutions (families, governments, businesses etc,.) are organized, the question isn't "Is power a good thing or a bad thing?" but rather "What is power, and how do I know who has it?"

Power is a Good Thing!

Because Christians tend to think power is evil, I begin by calling to mind the words of the Psalmist,

> "God has spoken this once, Twice have I heard this: That *power belongs to God*." (Emphasis mine) (Ps 62:11, NKJV)

These amazing words are the primer for the study of power because they show that power is a belonging or property of God! Now, if power is the 'belonging', property, or attribute of a holy God, then power cannot be evil and the study of power certainly isn't unchristian! Indeed, one can even go on to say that because power belongs to God, power and the study of power are good!

Having settled the issue of whether power is good or bad, we can now tackle the questions; what exactly is power, and how do I know the person or group that has it? Again, the Psalmist provides some answers to those weighty questions, saying,

> "Say unto God, "How terrible art thou in thy works! Through the greatness of thy power shall thy enemies submit themselves unto thee." (Ps 66:3, KJV)

These words mean that,

Power is the Ability to Get People to Do What they Don't Ordinarily Want to Do

" . . . *Through the greatness of thy power shall thy enemies submit themselves unto thee.*" Did you notice why God's enemies—people with an agenda contrary to his—had to tow his line? You guessed right; it was because God had power. His great power made them submit to his wishes. Therefore, we can say that, power is the ability to get people to do what they would ordinarily not want to do. Power pushes through, to a large extent, its own agenda. Power doesn't just get its own way, it gets its own way in spite of, and among, people who disagree or dissent. Power overcomes resistance. Stanford professor Jeffrey Prefer, in his excellent book, *Managing With Power*, drives the point home, saying "Power is the . . . ability to influence people, to change the course of events, to overcome resistance and to get people to do what they would not otherwise do."

Power is a Tool for Getting Things Done, for Helping You Experience Career Progress

" . . . Through the greatness of thy power shall thy enemies submit themselves unto thee." Why is God able to accomplish everything he desires? You guessed right again. It's because he has power! Power is a tool for getting things done—a thing the physicists acknowledge when they define power as "The ability to do work." If you work in a group and possess little or no power, then you can only achieve so much. And, this is important, because you can't get much work done, your career can begin to stagnate. In other words, people with power tend to make better career progress than people without power.

Power is Often Revealed in Conflict and Disagreement. You Don't Need Power Where there's a Consensus

" . . . through the greatness of thy power shall thy enemies submit themselves unto thee." Notice carefully that God's power was displayed in the context of disagreements and conflicts of interest—in his relationship with enemies who were opposed to his own agenda. Therefore, we can say that power is most needed when we deal with people who disagree with us. If people are agreed on the direction in which things must happen—if there's a consensus—then, not only is power not needed, it's also pretty difficult to discern which person or group has power.

Power is a 'Zero-Sum Thing': The More Power You Have, the Less I Have

By saying, in effect, that '[All] power belongs to God," the Psalmist let's the cat out of the bag—power is a zero-sum thing in which one person's gain is always another's loss. There's only so much of it to go round. Drawing from the realm of politics; the more powerful the opposition is, the less powerful the government or ruling party becomes and vice versa. Having seen what power is, we now come to the question: how do I know who has power? . . .

Litmus Tests for Power (How to Know Who is in Charge)

Power gets things done. Therefore, knowing who's boss, and knowing the social distribution of power among the different persons and units in a group is critical to getting things done and making career progress. I mean, if you don't know that the people in the office next door are the real powers behind the throne when it comes to new product approvals, then your new product idea may end up dead on arrival! To help you better discern the distribution of power in a group, I have borrowed ideas from the field of Chemistry—a subject famous for its myriad analytical tests which can conclusively detect the presence or absence of chemical compounds. Anyone who has taken a basic chemistry class can easily recall the Litmus test—acids turn Litmus paper red, while bases turn it blue. In other words, once blue litmus turns red, you can rest assured that an acid is present in the mixture. In this vein, the following three "tests" are what I call "the Litmus tests for power" . . .

Litmus Test #1: Power Over the Agenda

Agendas deal with what's on the table, what's not on the table, and who's initiatives or proposals are being accepted, modified, rejected, etc—a clutch of very political actions. Because power, as we've seen, always reveals itself in the context of opposing interests, and since power overcomes resistance, the first test of power is this: power often gets its own way and/or hinders its antagonists from having their own way. And, increasing power is often first noticed as an increased ability to get your own way or an increased ability to hinder the agendas of others. Social scientist Onajomo Akemu drives this point home, saying,

"Interests refer to what people want - to what's at stake for them by a decision or course of action. Depending on how an action affects their interests, people will support or oppose it. Managers often run into trouble because they fail to realize what's at stake for other individuals or groups in their proposed course of action. *The effectiveness of the support and opposition of others depends on the amount of power held by those units and individuals.* Understanding how to leverage interests and power is an essential base for taking action on organizations." (Emphasis mine)

These illuminating words mean that a prime way to discern who has power is to carefully observe which person or group of persons often gets its own way, or is more frequently able to hinder others from realizing their own agendas.

Litmus Test #2: Power Over Schedules and Calendars

Farming is an ancient and honorable profession that has evolved from subsistence farming to its modern-day large scale mechanized variant. The infusion of science-based methods has seen more and more of the variables of farming—tools, seedlings, fertilizers etc—come under humankind's control. Notwithstanding, there are factors critical to farming—rain, dew, the onset of the seasons—over which man still has little or no power. Indeed, seasons still have so much power that the farmer who chooses to plow or plant out of season is doomed! Why? Because seasons, coming and going as they please, wait for no one. All this helps us better understand the concept of power: the person who has control of the calendar or schedule—who others have to wait for—is often the person in power. The writer of Micah drives this point home, saying,

> "The remnant of Jacob will be in the midst of many peoples like dew from the LORD, like showers on the grass, which do not wait or linger for mankind. The remnant of Jacob will be among the nations, in the midst of many peoples, like a lion among the beasts of the forest, like a young lion among flocks of sheep, which mauls and mangles as it goes, and no one can rescue." (Mic 5:7–8, NIV)

These words offer conclusive proof that,

POWER PLAY

Being in Power is Synonymous With Having Control Over Other Peoples' Calendars

By saying " . . . *The remnant of Jacob will be . . . among many people . . . like a young lion among . . . flocks of sheep,*" the writer of Micah buttresses what I have been saying—the person in power is, like a young lion among sheep, able to get her own way and have the last word. But, by also saying "The remnant of Jacob will be in the midst of many peoples . . . *like showers on the grass, which do not wait for man or linger for mankind,*" he shows us another overlooked truth—people in power have power over other peoples' calendars! In other words, they can—like rain showers that determine when, and what kind of work, a farmer does—make others wait for them, hurry up for them, and even go before them. This is the reason some leaders, wanting to show who's boss, often keep their visitors waiting for long periods before seeing them! Again, Professor Pfeffer, in his book, *Managing With Power*, drives the point home, saying,

> "Causing others to wait, or not waiting yourself, is more than a symbol of your own power—it is also a tactic that can be used to increase your power. By being late, you call attention to yourself, and this very fact of visibility can produce influence. Also, making others wait for you forces them to consider your implicit power over them. When you do arrive, others may pay more attention to you in order to convince you to arrive on time in the future, which again reinforces their awareness of their dependence on you."

Waiting Often Reveals the Pattern of Power Distribution in a Group

" . . . The remnant of Jacob will be in the midst of many peoples . . . like showers on the grass, *which do not wait for man or linger for mankind . . .* " Waiting doesn't just show who's boss, it can also reveal the distribution of power in a group. For example, if A is boss of B, and B is in turn the boss of C, then it follows that when A communicates with B, the latter often replies immediately. On the other hand, when B communicates with A, the latter is at liberty to delay and reply at a time of his own choosing. Since this power relationship is replicated down the hierarchy, it means that one can map out the hierarchy of the group by simply tracking the time it takes to reply mails! Indeed, this is how counterterrorism experts at major Western intelligence agencies map out the hierarchy of many Islamist terror groups.

So, next time you are in a group setting, carefully observe who has power to call or postpone meetings, closely monitor arrival and departure routines, and faithfully measure the time intervals taken to respond to requests and queries. Your observations can quickly separate the men from the boys (and the women from the girls) and pinpoint the people in power!

Litmus Test #3: 'Power Distances'

It is fall 2021 as I write, and the COVID-19 Pandemic is still wreaking havoc worldwide. The pandemic has also popularized the phrase "social distancing"—helping people pay careful attention to the physical distance between them and others. But the truth is that long before social distancing gained its current traction, it had another more subtle manifestation in the power relationships between subordinates and bosses. How do I mean? Recently, as I watched the supreme leader (head of state) of a certain country on cable television, I noticed how far away his followers were from his own seat as he addressed them, and it dawned on me that when people deeply respect or fear you, they tend to keep their distance! In other words, there's often a defined physical space between leader and subordinate. The writer of Acts, in his narrative of how ordinary people behaved in meetings with the apostles, helps us see this truth, saying,

> "Now by the hands of the apostles (special messengers) numerous and startling signs and wonders were being performed among the people. And by common consent they all met together [at the temple] in the covered porch (walk) called Solomon's. And none of those who were not of their number dared to join and associate with them, but the people held them in high regard and praised and made much of them." (Acts 5:12–13, AMP)

These words reveal some interesting truths about power . . .

The More Highly Placed You are in an Organization, the Greater the Physical Distance Subordinates Place Between You and Them

By saying *"they all met together,"* the writer of Acts shows us that this was a general gathering of all believers—apostles and laypersons alike. But, by going on to say " *. . . And none of those who were not of their number dared to join and associate with them,"* he shows us that laypersons were careful to maintain a discreet physical distance between them and the apostles! Not done yet, the writer of Acts continues his discourse, saying " . . . *but the people held them [the apostles] in high regard . . .* " This last phrase hits the nail on the head; helping us see that the physical distance between leaders (apostles) and led (laypersons) arose from the respect the latter had for the former. By division, this also means that . . .

You Can Know Who's Boss by Carefully Observing the Physical Distances Between Different Persons

In any group, it does seem that leaders are the persons with the largest social space—as if people wittingly or unwittingly give them a wide berth! Therefore, one way to detect the leader or leading persons in any group is to simply (and surreptitiously) measure the physical space granted to that person or group of persons by others. But there's more to social distance as the following words of the writer of John's Gospel reveal . . .

> "After he said these things, Jesus became visibly upset, and then he told them why. "One of you is going to betray me." The disciples looked around at one another, wondering who on earth he was talking about. One of the disciples, the one Jesus loved dearly, was reclining against him, his head on his shoulder. Peter motioned to him to ask who Jesus might be talking about. So, being the closest, he said, "Master, who?" Jesus said, "The one to whom I give this crust of bread after I've dipped it." Then he dipped the crust and gave it to Judas, son of Simon the Iscariot." (John 13:21–26, MSG)

This amazing passage is a treasure trove of insights on the subject of power distances, helping us see that,

Not Only Does Physical Distance Reveal Who's Boss, It can also Reveal the Organizational Hierarchy!

"One of the disciples, the one Jesus loved dearly, was reclining against him, his head on his shoulder. Peter motioned to him to ask who Jesus might be talking about. *So, being the closest,* he said, "Master, who?" Taking Jesus—the big bossman—as the reference point for measuring power distances, these words of the writer of John's Gospel immediately help us see that the disciples (Jesus' associates) were seated according to their closeness to him—the disciple whom "Jesus loved dearly," being seated closest to Jesus, and so on.

In other words, not only does power distance reveal who's boss, it can also reveal the hierarchy or power distribution in a group. All of which brings us to our final point...

Informal Cultures Tend to Have Smaller Power Distances than Formal Cultures

"One of the disciples, the one Jesus loved dearly, was reclining against him, his head on his shoulder . . . " These intriguing words show another thing about the culture in Israel in Jesus' day—it was very informal and 'feminine'. Why? Easy. Because it allowed the open display of affection. For someone like me who grew up in a rather 'masculine' culture where affection isn't, as a rule, openly displayed, the picture of a disciple (whom Jesus loved dearly) reclining with his head on Jesus' shoulder makes me uncomfortable! But, and this is crucial, Jewish culture at that time permitted that kind of behavior—making for small power distances. For more formal (or 'masculine') cultures, power distances tend to be larger. To be clear, power distances occur in every social group, but the magnitude of that phenomenon is determined by the degree of formalism prevalent in that clime. Since all power distances are not the same, you might need to look more carefully to see the smaller power distances in groups with more informal cultures.

SOURCES OF POWER IN THE WORKPLACE

"Power, which psychologists often define as having greater control over valued resources in a relationship."—Marissa King

To better understand the sources of power, one need only look at the history of the country officially known as the Kingdom of Saudi Arabia. Hitherto of little consequence in world affairs, Saudi Arabia is today one of the leading powers in the Middle East, and a strategic ally of the United States. And how did that transformation come about? Easy. The answer lies in the words "crude oil." The discovery of large deposits of crude within her borders, and the increased importance of that commodity in the world economy, have given the Saudi government increased leverage in global affairs. In essence, Saudi Arabia's weight in international affairs can be traced to her ownership of significant deposits of an economically valuable resource—crude oil. All this helps us see that power has its roots in the ownership or control of resources critical to the well-being of others. In other words, people who control or own resources—information, intellectual capital, economic assets, relational assets, etc—crucial to the functioning or wellbeing of others tend to become powerful. The writer of Genesis, in his account of how Issac blessed his son Jacob, corroborates this line of thought, saying,

> "May God give you of heaven's dew and of earth's richness- an abundance of grain and new wine. May nations serve you and peoples bow down to you. Be lord over your brothers, and may the sons of your mother bow down to you. May those who curse you be cursed and those who bless you be blessed." (Gen 22:28-29, NIV)

Power Flows from the Ownership and Control of Critical Assets

Before saying " . . . May nations bow down before you and peoples serve you. Be lord over your brothers . . . "—a clear reference to the unequal relationships associated with power—Isaac had to say "May God give you of heaven's dew and of earth's richness- an abundance of grain and new wine." These words mean only one thing; Jacob's power over his brothers was rooted in his control of the economic factors which determined productivity in an agrarian economy—land, grain, new wine, etc. In other words, power comes from the control or ownership of productive resources—material, intellectual or relational. Or, to put it bluntly, power has its roots in the control of resources crucial to the wellbeing of others. The persons or groups with control or ownership of those assets tend to become powerful—able to impose their views, agendas, culture, and way of life on others. But, the writer of Genesis is not done speaking about power and the unequal relationships it can gender. He goes on to say that,

> "Isaac answered Esau, "I have made him [Jacob] lord over you and have made all his relatives his servants, and I have sustained him with grain and new wine. So what can I possibly do for you, my son?" (Gen 27:37, NIV)

These amazing words show us that,

Section 1 | Managing 'Up'

Power Often Shifts as the Sources of Power Wax and Wane

"I have *sustained* him with grain and wine . . . " The key word in this sentence is "sustained"—the root of the word "sustainable"—meaning that which is long lasting. The idea is that you remain powerful only as long as the assets you own or control are mission-critical to the success of others. In simple terms, if people no longer need or depend on the assets you control, your power over them will wane. Again, Professor Pfeffer drives the point home, saying,

> " . . . *power can often be increased* by finding underutilized resources and exploiting them. Resources are useful in the development and exercise of influence only to the extent one has discretion over them, and only to the extent that the dependence of others can be developed." (Emphasis mine)

If power can, in the words of Professor Pfeffer "*be increased*," then it follows that power can also be decreased. Acquiring, maintaining and increasing power demand that you own or control an asset that others need not just today, but also tomorrow. Anything less than that will see your power decrease over time.

Putting it Into Practice

In many cases, control over seemingly "mundane" organizational resources like jobs and money can help you acquire power. In other cases, the sources of power are a little more arcane. If, for example, you work in an industry where technology is the mission-critical factor, then expect engineers and technologists—who best understand technology—to be powerful. But if, with the passage of time, consumers feel shortchanged and put pressure on the government to increase regulatory oversight of the industry—making regulation mission-critical for success—then one wouldn't be too surprised to see a new set of people in power; people who, because they are trained in law and environmental science, can best navigate regulatory matters. Whatever, the steps to acquiring power are twofold: first gain control or ownership of a mission-critical resource, then take steps to make sure that those resources are always needed by the people you serve.

BUILDING A POWER BASE

Because power often gets things done in spite of, and/or among, people who oppose it, the exercise of power is inherently 'political'. And, this is crucial, people steeped in the meritocratic ethos of "May the best man/woman/proposal win," normally shrink from political behavior. The latter are often driven by the belief that "If my proposal is the best, it will automatically be approved by the board." They forget that there might be others with alternate or opposing interests who also want their own proposals approved by the same board. And, this is also crucial, they are astonished when other peoples' proposals are selected in place of theirs! Former Yahoo! executive Tim Sanders, in his bestselling book, *Love Is the Killer App*, explains why ostensibly good proposals are sometimes rejected, saying,

> "Think about business that you've lost or promotions someone else grabbed, or competitive one-on-one situations where a rival triumphed. Calculate the size of the winner's network versus yours. For the most part, the winners are those with the largest networks, the most powerful connections, and the ability to call in their reserves at the moment of truth."

> *" . . . the winners are those with the largest networks, the most powerful connections . . . "* These insightful words hit the nail on the head, showing that, deliberately cultivating a power base or network can help further your career. To put it bluntly, having a good proposal is often not enough; you also need to build a coalition or power base to help push your own agenda. The question becomes, "Just how does one build a power base?" In his excellent book, *Managing With Power,* Stanford professor Jeffrey Pfeffer shows us just how to build a power base, saying "Having resources is an important source of power only if you can use those resources strategically to help others whose support you need." In other words, you build your power base whenever you use the resources at hand to help others whose support you will probably need in the future. Interestingly, Jesus, in his Parable of the Unfaithful Steward, corroborates this line of thinking, saying,

> "And I tell you, make friends for yourselves by means of unrighteous mammon (deceitful riches, money, possessions), so that when it fails, they [those you have favored] may receive and welcome you into the everlasting habitations (dwellings)." (Luke 16:9, AMP)

Much reflection on these words has helped me see that . . .

Section 1 | Managing 'Up'

Leaders Build their Power Bases by Sharing Resources

"Make friends for yourselves by means of unrighteous mammon [money] . . ." The long and short of this parable is this: the unfaithful steward built his power base by using his master's resources—a source of power under his control—to help others who, in turn, would be obliged to help him in future. By saying "Make friends for yourselves by means of unrighteous mammon . . . .so that *when it* [the unrighteous mammon] *fails*, they [those who are favored] will receive you," Jesus reveals a great truth: money or material resources can fail. Material resources "fail" whenever those resources *alone* cannot help you get the job done—which happens whenever you also need the cooperation of others to get things done—the very reason you have to build a power base. Leaders build coalitions, recruit allies, and make friends by sharing their resources with others. Sharing resources with others activates what psychologists refer to as the norm of reciprocity—people tend to feel obligated to help those who have helped them in the past.

Putting it Into Practice

Although many are aware that God promised to make David king of Israel, what they may not know is that David had to deliberately cultivate a power base before he could see that promise fulfilled! The writer of First Samuel makes this clear, saying,

> "When he arrived at Ziklag, David sent part of the plunder to the leaders of Judah, who were his friends. "Here is a present for you, taken from the LORD's enemies," he said." (1Sam 30:26, NLT)

David "Oils His Machine"—Sending Some War Booty to the Leaders of Judah!

"*David sent part of the plunder to the leaders of Judah . . .* " Here we see David (a student of power) "oiling his machine"—deliberately cultivating a power base long before becoming king—by sharing his resources (war booty) with the leaders of Judah. Appparently the norm of reciprocity was valid in biblical Israel because the writer of Second Samuel goes ahead to say that,

"Then Judah's leaders came to David and crowned him king over the tribe of Judah. When David heard that the men of Jabesh-gilead had buried Saul," (2Sam 2:4, NLT)

The Leaders of Judah—David's Power Base—Reciprocate by Helping David Become King of Judah!

By saying *"Then Judah's leaders came to David and crowned him king over the tribe of Judah,"* the writer of Second Samuel let's the cat out of the bag—it was the same leaders of Judah who had received some war booty from David that helped him become king of Judah! Sharing resources as a way of building a power base is an 'ongoing thing' for the best leaders, a 'yesterday thing' for average leaders, and a 'never-done-it-before thing' for the also-rans. To build an effective power base, you should . . .

Share "What" You Know

Knowledge is an intellectual resource. Don't hoard what you know. If someone, a colleague or partner, is hard-pressed about getting a job done and you know how that job can be done, by all means tell the person what you know. But before you can 'share', you must first 'know', so building your power base begins with personal development, with taking time to improve yourself. Read books and attend seminars so that you can have something to share.

Share "Who" You Know

Who you know is a relational resource. To keep building your power base you must be willing to share your "contacts", people you think can be helpful to others (I take a deep dive into this topic in Chapter 10, "Managing Your Personal Network"). Sharing "who" you know always begins with asking yourself this question, "Is there someone I know that I think this person should know?"

Share What You Have

If you have or control any kind of material resources (e.g., access to jobs etc), then you can build your influence network by sharing those resources with people who need and appreciate them.

Wrap Around

If managing 'up' is about managing your relationships with people who have power over your career, then it's nigh impossible to climb the corporate ladder (manage 'up') without first "accepting the hierarchy." But, and this is crucial "accepting the hierarchy," is difficult if you don't take the time and make the effort to understand how power operates in hierarchical organizations.

Chapter 3

Managing Your Boss

WHO EXACTLY IS A BOSS?

EVERYONE, FROM THE MIGHTIEST CEO to the lowliest workman, has a boss or group of persons who serve the function of boss. Bosses are crucial to the workplace because they are the human channels for ensuring that the work being done is in accordance with the mission, vision and values of the organization. In this sense, bosses are representatives of higher authorities in the groups they lead—representing the interests of higher-ups in their dealings with subordinates and associates. This is the reason subordinates who have poor relationships with direct supervisors often find it difficult to experience career success. I mean, the impression higher-ups—who hold the power to reward and punish—form of you is deeply colored by the reports they receive from your direct supervisor! In this very classical sense, bosses are like relay stations—receiving and then relaying information from higher-ups to workers, and conveying feedback from "below" to higher-ups. The writer of Luke's Gospel, in his now-famous story of how Jesus healed a Roman centurion's sick servant, drives the point home, saying,

> "I am a man under orders; I also give orders. I tell one soldier, "Go," and he goes; another, "Come," and he comes: my slave, 'Do this,' and he does it." (Luke 7:8, MSG)

These words show that,

Section 1 | Managing 'Up'

A Boss is, First and Foremost, a Representative of Higher-ups

"*I am a man under orders; I also give orders* [that ostensibly agree with the ones I have received] . . . " Those words say it all: the centurion was a mid-level boss who gave orders to men under him. By division, the orders he gave had to be in agreement with the ones he had received, or he would be an agent of confusion in the organization. Like I said before, it is this representative or liaison function that makes bosses so crucial to workplace success, because employees who don't get along with their immediate bosses tend to be seen in a bad light by higher-ups.

Bosses are Coordinators and Supervisors—Nerve Centers of the Units they Head

Because the orders the centurion gave had to be in tandem with the ones he received, and because he was a channel through which feedback from "below" flowed "upstairs," the centurion became the nerve center or hub of the organization. His position gave him unique access to information on what ought to be done and what was actually being done—information which helped him coordinate or ensure that the work done by the soldiers under him was in line with the information (orders) he'd received from higher-ups.

Bosses Control and Direct the Behavior of Others

"*I tell . . . one, "Go," and he goes . . .* " The Centurion controlled the behavior of his subordinates by means of the information he communicated to them. In this sense, a boss is a person who has the right or authority to direct the behavior of others (subordinates or associates). That said, bosses aren't all-powerful. By saying "I tell one, "Go," and he goes," the writer of Luke's Gospel reveals a major limitation of bosses,

Control May Produce Compliance, But Compliance Isn't Necessarily Commitment!

The soldier who "goes" at the command of the centurion is only expected to "go" (compliance); he is not expected to go the *extra mile* (commitment)—even though he probably can. In other words, while control can produce compliance, it cannot produce commitment. This is because compliance is a thing of the 'head', while commitment is a thing of the 'heart'. To get people committed, bosses must move from authority to influence (more on this in Section 3, where I deal with Managing 'Down'). In his excellent book, *Managing*, management teacher Henry Mintzberg said that "I define managers as being able to control insiders but having to convince outsiders. Employees, after all, are paid to accept managerial authority." His wise words drive home the point; control, compliance and commitment—the direction of the behavior of others in ways that help achieve the organization's goals—are at the heart of being a boss. While increasing democratization has reduced the influence of "command and control" and hierarchical thinking in today's workplace, the truth is that, however you look at it, bosses are still symbols of power and authority—the very reason I placed this chapter right after the one on power!

Having seen what bosses do, we can now turn our attention to the nitty-gritty of managing your boss, what I refer to as . . .

WINNING WITH YOUR BOSS

Recently I did some business with persons living in the United States. Because Nigeria (my country of residence) is a clear nine hours ahead of the western seaboard of the US, doing business with those persons put me under severe strain because I had to keep working and taking calls when most offices here in Nigeria were closed for the day! Seemingly unaware of this time zone differential, my international partners kept plying me with work during my rest period. Success at that kind of partnership meant that I had to adjust my work schedule to theirs—a stressful, but ultimately rewarding experience (my partners loved it that I was available whenever they needed me). Much reflection on that experience has helped me see that, subordinates and associates are more likely to "manage" bosses when their own schedules and styles complement those of the latter. Interestingly, Jesus' teaching agrees with this principle . . .

> "Be dressed ready for service and keep your lamps burning, like servants waiting for their master to return from a wedding banquet, so that when he comes and knocks they can immediately open the door for him. It will be good for those servants whose master finds them watching when he comes. Truly I tell you, he will dress himself to serve, will have them recline at the table and

will come and wait on them. It will be good for those servants whose master finds them ready, even if he comes in the middle of the night or toward daybreak." (Luke 12:35–38, NIV)

Winning with Your Boss Begins With Adapting Your Schedule and Style to Her's

"Be dressed ready for service and keep your lamps burning, like servants waiting for their master to return from a wedding banquet, *so that when he comes and knocks they can immediately open the door for him . . .* " Although they didn't know when the master would return, although the master was out partying at a wedding, and although the master arrived late, the servants immediately opened the door when he eventually showed up. The servants put off sleep and rest in order to better attend to their master. The servants *adapted* their schedules to their masters'. In effect, the schedules of the servants complemented those of the master. Managing your boss begins when your schedule and style complements her own. No wonder management teacher Peter Drucker, said that,

> "Bosses are neither a title on the organization chart nor a "function." They are individuals and are entitled to do their work in the way they do it best. It is incumbent on the people who work with them to observe them, to find out how they work, and to adapt themselves to what makes their bosses most effective. This, in fact, is the secret of "managing" the boss."

"Adapting" Involves Extending Your Schedule

After all is said and done, managing your boss begins when you adapt your schedule and style to hers'. But, by saying "keep your lamps burning, like servants *waiting for their master to return from a wedding banquet,*" Jesus shows us that the best associates are willing to keep working while their boss is out partying or resting. Therefore, 'adapting' includes another component—a willingness to work longer than the boss. This willingness to put in longer hours than the boss helps the associate develop expertise, an expertise which can provide an answer or solution immediately the master asks or "knocks on the door."

In this light, "adapting" is really made up of two components—*changing* your schedule to complement that of your boss, and *extending* your schedule in ways that make you stay longer at a task than her. The former makes you compatible with your boss, while the latter helps you contribute to her performance. Both are like the two sides of a coin, or like a person's right and left hands—equally necessary.

Winning with Your Boss Continues with Not Placing Any 'Subordinate-imposed Burden' on Her

By saying "... *keep your lamps burning, like servants waiting for their master to return from a wedding banquet,*" Jesus helps us see that the best subordinates, by changing and extending their own schedules, take some of the 'load' from their boss's shoulders—helping the latter work shorter hours (if this wasn't so, the master wouldn't have been able to attend a wedding in the first place!). By division, subordinates who don't change and extend their own schedules automatically impose a burden on their bosses—leaving the latter overworked and stressed out. In this sense, if your boss is overworked, stressed out, unable to take any breaks, and working longer hours than you, you just might be imposing a burden on her! William Oncken and Donald Wass, in their best-selling Harvard Business Review article, *Management Time: Who's Got the Monkey*, explore this phenomenon by asking the question "Why is it that managers are typically running out of time, while subordinates are typically running out of work?" They found out that a key reason managers (in our context, bosses) are overworked is that they are unwitting victims of what they referred to as subordinate-imposed time—a situation where "... managers spend more time dealing with subordinates' problems than they even faintly realize." It is this doing the work of subordinates (in addition to their own work) that really gets bosses overworked and exhausted. The writer of Hebrews corroborates all this, saying ...

> "In fact, though by this time you ought to be teachers, you need someone to teach you the elementary truths of God's word all over again." (Heb 5:12, NIV)

To bring out the "management meaning" of this passage, I have paraphrased it thus "In fact, though by this time you [my 'subordinates'] ought to be teachers [influencing and helping others], you need someone [me, your 'boss'] to teach you the elementary... [principles] ... all over again..." This paraphrase show us that a key reason bosses are overworked is, you guessed right ...

Subordinate-imposed Time

"... though by this time you [my subordinates] ought to be teachers [influencing and helping others], *you need someone* [me, your boss] *to teach you ... all over again ...* " There it is in black and white; if a boss has to constantly help subordinates complete their own legitimate tasks, then that boss would end up carrying, not only her own workload, but also the workload of her subordinates—leaving her tired, overworked, and with little discretionary time. When a subordinate can't or won't get the job done by himself the first time, then the boss may be tempted to lend a helping hand or, worse still, find herself taking over the task. Every time this happens, the boss is overloaded with work, while the subordinate is 'freed'. The boss has unwittingly become the latest victim of subordinate-imposed time—working late and on weekends—while the subordinate has time enough for his own family. In this sense, the boss is actually working for the subordinate! The problem with subordinate-imposed time is that it can set-off a vicious cycle of dependency—the more the boss helps the subordinate get the job done, the less the latter is able to do things without help, and the more he needs help to get things done. If you're a subordinate or associate, you need to know that ...

The Best Way to Not Impose a Subordinate-imposed Burden on Your Boss is to Get the Job Done the First Time!

"... though by this time you [my 'subordinates'] ought to be teachers [influencing and helping others], you need someone [me, your 'boss'] to teach you ... all over again ... " You show that you value your boss's time when you're *not* the employee who must be put through the basics of the task more than once. Don't be the person who must be nursed and carried by other staff members again and again before the task can get done. Get it done the first time. The people who don't need to be carried by their boss not only free the latter to engage in higher value tasks, they also show that they are candidates for promotion. Strive to get it right the first time.

Managing Your Boss

Winning with Your Boss Berths Ship when You Know How to be the Bearer of Bad News!

By saying "Be dressed ready for service . . . so that when he [the boss] comes and knocks they [subordinates] can immediately open the door for him," Jesus reveals the third leg of the tripod of factors that make a person an effective subordinate—the ability to deliver feedback. Knocking a door is a metaphor for asking questions and demanding answers. In contrast, quickly opening the door is symbolic of the ability to swiftly give relevant information or answers. Therefore, Jesus' words mean that the best associates know the answers to the questions on the boss's mind and are able to quickly provide her the necessary feedback. But, and this is crucial, since some feedback are essentially 'bad news'—information about projects gone awry or targets not met—knowing how to deliver feedback is just as important as having the right feedback.

Anyone who has worked for even one day in an organization knows that nobody wants to be the one who tells the 'bad news' to the boss! No one wants to be the person who lets his senior leader know that things are not as rosy as expected. And the reason is clear: in most groups, there is an unstated policy of shooting the messenger or blaming the bearer of bad tidings for the bad tidings. Bring too many reports of doom and gloom to the boss, and very soon you'll find that no one wants to associate with, or promote, you! Robert Cialdini and Co., in their excellent book, *Yes! 50 Scientifically Proven Ways to Be Persuasive,* show how the best associates deliver bad news, saying,

> "Does fear persuade or paralyze? . . . For the most part research has demonstrated that fear arousing communications usually stimulate the audience to take action to reduce the threat. However, this general rule has an exception: when the fear producing message describes danger but the audience is not told of clear, specific, effective means of reducing the danger, they may deal with the fear by "blocking out" the message or denying that it applies to them."

Professor Cialdini and his colleagues are spot on: prophets of doom, naysayers and all other such bearers of bad tidings are generally unwelcome except they also—with their 'bad news'—bring " . . . clear, specific, effective means of reducing the danger . . . " The writer of Genesis, in his account of a terrible famine in the time of Pharaoh, king of Egypt, buttresses this point, saying,

Section 1 | Managing 'Up'

> "Then Joseph said to Pharaoh, "The dreams of Pharaoh are one . . . God has revealed to Pharaoh what He is about to do . . . seven years of famine will follow . . . the famine will ravage the land . . . "
> (Gen 41:25-32, NIV)

Sir, Something Terrible is About to Happen!

Joseph was in a terrible position. He had just been hurriedly released from prison to interpret the king's dream. As he listened to Pharaoh recount the dream, he realized that Pharaoh's dreams pointed to an upcoming famine that would be so severe, it could wipe out Egypt! How do you tell this kind of news to a leader who could order your beheading for bringing such heavy tidings? The writer of Genesis shows us just how Joseph nimbly sidestepped that deathtrap, saying,

> "And now let Pharaoh look for a . . . wise man and put him in charge of the land of Egypt . . . to take a fifth of the harvest . . . during seven years of abundance . . . This food should be held in reserve for the country, to be used in the seven years of famine . . . *The plan seemed good to Pharaoh and to all his officials* . . . Then Pharaoh said to Joseph . . . You shall be in charge . . . " (Emphasis mine)
> (Gen 41:33-39, NIV)

Tell the "Good" News Immediately After the "Bad" News

Every time you have "bad" news to tell or difficult feedback to give, you can make it more palatable to people in authority by simultaneously telling some "good" news—by showing clear and specific steps about how things can still be turned around or mitigated. Notice that, although Joseph began with the brutal facts—hard times and a famine lay ahead—he immediately followed up the heavy tidings with a plan (" . . . now let Pharaoh look for a man . . . to take a fifth of the harvest . . . ") to help the king turn things around. Subordinates of lesser ability would have simply told the brutal truth—and gotten mauled, marked for demotion, and maltreated. The best subordinates do more than tell the "bad" news, they also show people the solutions or plans for mitigation—and they get promoted! And that's because . . .

Telling the "Good" News Immediately After the "Bad" News Points at the Solution and Takes Peoples' Eyes Away from the "Bad" News.

"*The plan seemed good to Pharaoh and to all his officials.*" After listening to Joseph, Pharaoh and his officials came away with one thing; Joseph's plan to tackle the upcoming famine was good! Telling the "good" news (how the problem can be solved or mitigated) helps people more easily accept the "bad" news, and makes them see your as a savior, and not just as a doomsday prophet or naysayer whose message must be denied, or person, attacked. Although feedback is a tool for separating good leaders from bad ones, *giving* feedback reveals the competence of the giver of the feedback, while the other side of the coin—*receiving* feedback—reveals the character and competence of the receiver of the feedback. The best bosses are able to separate negative feedback (bad news) from the giver of the feedback, while the worst bosses conflate the two. The worst bosses are the ones with a "shoot the messenger" mentality. And, in the next chapter, it is to 'managing' difficult bosses that we turn our attention . . .

Chapter 4

Managing a Difficult Boss

WHAT IS THE VALUE OF A DIFFICULT BOSS?

"One of the ways God deals with selfishness is to send you someone more selfish than you to take care of."—STEVE FARRAR

SELFISHNESS IS A CHARACTER quality that's discouraged and reviled everywhere, with selfish persons being either unwelcome or even shown the door in most work groups. And the reason isn't far-fetched: selfishness—the social equivalent of a physical spanner thrown into the works—undercuts the work and spirit of teams, groups, and organizations. I often half-jokingly say that difficult bosses and babies are probably the most selfish persons one can ever meet, which is why I paraphrase Steve Farrar's quote above as "One of the ways God deals with selfishness is to send you someone [a baby or difficult boss] more selfish than you!" In this light, one can even say that difficult bosses may just have some positive developmental value in the lives of subordinates! On a more serious note, I have learned plenty of lessons from books, conferences, and the personal examples of the many superb leaders I have come in contact with, but the most enduring lessons I have learned have come from interacting with "difficult" bosses. It seems like the lessons learned from working with the latter tend to be "stickier" and more memorable—as if difficult bosses played some special role in my development as a leader!

Another reason for my zeroing in on difficult bosses is that, while 'managing your boss' (the subject of the last chapter) is par for the course for anyone who wants to taste career success, managing a difficult boss is necessary to avoid career derailment. The one protects from the 'low' of career failure, while the other is a prerequisite for reaching the 'high' of career success. One is a drag or 'pull', while the other is a filip or "push." The writer of Second Samuel, in his account of David's preparation for leadership, reveals both the developmental value of difficult leaders and their ability to derail the careers of subordinates, saying,

> "Then all the tribes of Israel went to David at Hebron and told him, "We are all members of your family. For a long time, even while Saul was our king, you were the one who really led Israel. And the LORD has told you, `You will be the shepherd of my people Israel. You will be their leader.'"" (2Sam 5:1-2, NLT)

David Goes to School!

" . . . *even while Saul was king, you* [David] *were the one who really led Israel.*" Everyone knows the story of David—a man anointed to be king of Israel around the tender age of seventeen. Now, since seventeen-year olds don't ordinarily have the skills to lead kingdoms, it was necessary that David go to school. The school for leaders wasn't a classroom or conference—although those things are good—it was a job working for a very difficult boss called King Saul. Therefore, we can say that, in the economy of God . . .

Working with a Difficult Boss Can be a Good Way to Learn Leadership!

"For a long time, *even when Saul was our king* . . . " King Saul was the quintessential difficult boss—insecure and intensely jealous; he simply couldn't stand it when, on returning from the battlefield, the young women sang "Saul has killed his thousands, and David, his ten thousands." Saul was also moody, physically abusive, and murderous—making multiple attempts on David's life. Yet we see that it was in that cauldron that David learned to lead! Some of the lessons David learned are that . . .

Section 1 | Managing 'Up'

You Don't Have to be Boss to Provide Leadership (Leadership is Influence)

" . . . even when Saul was our king, *you were the one who really led Israel.*" There it is in black and white: although Saul was king and top dog, there was still enough wiggle room for subordinate David to provide leadership to the people. Why? Because leadership isn't all about position. It's majorly about influence, and any smart conscientious person can influence others. In theory, almost everyone knows this; but it takes working for a difficult boss to actually develop the skills to put it into effect.

Effective Subordinates Can Work with Difficult Bosses and Still Make a Mark

There are no perfect bosses anywhere, and effective leaders exercise influence in spite of working for bad bosses. Saul, David's boss, was an impulsive and physically abusive man, yet David made his mark in Israel—with the people acknowledging his leadership and influence. Working for a difficult boss is bad enough, but it shouldn't stop you from making your mark. The question becomes: how exactly was David able to make his mark while serving Saul? And the answer is . . .

Effective Subordinates Strive to Work from their Areas of Strength

> "In the past, while Saul was king over us, *you were the one who led Israel on their military campaigns . . .* " (Emphasis mine) (2Sam. 5:1–2, NIV)

David provided leadership in just a single sphere of service—military campaigns. That sphere of service happened also to be his area of natural strength. The moral of all this is that you'll find it easier to manage a difficult boss if you 'stick to the knitting', if you go as much as possible with your strengths, and if your strengths complement your boss's weaknesses.

4 TYPES OF DIFFICULT BOSSES

Although working with a difficult boss can be a good school to learn leadership, as anyone who has had to cope with one knows, it's also very enervating. And the reason isn't farfetched—there are different types of difficult bosses, so much so that, what you learn dealing with one is often inapplicable to others. It does seem like Leo Tolstoy's now-famous words in his novel *Anna Karenina* "All happy families are alike; each unhappy family is unhappy in its own way," apply to difficult bosses! While all 'good' bosses are seemingly alike, the 'difficult' ones tend to be difficult in many annoyingly different ways! Since the term "boss" is synonymous with authority; and since authority is itself synonymous with what a person does with power—with staying within the limits and boundaries of acceptable behavior—there are (drawing heavily from the work of Katherine Crowley and Kathi Elster) four broad types of difficult bosses; the ones who cross all the lines, those who don't let you cross any line, those who let you cross all the lines, and those who simply sit on the lines! The first type are the control freaks, the second are insecure, the third are ambivalent (shying from confrontation of any kind), and the fourth are checked out—unconcerned about anyone but themselves. Notice carefully that I am defining a difficult boss strictly in terms involving the use of the legitimate power she has over her subordinates.

The Insecure Boss (You Aren't Allowed to Cross Any Line!)

Because this boss is basically insecure, her power is a tool to cut everyone down to size. She doesn't let anyone "cross any line." She uses her power to cut down talented subordinates, and pooh-pooh their suggestions and projects—all because she actively seeks to be the "only star in the firmament." Like I said before, King Saul is the quintessential insecure leader, and the writer of First Samuel tells his depressing leadership story, saying,

> "But something happened when the victorious Israelite army was returning home after David had killed Goliath. Women came out from all the towns along the way to celebrate and to cheer for King Saul, and they sang and danced for joy with tambourines and cymbals. This was their song: "Saul has killed his thousands, and David his ten thousands!" This made Saul very angry. "What's this?" he said. "They credit David with ten thousands and me with only thousands. Next they'll be making him their king!" So from that time on Saul kept a jealous eye on David." (1Sam 18:6–9, NLT)

Section 1 | Managing 'Up'

The Insecure Boss is a Highly Competitive Individual Who Can't Stand Being Outshined

"*Saul has killed his thousands, and David his ten thousands!" This made Saul very angry.*" Notice what made Saul very angry—it was the supposedly greater acclaim in which subordinate David was held. Insecure bosses can't stand, or even share the spotlight with, capable associates. Why? Because, they, like Saul, see every capable associate as a competitor for their own position ("What's this?" he [Saul] said. "They credit David with ten thousands and me with only thousands. Next they'll be making him their king!"). These bosses like being held in the highest esteem by others (and I deliberately use the term "highest," because they are often highly competitive individuals). They can't stand anyone being more renowned than them, and often become verbally, emotionally, or even physically abusive if indeed a subordinate is held in esteem by others. In their insecurity, they set their subordinates up for a fall by giving them impossible tasks. In fact, Saul, in the vain hope that David would be killed in battle, gave the latter the seemingly impossible task of getting the foreskins of a hundred Philistine soldiers!

The Control Freak (She Crosses All the Lines!)

Control freaks, as the term implies, cross all the lines—not knowing or respecting the conventional interpersonal boundaries—and intrude into the lives and conducts of subordinates. Nothing is too small to escape the eye, ear, or hand of this kind of boss. The words of Katherine Crowley and Kathi Elster, in their excellent book, *Working for You Isn't Working for Me*, best illustrate the mindset of these leaders,

> "In order to feel in control, this kind of boss needs to know everything that is going on at all times. Because they don't like looking bad or being caught off guard, Control Freaks take every precaution to make sure that they are informed and aware of all activities under their domain. A Control Freak boss will want to know the status of every project at all times. He or she wants to approve every decision. The worst thing you can do to these authority figures is surprise them."

Unbeknown to many, Job—the same Job who suffered the hellish loss of all his possessions—is the archetypal control freak. The writer of Job begins his narrative of Job's unsavory leadership, saying,

> "His [Job's] sons used to take turns holding feasts in their homes, and they would invite their three sisters to eat and drink with them." (Job 1:4, NIV)

These words reveal a little appreciated fact . . .

Job's Sons Were Grown Independent Men!

"*His* [Job's] *sons used to take turns holding feasts in their homes.*" There it s in black and white: everyone of Job's seven sons had his own home! In other words, Job's sons were grown independent men. The writer of Job continues his narrative, saying,

> "When these celebrations ended—and sometimes they lasted several days—Job would purify his children. He would get up early in the morning and offer a burnt offering for each of them. For Job said to himself, "Perhaps my children have sinned and have cursed God in their hearts." This was Job's regular practice." (Job 1:5, NLT)

These amazing words show that, although Job's sons were grown independent men with their own households, Job still controlled them. How do I mean?

Controlling Leadership Crosses the Line—Seeking to Manage a Subordinate's Relationship with Third Parties

"[Job] would get up early in the morning and offer a burnt offering for each of them. For Job said to himself, "*Perhaps my children have sinned and have cursed God in their hearts." This was Job's regular practice.*" Although his sons were grown independent men, Job felt that they were unable to maintain healthy relationships with third parties (in this case, God). So what did Job do? He continuously monitored his sons and continually called them for sanctification rituals. In effect, Job was micromanaging his grown sons—never letting them operate independently and treating them like children!

Section 1 | Managing 'Up'

Controlling Leadership Crosses the Line—Seeking to Determine and Define What Subordinates Think

"Perhaps my children have sinned and cursed God in their hearts." When it comes to controlling behavior, Job gets the silver cup! Imagine, he was all worked up over the unspoken and unarticulated thoughts of grown men! Controlling leaders love to tell their people what to think—not merely how to think. Since thinking is the foundation of action, when you're overly concerned about someone's thoughts, you're one short stop away from concern for their actions. Simply put, controlling leaders want to be in the know about your every thought, plan or action. These words of the writer of Job show that management teacher Stephen Covey was spot on when he said "If our paradigm is one of control, we assume that people have to be tightly supervised if they're going to produce or perform well." Job's paradigm was one of control, so he tightly supervised ("snoopervised?") and micromanaged his sons. Underlying all his micromanagement was this thought: my sons are still children and immature.

The Ambivalent Boss (She Lets You Cross All the Lines!)

Ambivalent bosses prefer to let sleeping dogs lie, and studiously avoid conflict and confrontation. Bad behavior often blossoms unchecked under these spineless leaders. Again, Katherine Crowley and Kathi Elster put it beautifully, saying,

> "Ambivalent leaders don't like getting their hands dirty. They may like the status of managing people, but they do not want to handle any interpersonal difficulties between their employees. Ambivalent leaders are skilled avoiders of confrontation, disagreement, argument, and other forms of conflict."

David, Israel's most famous king, is the poster boy for ambivalent bosses. David always shied from the difficult work of confronting wrongdoing among his sons or close associates—preferring to let the matter slide, to kick the can down the road or, even worse, to pray that God punish the wrongdoer! The writer of Second Samuel, while narrating the events that occurred when Joab (David's army chief) murdered his Israelite rival Abner, reveals this dark side of King David, saying,

"When Abner arrived at Hebron, Joab took him aside at the gateway as if to speak with him privately. But then he drew his dagger and killed Abner in revenge for killing his brother Asahel. When David heard about it, he declared, "I vow by the LORD that I and my people are innocent of this crime against Abner. Joab and his family are the guilty ones. May his family in every generation be cursed with a man who has open sores or leprosy or who walks on crutches or who dies by the sword or who begs for food!" . . . Then King David said to the people, "Do you not realize that a great leader and a great man has fallen today in Israel? And even though I am the anointed king, these two sons of Zeruiah—Joab and Abishai—are too strong for me to control. So may the LORD repay these wicked men for their wicked deeds." " (2Sam 3:27-39, NLT)

Imagine! An innocent man—who also happened to be his guest—was murdered by his subordinates. Yet, all King David could say were the following mealy-mouthed words " . . . And even though I am the anointed king, these two sons of Zeruiah—Joab and Abishai—are too strong for me to control. *So may the LORD repay these wicked men for their wicked deeds.*" In effect, because the lily-livered king couldn't confront his subordinates, he shifted the responsibility to punish them to God! Although David was a giant-killer who courageously confronted and killed Goliath, he was weak-kneed when it came to drawing the line in the sand and confronting wrongdoing among his close associates (call to mind his unwillingness to confront his son Absalom after the latter murdered his half-brother Amnon).

The Checked Out Boss (She Prefers to Sit on the Lines!)

Although selfishness—in the form of the abuse or misuse of power—colors the performance of all difficult bosses, this behavior comes to a head with the Checked Out boss. The latter is only passively concerned with the overall interests of her organization—while actively putting her own interests first. Indeed, it is this crass unwillingness to use their powers to further the legitimate interests of the groups they head, and their willingness to put their own interests right, front and center, that hallmark Checked Out bosses. The latter always blow hot and cold—'hot' for their own personal interests, and 'cold' for the interests of their groups (and group members) which they neglect. Again, Katherine Crowley and Kathi Elster put it beautifully, saying, "Checked out bosses are preoccupied with non-work related personal matters . . . He or she is not capable of managing you or anyone else effectively." Solomon, Israel's wisest king, is the poster boy for the Checked Out boss. His discouraging story is narrated by the writer of Second Chronicles,

> "And it came to pass at the end of twenty years, wherein Solomon had built the house of the Lord, and his own house; That the cities which Huram had restored to Solomon, Solomon built them and caused the children of Israel to dwell there." (2Chr 8:1–2, NKJV)

Solomon the Selfish!

" . . . at the end of twenty years . . . " Only after twenty years did Solomon deem it fit to begin building dwelling cities for the ordinary citizen of Israel! He spent seven years building the temple (1 Kings 7:1) and, wait for it, thirteen years building his own house. For twenty years Solomon did little about the welfare of the people—-the remote cause of the future break up of the kingdom. Clearly, Solomon's leadership was at best selfish, and at worst, lousy. As if this wasn't bad enough, as I read Paul Kennedy's excellent book, *The Rise and Fall of the Great Powers*, I came across a section where Dr. Kennedy spoke about how the influx of silver from Spain's American colonies produced a debasement of silver currency in Spain itself

> "The flow of American silver [silver from Spanish colonies in the Americas] was bound to cause economic problems (especially price inflation) which no society of the time had the experience to handle . . . "

These words not only drove home the point that an overabundance of silver in an economy that uses that metal as its currency can produce a dangerous hyperinflation, they also called to mind the damaging effects of King Solomon's stupendous personal wealth on Israel's economy. Listen to the writer of First Kings,

> "King Solomon made silver as common in Jerusalem as stones . . . " (1 Kgs 10:27, NKJV)

Managing a Difficult Boss

Solomon's Stupendous Wealth—Poorly Managed—Produces Hyperinflation in Israel!

"*King Solomon made silver as common as stones . . .* " As everyone knows, stones, because they are in such plentiful supply, are essentially worthless. Because Solomon's stupendous wealth made silver as abundant as stones in Israel, that metal became essentially worthless. The problem with this is that, like the influx of silver from the Americas which debased Imperial Spain's currency, Solomon's wealth also produced hyperinflation. What was probably good for Solomon—being stupendously wealthy and having plenty of silver—must have been terrible for the ordinary people of Jerusalem. How do I mean? You see, silver coins were the currency of Israel (remember that Jesus was sold for 30 pieces of silver) and, by making silver as common as stones, Solomon was actually debasing the currency in peoples' pockets. In modern day terms, we would say Solomon's economic policies (his poorly managed wealth) caused hyperinflation—plenty of money chasing few goods, leading to high prices. This harsh economic climate was what led the people to say that the rule of Solomon didn't benefit them and to insist that Rehoboam, Solomon's son and successor, give them some relief. *The key thing in all this is not that Solomon was wealthy, but that he—the quintessential Checked Out boss—didn't even bother to use his power as manager of the economy to mitigate the negative effects of his wealth.*

Having seen the four broad types of difficult bosses, the question becomes "How exactly do I manage a difficult boss?" The answer begins with putting into practice the words of the writer of Proverbs,

> "By long forbearance a ruler is persuaded, and a gentle tongue breaks a bone." (Prov 25:15, NKJV)

Managing a Difficult Boss Requires Lots of Forbearance

"*By long forbearance a ruler [boss] is persuaded* [influenced] . . . " Did you notice that it is not just forbearance, but *long* forbearance that gives a subordinate the power to persuade or influence her boss? Most subordinates think that influencing uplines begins with 'smarts'—with showing the boss just how good at the job they are—but these words of the writer of Proverbs take a hammer to that kind of thinking. They show that it is "long forbearance" that's the first rung on the ladder to influencing a boss. Merriam

Section 1 | Managing 'Up'

Webster dictionary defines forbearance as " the quality of someone who is patient and able to deal with a difficult person or situation without becoming angry." In other words, by using the term 'forbearance', the writer of Proverbs is really talking about managing a *difficult* boss! Interestingly, the writer of Romans, in his treatment of the great theological themes of forgiveness and repentance, sheds more light on the word 'forbearance', saying,

> "Whom God set forth as a propitiation by His blood, through faith, to demonstrate His righteousness because in his forbearance, God had passed over the sins previously committed." (Rom 3:25, NKJV)

His words drive home the point . . .

To Forbear is to Overlook a Person's Faults and Failings

" . . . *because in his forebearance, God had passed over [overlooked, covered] the sins that were previously committed.*" There it is in black and white: to forbear is to overlook the faults of another without getting all worked up, critical, or angry. Effective subordinates—the ones who end up hugely influencing difficult uplines—are those who are best able to do a tough thing; overlook the failings of their bosses. Forbearance consists of two deeply interwoven actions—acceptance, and adjustment.

- Acceptance: this certainly isn't the same thing as condoning or approving the boss's failings. It is simply taking a realistic view of the whole situation. Writers Katherine Crowley and Kathi Elster put it beautifully, saying "Acceptance (as we are using it) is not approval. Acceptance is the recognition of reality—the sobering truth about the person whom you call boss." In essence, acceptance is coming to grips with the real situation of things.

- Adjustment: this is the consequence of acceptance, and involves steps you take to make up for the boss's deficiencies. Again, Katherine Crowley and Kathi Elster drive the point home, saying

  > "Accepting that the boss behaves a certain way is not approving of, agreeing with, or condoning the behavior. Acceptance allows you to take the person at face value and not get emotionally charged by his or her actions. If, for example, your boss is habitually late,

and you can accept this fact, you'll find ways to deal with it. But if you resist reality, if you insist that the boss should not be tardy and demand better time management from this person, you'll become increasingly frustrated and angry."

Managing a difficult boss can be a pretty enervating experience—draining your energy and dominating your life. But by applying the principle of forbearance, you can take control of the situation and literally take your life back.

Acceptance and Adjustment Transform Managing a Difficult Boss into a Prime Leadership Development Experience

Acceptance and adjustment—the tools for managing a difficult boss—require great patience and skill. Since, patience is the fruit of mature character and skill, the result of competence, it comes as no surprise that people who successfully manage a difficult boss often move up one notch in their development as leaders.

Wrap Around

Because difficult bosses are par for the course when you manage 'up', knowing the different types of difficult bosses (and knowing how to manage them) is one way to avoid career derailment. But, and this is crucial, difficult bosses also have some developmental value—helping you develop patience and skill at managing people, and helping you see that you can still exert some influence even when you're not the boss.

Chapter 5

Managing Career Transitions (1)

IF A TRANSITION IS a change from one phase to another, then a career transition can be defined as a change in work roles. Since jobs are the building blocks of careers, a change in work roles often shows up as a change in jobs—as a movement from one job (or type of job) to another. For those in organizations, career transitions can be *vertical*—movement up or down the hierarchy—as in promotion or demotion. Paradoxically, experiencing no movement at all may also signal a career transition—as in stagnation and being passed over for promotion. The second type of transition is majorly about *centrality*—movement toward, or away from the small core of persons who actually run the group—signalling inclusion, exclusion or membership. *Horizontal* or lateral movements are hallmarks of the third type of career transition. These are shifts to jobs at the same level of responsibility within the hierarchy, but within other specialties or functions. But, we are not done yet. A change in boss often signals the fourth type of career transition. Why? Because a new boss can significantly redefine your work role and change the context within which you operate. Job loss and retirement are the fifth type of transition. They are probably the most stressful career transitions because they involve movement out of the groups, organizations, or even professions to which a person belongs. Crucially also, since the first four types of transition involve movement to new work roles, they are all essentially about starting new jobs—a thing heavily tinged with risk and uncertainty. Indeed, as we shall see, it is because promotions—the most

Managing Career Transitions (1)

coveted career transition—involve the heightened risk and uncertainty associated with new work roles, that they are often harbingers of failure!

Managing career transitions is mission-critical to career success, not only because everyone will sooner or later face one type of transition or the other, but also because most career meltdowns tend to occur at, or around, the time a person is experiencing a career transition. Indeed, a career transition is where the proverbial rubber meets the road—the point in time where you may have to simultaneously manage up, manage across, manage down and manage yourself. And all of that happens as you face the extreme pressure and uncertainty that are par for the course during transitions. For this reason, and because the subject material is so broad, I have decided to dedicate all of three chapters—this, and the following two—to managing career transitions.

WILDERNESS: WHAT TO DO WHEN YOU FALL OUT OF FAVOR OR DON'T GET THE PROMOTION YOU THINK YOU DESERVE

"Here I am, after almost thirty years in the House of Commons, after holding many of the highest offices of state. Here I am, discarded, cast away, marooned, rejected and disliked." — WINSTON CHURCHILL (speaking to an acquaintance)

Although promotions are out and out the most coveted of all career transitions, they certainly are not the most frequently encountered type of transition. That prize goes to what I refer to as "the wilderness experience"—being passed over for promotion, or being excluded from the inner circle of persons who run the show. Indeed, because being passed over for promotion or being excluded from the inner circle that runs the show are really only forms of demotion, 'managing the wilderness' is akin to managing demotion. The career of former British Prime Minister Winston Churchill during the period 1932 to 1940—when he was rejected, out of favor, and looked a complete failure—provides probably the clearest example of a wilderness experience. Historian William Manchester in, *The Last Lion: Winston Spencer Churchill,* his excellent biography of Winston Churchill, quotes the despondent Prime Minister as telling an acquaintance "Here I am, after almost thirty years in the House of Commons, after holding many of the highest offices of state. Here I am, discarded, cast away,

Section 1 | Managing 'Up'

marooned, rejected and disliked." Yet on June 4, 1940, Churchill literally came back from the dead; becoming prime minister and eventual hero of World War 2. How did this out-of-favor politician survive the wilderness? More to the point, how can leaders today survive the "wilderness"—those periods in their careers when they or their offerings are rejected or not well received by others? I believe we can find some answers to those questions by studying the life of an unnamed queen of the Babylonian empire whose story is chronicled in the book of Daniel. The writer of Daniel begins his narrative of that remarkable woman's travails by saying,

> "Belshazzar the king made a great feast for a thousand of his lords, and drank wine in the presence of the thousand. While he tasted the wine, Belshazzar gave the command to bring the gold and silver vessels which his father Nebuchadnezzar had taken from the temple . . . in Jerusalem, that the king and his lords, his wives, and his concubines might drink from them . . . " (Dan 5:1–3, NKJV)

A King Throws a Party!

By throwing a party with a guest list of over a thousand well-connected persons, Belshazzar was having a ball fit for a king. No surprise at that because Belshazzar was not only a king, he was also a descendant of the famous Babylonian king, Nebuchadnezzar. Now everyone knows that oriental kings, who are free to do as they please, can also party! But the strange thing about this party is that,

A King Throws a Party and Doesn't Even Invite His Own Queen!

"Belshazzar . . . made a great feast for a thousand of his lords . . . [and] his wives, and his concubines . . . " A cursory look at the guest list shows that invitees came from two broad groups—work associates (numbering a thousand lords or noblemen), and members of his harem (numerous wives and concubines). But, a closer look at the second group—guests who were members of the king's harem—reveals an alarming fact; the king did not invite his queen! For some reason, Belshazzar overlooked his queen when he was drawing up his guest list. My guess is that she was out of favor and in the political wilderness! The writer of Daniel confirms this line of thinking, saying,

MANAGING CAREER TRANSITIONS (1)

> "They drank wine, and praised the gods of gold and silver, bronze and iron, wood and stone. In the same hour the fingers of a man's hand appeared and wrote opposite the lampstand on the plaster of the wall of the king's palace; and the king saw the part of the hand that wrote. Then the king's countenance changed, and his thoughts troubled him, so that the joints of his hips were loosened and his knees knocked against each other." (Dan 5:4-6, NKJV)

The Handwriting on the Wall!

As the king and his guests partied, a mysterious hand proceeded to write an encrypted message on the wall. A flummoxed king hurriedly called his counselors to read the handwriting on the wall, but the latter were unable to decipher the writing. In the ensuing commotion, enter the queen. Listen again to the writer of Daniel,

> "The queen, because of the words of the king and his lords, came to the banquet hall. The queen spoke, saying, "O king, live forever! Do not let your thoughts trouble you, nor let your countenance change. There is a man in your kingdom in whom is the Spirit of the Holy God. And in the days of your father, light and understanding and wisdom . . . were found in him; and King Nebuchadnezzar your father—your father the king—made him chief of the magicians, astrologers, Chaldeans, and soothsayers. Inasmuch as an excellent spirit, knowledge, understanding, interpreting dreams, solving riddles, and explaining enigmas were found in this Daniel, whom the king named Belteshazzar, now let Daniel be called, and he will give the interpretation."" (Dan 5:10-12, NKJV)

In effect, these words mean that,

An Out-of-Favor "Employee" Provided the Solution to Her Organization's Problem

By saying *"The queen, because of the words of the king and his lords, came into the banquet hall,"* the writer of Daniel helps us see that the queen—an ostensibly influential member of the king's household—was not invited to the party! But by going on to say " . . . *The queen spoke, saying, "There is a man [Daniel] in your kingdom . . . now let Daniel be called,"* he shows us that, although she was probably out of favor and was not even invited to a meeting of the top leaders in her own organization, this amazing woman still provided the solution to her organization's problem. What lessons can people who face the "wilderness" draw from the behavior of this remarkable woman? I believe we can draw the following lessons . . . When you go through the wilderness . . .

Don't Hold Any Grudges (Stay Emotionally Fit)

Being passed over for a promotion or being left out of the loop can be hugely demoralizing, and can even make one bitter and resentful. Notwithstanding, here we see a queen who had suffered this very public slight, come hastily into the banquet hall to help the same organization which had so publicly slighted her. When passed over for a promotion or when excluded from the inner circle, work very hard to manage your emotions and avoid any kind of bitterness and resentment. Not bearing any grudges means that you are still willing to be of service to the people who rejected you.

Keep Growing and Learning (Stay Professionally Fit)

Because she had the answers, this out-of-favor queen was able to provide a solution to her leader, the king. But, and this is crucial, to have the answer, she first needed to possess a firm grasp of the history and performance of her organization. The temptation facing out-of-favor persons is to wallow in self pity, to sulk in silent resignation, to throw up their hands in despair, and to stop growing and learning. If you give in to this temptation, you will ultimately slide into irrelevance.

Putting it Into Practice

In 1985 Steve Jobs was kicked out of Apple—the company he co-founded—and found himself in the wilderness. How did he handle his time "out of favor'? Management writer Jim Collins, in his co-authored book, *Great By Choice*, said that,

> "The same point holds for Steve Jobs . . . *When banished to the high-tech wilderness* in 1985 after being ousted from his own company, Jobs never stopped developing, growing, learning, pushing himself. He could have taken his fortune and retired to a life of ease and

comfortable irrelevance. *Instead... In the 12 years away from Apple, Jobs turned himself from a creative entrepreneur into a disciplined, creative company builder."* (Emphases mine)

This illuminating passage drives home the point: "managing the wilderness" depends on the maintainance of emotional and professional fitness. If you are out of favor in any way, see it as a period of introspection and growth that can lead to an improvement in your person and performance. Your time will come because seasons change!

In the final analysis, the wilderness—the season when a person is misunderstood, rejected, or out of favor—is a time of testing. It tests your emotional maturity and your ability to keep growing and learning. But leaders who, like the Babylonian queen, work on themselves in the wilderness, can expect to come out better able to add value to others. The wilderness is really only an ivy league university! Having dealt with the most frequent type of career transition, we can now turn our sights to the most coveted type—promotion...

High-Risk Vs Low-Risk Promotions (2 Kinds of Promotion)

Like I pointed out before, because promotion can involve a change in work roles, and because where there's change, there you also find uncertainty, some promotions are risky. I mean, who hasn't heard of the excellent factory-hand who got promoted to shop-floor manager and flopped. But the question in all this is; why are some promotions risky, and others less risky? As I reviewed Peter Drucker's excellent book, *Management: Tasks, Responsibilities And Practices*, I came to better understand why some promotions are risky, and others less risky. In that book, Professor Drucker said that,

> "Promoting any high-performing operating person to a staff job where they no longer apply the day-to-day skills that helped make them become a success is... a high-risk decision. And so is promoting a high-performing staff person into an operating job."

His words mean that...

Section 1 | Managing 'Up'

*There are Two Broad Kinds of Promotions—
High-risk Promotions and Low-risk Promotions*

" . . . *promoting any high-performing operating person to a staff job . . . is a high-risk decision* [promotion]." The import of those words is clear: some promotions ("high-risk" promotions) are inherently riskier than others ("low-risk" promotions). Crucially, those words also help us see that low-risk promotions occur whenever a person is promoted to a job that is significantly similar to her last one (e.g., staff job to staff job, or operating job to operating job). In contrast, high-risk promotions occur whenever a worker is promoted to a job that is significantly different from his last one (e.g., staff job to operating job, or vice versa). The increased risk of failure associated with high-risk promotions stems from the fact that the day-to-day skills which helped the worker succeed at a 'lower' job are of little value in the 'higher' job. Therefore, if the newly promoted individual does not, or cannot, quickly learn the requisite skills needed to do her new job, she is bound to fail. Imagine my surprise when I saw these principles writ large in Jesus' teaching on the Parable of the Unjust Steward . . .

> 'Whoever can be trusted with very little can also be trusted with much, and whoever is dishonest with very little will also be dishonest with much. So if you have not been trustworthy in handling worldly wealth, who will trust you with true riches?" (Luke 16:10–11, NIV)

The "little-much" principle that Jesus elucidates in this parable has been the bedrock of promotion for a long time, and rightly so. If a person is faithful in performing her duties at a lower-level job, she should be promoted to a higher level one. The assumption being that, success at *any* lower-level job qualifies a person for promotion to higher-level work. But a closer look at Jesus' words reveals a more nuanced truth . . .

Success at a Lower-level Position is the Prerequisite for Promotion to a Similar Higher-level Job (Low-risk Promotions)

By saying "if you have not been trustworthy in handling *worldly wealth*, who will trust you with *true riches*?" Jesus is actually talking about two different jobs with roughly similar contents and functions—wealth or resource management. That is, the lower-level ("little") position, and the higher-level ("much") position are both concerned with wealth management. For example, a person who profitably manages $20 can be safely promoted to manage $100. Why? Because the difference between old job and new job is in degree, not in kind. And, this is crucial, the skills that make for success with the "$20 budget job" are readily applicable to the "$100 budget job"—making the promotion a low-risk one. In other words, when it comes to low-risk promotions, the skills needed to succeed at the "higher" job are developed and tested on the "lower" one. By division, this means that . . .

High-Risk Promotions are those Promotions Which Move a Person from a Low-level Job to a Different Kind of High-level Job

This is the corollary of Jesus' teaching in the Parable of the Unjust Steward. People who succeed at lower level jobs will be less likely to succeed at higher level jobs if the latter are significantly different from the ones they were originally engaged in. Why? Because the skills needed to excel at the one are different from those needed to excel at the other. In other words, promotions are high-risk whenever the lower-level job a person worked at doesn't prepare her for the higher-level one to which she has been promoted!

Putting it Into Practice

The tragic story of Gedeliah the son of Ahikam, an accomplished secretary and midlevel administrator, who Nebuchadnezzar king of Babylon made governor of Judah, drives the point about low-risk and high-risk promotions home. The writer of Jeremiah begins his narrative of the misfortune that befell Gedeliah, saying,

> "When all the army officers and their men . . . heard that the king of Babylon had appointed Gedeliah . . . as governor over the land . . . they came to Gedeliah at Mizpah . . . Gedeliah . . . took an oath to reassure them and their men. "Do not be afraid to serve the Babylonians," he said, "Settle down in the land and serve the king of the Babylon and it will go well with you." (Jer 40:7–9, NIV)

A Midlevel Administrator is Appointed to High Political Office

After a bruising siege of Jerusalem, the rampaging Babylonian army captured the king of Judah, executed many of Israel's leaders, burnt down the city of Jerusalem, and destroyed its wall. Nebuchadnezzar king of Babylon then proceeded to appoint a pliant Gedeliah—hitherto a midlevel secretary—to the high office of governor of Judah! The plot thickens as the writer of Jeremiah continues his narrative, saying,

> "Jonathan son of Kareah and all the army officers still in the open country came to Gedeliah at Mizpah and said to him, "Don't you know that Baalis king of the Ammonites has sent Ishmael son of Nathaniah to take your life?" But Gedeliah didnot believe them. Then Jonathan . . . said privately to Gedeliah . . . "Let me go and kill Ishmael . . . and no one will know it. Why should he take your life and cause all the Jews who are gathered around you to be scattered and the remnant of Judah to perish?" But Gedeliah . . . said to Johanan . . . " Don't do such a thing! What you are saying is not true." (Jer 40:13-16, NIV)

A Newly-Appointed Governor is in Over His Head!

"*Don't you know* that Baalis king of the Ammonites has sent Ismael . . . to kill you?" There it is in black and white: Governor Gedeliah should have known all about Israel's tenuous relationship with an enemy foreign power like the Ammonites who, to destabilize Israel, had sent an assassin named Ishmael to kill him. In erffect, a prerequisite for success in the office of governor was the mastery of politics and international relations. But Governor Gedeliah, because of his background as a midlevel administrator, was out of his depth when it came to high-wire politics and diplomacy. That deficiency was to cost him his life. Listen again to the writer of Jeremiah,

> "In the seventh month Ishmael son of Nethaniah . . . who was of royal blood and had been one of the king's officers, came with ten men to Gedaliah . . . at Mizpah. While they were eating together there, Ishmael son of Nethaniah and the ten men who were with him got up and struck down Gedaliah . . . with the sword, killing the one whom the king of Babylon had appointed as governor over the land. Ishmael also killed all the Jews who were with Gedaliah at Mizpah, as well as the Babylonian soldiers who were there." (Jer 41:1-3, NIV)

Managing Career Transitions (1)

A Newly-Appointed Governor is Murdered!

Ishmael son of Nethaniah and the ten men who were with him got up and struck down Gedaliah . . . " There it is in black and white: Governor Gedaliah was assassinated by Ishmael—the very man he had been warned about! Because he didn't have a firm grasp of international relations, and because he possessed almost no insight into his country's local politics, Governor Gedaliah was murdered in cold blood. His inability to manage his promotion meant that many of the people he led were later brutalized, killed, and scattered by a vengeful Babylonian army. But, and this is crucial, the root cause of this tragedy is all too familiar. It was because . . .

Gedeliah's Promotion was a High-Risk Promotion

Gedeliah's promotion to governor was a high-risk one because his previous job as a midlevel administrator didn't prepare him for the demands of the office of governor. To further complicate matters, Gedeliah's refusal to learn on the job—as signified by his refusal to accept and act on confidential intelligence from his army commanders—sealed his fate. This tragic story is a pointer to the pitfalls of high-risk promotions. While a failure to manage your promotion may not lead to anyone's death, it certainly can lead to embarrassment, disappointment, and the waste of organizational resources. Which is why, in the next part of this chapter, I take a deep dive into what exactly newly promoted leaders must learn if they want to succeed . . .

NOW YOU'VE LANDED YOUR DREAM JOB! (MANAGING HIGH-RISK PROMOTIONS)

"Instead of facing an oft-termed honeymoon period . . . a new CEO faces relative vulnerability. This early lack of power is reflected in the disproportionate number of CEOs whose tenures last 3 years or less."—Donald Hambrick and Gregory Fukutomi

If stepping into any kind of new job isn't easy, then stepping into the shoes of senior leader in an organization must be extremely difficult. Management researchers Donald Hambrick and Greg Fukutomi, in their Academy of Management Review article, *The Seasons of a CEO's Tenure*, shine a light on the hidden 'banana peel' in the path of newly promoted leaders, saying "A new executive, even one internally appointed, enters the position at a disadvantage in terms of knowledge of the task at hand; pertinent facts, contacts, trends, and issues are not yet well understood." These sobering words highlight an under-appreciated fact: regardless of all the 'champagne popping' and celebration, leaders who step into new positions do so at a disadvantage! The writer of Second Chronicles, in his narrative of the challenges faced by a newly appointed King Rehoboam—who succeeded his famous father Solomon and immediately faced a stern leadership test—helps us see exactly what factors put new managers at a disadvantage, saying,

> "Then [when Rehoboam had just become king] worthless rogues gathered to him, and strengthened themselves against Rehoboam the son of Solomon, when Rehoboam was young and inexperienced and could not withstand them." (2Chr 13:7, NKJV)

These eye-opening words show that,

Rehoboam's Newness to the Job Made him Vulnerable!

The story is the stuff of many a Sunday School teaching. Young king Rehoboam, on stepping into the shoes of his father Solomon, immediately faces an existential challenge from an entrenched opposition. The latter demand that the new king immediately undo the harsh tax regimen instituted by his father Solomon, failing which, they would break up the kingdom. Predictably, an inexperienced Rehoboam failed this test, and the rebels broke away—forming an independent kingdom in northern Israel. By saying *"Then* [when Rehoboam was new to the job] *worthless rogues ... strengthened themselves against him ... when* [he] *was young and inexperienced, "* the writer of Second Chronicles hits the nail on the head, helping us see that Rehoboam was overwhelmed chiefly because of his inexperience—confirming the words of Hambrick and Fukutomi "A new executive ... enters the position at a disadvantage ... "

The question becomes: why are newly promoted leaders at such a disadvantage? As I read management teacher Henry Mintzberg's excellent book, *The Nature of Managerial Work*, I stumbled on the following words,

> "The manager is the nerve center of his organization, with unique access to a wide variety of internal and external contacts that provide privileged information. But most of this

information is not documented, and much of it is unsubstantiated and non-quantitative."

If a leader is *"the nerve center of his organization, with unique access to a wide variety of internal and external contacts that provide privileged information,"* then it's no surprise that newly appointed leaders are at a great disadvantage. And here's why; it's because newly appointed leaders haven't had the time to develop the relationships and cultivate the contacts that can grant them access to privileged information. The writer of First Kings, in his narrative of king Rehoboam's troubles, brings this truth home powerfully, saying,

> "Rehoboam went to Shechem, for all Israel had gone there to make him king . . . "Your father put a heavy yoke on us, but now lighten the harsh labor and the heavy yoke he put on us, and we will serve you." Rehoboam answered, "Go away for three days and then come back to me." So the people went away . . . " (1Kgs 12:1–5, NKJV)

A Newly Appointed Leader Lacks the Information Needed to Make a Crucial Decision!

"Rehoboam answered, *"Go away for three days and then come back to me."* Those words say it all. When confronted with the question of easing the harsh economic policies of his predecessor Solomon, Israel's brand new leader didn't have the information needed to make that weighty decision—a major change in economic policy—at his finger tips. The new king did what most leaders in his shoes would have done—ask for time to think and consult. Rehoboam's dilemma is probably replicated in the lives and experiences of many newly appointed leaders. Rehoboam's dilemma can only mean one thing . . .

New Leaders are Vulnerable Because they Lack the Information they Need to Make key Decisions

Having to deal with such a hot button issue may have made Rehoboam vulnerable, but having to deal with that hot button issue *at a time he knew very little about it* was what made him exquisitely vulnerable. By the way, it's this vulnerability that makes new leaders ready captives to people with vested interests—people whose interests are often at odds with the overall interest of the organization. So how do new leaders solve this leadership challenge of not knowing enough about the inner workings of their organizations? The writer of First Kings shows us exactly how Rehoboam attempted to navigate that delicate challenge, saying,

> "Then King Rehoboam consulted the elders who had served his father Solomon during his lifetime. "How would you advise me to answer these people?" he asked."... But Rehoboam rejected the advice the elders gave him and consulted the young men who had grown up with him and were serving him. He asked them, "What is your advice? How should we answer these people who say to me, 'Lighten the yoke your father put on us'?" (1Kgs 12:6–9, NKJV)

These words mean that,

Newly Appointed Leaders Often Attempt to Manage their Ignorance of the Workings of their Organizations by Quickly Cultivating Multiple Sources of Information

Rehoboam attempted to cure his ignorance of how Israel's government worked by seeking advice from two different sources—his father's counselors and his own peers. His example illustrates just how new leaders attempt to make sense of their new jobs—they quickly reach out to others for advice. Former Corning CEO, James R. Houghton, pithily describes this process, saying "[Leadership] is capturing reliable information through a network of sources so that judgments can be formed." Therefore the effective management of promotion requires that newly appointed leaders do two things . . .

1. Quickly build relationships and cultivate diverse contacts in order to obtain the information they need to make decisions and run the enterprise and,

2. As much as possible, avoid making any crucial decisions when they'we've just stepped into office.

Again, the wise words of Professor Mintzberg drive home those two points "Clearly the manager must devote considerable time at the start of a new job to developing liaison contacts, to building his own information channels, to collecting information about his new organization and its environment." Therefore, if you've just being promoted to a new position, most of your time should be devoted to developing contacts, to building your own information channels to help you "make sense" of what's happening, and to, as far as is possible, avoid making any key decisions. Notwithstanding, whether you're an 'outsider' new to the organization or an 'insider' newly promoted from within, managing promotion can be boiled down to keeping tabs and obtaining information on two generic factors . . .

- The Context: what exactly are the reasons for the removal from office of your predecessor? What are the pressing issues facing key stakeholders? What is expected of you? Rehoboam, on taking office, never cared to find out the key issues bothering the people. His blindness to their economic hardship left him vulnerable.

- The Contacts: who are the persons with the most reliable information on what's happening in the organization? These "contacts" can help you better understand the "context." Rehoboam chose to sideline the right contacts (his father's advisers), and to listen to the wrong contacts (his peers). He paid dearly for that mistake.

Chapter 6

Managing Career Transitions (2)

CHANGE OF GUARDS (MANAGING A NEW BOSS)

ONE OF THE MOST challenging career transitions you can face is the transition from an 'old' boss to a newly appointed one. That transition is even more difficult if you've successfully "bonded" with, or become comfortable working for, your previous boss. Bonding with an old boss is synonymous with becoming conversant with her expectations and her style of work. For example, if the old boss was a "reader," then you probably have learned to present detailed written situation reports. In other words, the key challenges associated with 'managing' a new boss revolve around the new work-roles that have to be learned, and the new styles of work that have to adapted to. Researchers Nigel Nicholson and Michael West, in the *Handbook of Career Theory*, drive the point home, saying

> "Work role transitions are any major change in work role requirements or work context. This definition aims to encompass . . . the . . . times when the job itself changes around the immobile incumbent, such as . . . when there is a redefinition of the role through the succession of a new boss . . . "

Those words hit the nail on the head: a key challenge associated with 'managing' a new boss is the fact that the latter often redefines or redesigns the work you are expected to do. It is this redefinition of work roles that's at the heart of the difficulties and uncertainties associated with managing a new boss.

Managing Career Transitions (2)

In the Scripture record, one person who famously had to navigate this kind of career transition was Princess Michal, daughter of King Saul. Michal had flourished under the leadership of Saul—something that wasn't hard to do seeing that Saul was her father! But now she had to deal with David, the new head honcho who, believe it or not, also happened to be her husband! The writer of Second Samuel begins his narrative of Michal's intriguing story, saying,

> "But as the Ark of the LORD entered the City of David, Michal, the daughter of Saul, looked down from her window. When she saw King David leaping and dancing before the LORD, she was filled with contempt for him." (2 Sam 6:16, NLT)

This passage is a treasure trove of insights, helping us see that,

A Change of Guards Can be Hard to Manage if You have too much Invested in the 'Ancien Regime'!

"*...the City of David, Michal, the daughter of Saul...*" These words paint a clear picture of the earthshaking change that had occurred in Israel. Where once Saul had reigned, there King David now held court. Once, the capital of Israel had been in Saul's hometown of Gibeah, now it was in a place tellingly referred to as "the City of David." Although that kind of change is hard enough for anyone to absorb, it must have been harder still for Michal. Why? Easy. Because she was connected to the 'old', but had to be involved with the 'new'. She was the daughter of Saul (the old boss) who had to live in the city that was named after the new head honcho—David. To further complicate matters, Michal was also the wife of David! Which is why...

A Changeover from 'Old' Boss to 'New' Boss can Leave You Feeling Alienated and Out of Place

By saying "*...Michal...looked down from her window* [and] *saw King David leaping and dancing,*" the writer of Second Samuel reveals the huge sense of alienation that Michal must have felt. Imagine, she was a virtual bystander, watching from, of all places, her window, as the new head honcho mixed it up with the crowd. But, and this is crucial, Michal's sense of alienation was the proverbial calm before the storm—laying the groundwork for a

Section 1 | Managing 'Up'

confrontation with David. Listen, as the writer of Second Samuel continues the story of Michal, saying,

> "When David returned home to bless his family, Michal came out to meet him and said in disgust, "How glorious the king of Israel looked today! He exposed himself to the servant girls like any indecent person might do!" David retorted to Michal, "I was dancing before the LORD, who chose me above your father and his family! He appointed me as the leader of Israel . . . Yes, and I am willing to look even more foolish than this . . . So Michal, the daughter of Saul, remained childless throughout her life." (2Sam 6:20–23, NLT)

An "Employee" Enters into Conflict with the New "Boss," and Bungles the Change of Guards!

"When David came home . . . Michal came out to meet him and said in disgust, "How glorious the king of Israel looked today! He exposed himself . . . like any indecent person might do!" There it is in black and white: what made Michal mad was David's leaping and dancing in public! She felt that David's behavior or style—unlike that of Saul, his predecessor—was beneath the stately dignity which a king should display in public! David never forgave Michal for this comparison with Saul his predecessor, choosing never to have sexual relations with her again—the reason Michal "remained childless throughout her life." As an aside, this incident highlights one of David's major character flaws—an unwillingness to overlook perceived slights (in Chapter 1, we saw a vengeful David instructing his successor Solomon, to execute Shimei, a man who had slighted him many years before). David's thin-skin may have been due to his early childhood deprivation and rejection as a humble shepherd boy. But, to return to our main point, people (like Michal) who mismanage a change of guards, can become alienated, slide into irrelevance, and enter into conflict with the new boss—a career threatening triad of events. To prevent this, you need to always keep in mind the following truths . . .

There Will be a Difference in Style

David governed differently from Saul. David was artistically inclined and loved to mingle with commoners (making him more willing to dance in public), while Saul was more aloof and concerned with maintaining his 'kingly' aura. The fact is that no one style is right or wrong.

There Will be a Difference in Substance

David's leadership emphasized military conquest and the priestly ministry. He even went as far as designing musical instruments and writing out the order of worship for the Levites. Saul didn't care for things like that. The fact is that no one substance or emphasis is right!

You Need to Manage Your Expectations Carefully and be Willing to Adapt

Never expect the new boss to behave like the old and never think that just because a new boss isn't behaving like the old, he or she must be wrong or, more ominously, he or she must be a bad person. Crucially also, you must be flexible—ready for any redesign or redefinition of your work roles. Michal's inability to manage her expectations, and to adapt to David's style, ultimately wrecked her ability to manage the change of guards. In a very symbolic sense, Michal's bungling of her relationship with her new 'boss' made her lose her 'job'! And, it's to the subject of job loss that we next turn our attention . . .

MANAGING A JOB LOSS

A job loss is a career transition that causes a worker to temporarily exit the workforce. The increasing pace of technological change coupled with changes in the work values and expectations of upcoming younger generations have combined to significantly increase the occurrence of this work transition. Just take a look around, and you'll see job losses by whatever name called—job hopping, terminations, dismissals, voluntary departures, etc. Because employment contracts presume a meeting of minds or some degree of agreement between employer and employee, the roots of a job loss often lie in a disagreement between both parties. Speaking of agreements, the writer of Amos has this to say,

> "Can two [persons] walk together, unless they are agreed?" (Amos 3:3, NKJV)

Half jokingly, I often paraphrase these words as "Can two persons work together for a long time, unless they are agreed and have a lot in common?" This paraphrase drives home the point: the more points of agreement you have with an employer, the longer you tend to work for her. But, and this is important, it also follows that the disagreements which lead to early-career job terminations, tend to be different in kind from those which lead to job losses in the later stages of a person's work-life. Therefore we can say that . . .

1. Agreements are crucial, and people who aren't in agreement can't even begin to walk or work with each other. From a work perspective, you need to have some degree of agreement with an employer before you even begin to work for her.

2. The more two persons or parties are in agreement, the farther the distance they can walk together. In effect, the more you and I agree, the more long-lasting our relationship will be. From a work perspective, the more you are in agreement with an employer, the longer you tend to work for him.

3. Disagreements occurring at the early stage of a relationship tend to be different in kind from those occurring at the middle or later stages. From a work perspective, since it is disagreements between an employer and an employee that are the root causes of job loss, the reasons for early-career job losses should be different from those for middle-, and late-career stages.

There are 3 Broad Kinds of Job Loss—Early-Career-, Mid-Career-, and Late-Career Job Loss

The implication of #3 above is that there are actually 3 broad kinds of job loss—early-career-, mid-career-, and late-career job loss. Because the reasons for these three kinds of job loss are different, the tools for managing them must necessarily be different. I define early-career as the period 1–5 years after leaving school/training or beginning work, mid-career as 5–20 years after school/training, and late-career as the period 20 or more years after school/training. To be clear, these time periods are the products of rules of thumb. Indeed, some experienced workers who move to new employers often have an early-career-like experience where they struggle to 'fit in' at their new workplaces!

Managing Early-Career Job Loss

Again, our jumping off point is my paraphrase of the probing question posed by the writer of Amos "Can two persons work together for a long time, unless they are agreed and have a lot in common?" Like I said before, this paraphrase drives home the point: the more points of agreement between an employer and an employee, the longer and more fulfilling their working relationship will be. The converse is also true; the less an employer and employee have in common, the shorter—and rockier—their working relationship. All this helps us see that, not only are disagreements between employer and employee the real reason for job losses, the disagreements which cause early-career job losses tend to be different from those causing late-career terminations. Ram Charan, Stephen Drotter, and James Noel, in their book, *The Leadership Pipeline*, corroborate this line of thinking, saying,

> "Most people who early in their career leave, or are asked to leave organizations don't fit. Although some people depart because they don't lack the talent for a specific job, most simply lack the beliefs, values, and ability to conform to an established style of working."

In effect, it's a disagreement—a lack of 'fit'—between employer and employee that's the prime reason for early-career job loss. This lack of fit is often because the employee lacks the necessary ability to perform or her values are at odds with those of her employer. The implication is that an early-career job loss should push you to ask yourself the questions: what kind of organization am I best suited to work for? Or, with what kind of persons do I do my best work? In simple terms, early-career job losses are failures that are best managed by looking inwards and attempting to gain insight into your strengths, weaknesses, and values. Therefore, we can say that self awareness is the principal tool for managing early-career job losses. And, it is to that subject that we now turn . . .

Section 1 | Managing 'Up'

SELF-AWARENESS

"Through . . . self-awareness . . . we become conscious of areas of weakness, areas for improvement, areas of talent that could be developed; areas that need to be changed or eliminated from our lives."—STEPHEN COVEY

Years ago, golf legend Tiger Woods was in the news for the wrong reasons, for that most human of failings—sexual infidelity. Regrettably, his marriage imploded and commercial sponsors deserted him in droves. As I write, Mr. Woods has turned the corner and regained some of the form that once saw him dominate golf. Although, at that time, many were quick to condemn him, a few commentators pointed out the striking similarities among the women with whom he was allegedly involved. All were blonde white waitstaff. It does seem that Tiger has a weakness for white blonde waitresses; a weakness of which he wasn't even aware. In a sense, because Mr. Woods didn't know himself, his greatest enemy went unnoticed! As a teacher, that incident got me thinking; was this an isolated case? Is it possible that leaders have weaknesses of which they are not even aware? Conversely, do we have strengths and abilities that lie unnoticed and untapped? Notice carefully that all these questions have to do with self-knowledge. The Psalmist throws some light on the subject saying,

> "For I have kept the ways of the Lord, And have not wickedly departed from my God . . . I was also upright before Him, and I *kept* myself from *mine iniquity*." (Ps 18:21–23, KJV) (Emphasis mine)

Self-Awareness is Insight into Oneself, into Personal Weaknesses and Strengths.

In this beautiful Psalm—which was written shortly after his infamous adultery with Bathsheba—King David reached an "Aha" moment, a moment where he noticed that he was "naturally" prone to a certain weakness which he referred to as "*mine iniquity.*" David finally realized that he was prone to sexual infidelity and, crucially, began to take steps to protect himself from that weakness. How do I know this? Easy. The word "kept" in the phrase "I *kept* myself from mine iniquity," can also be translated as "protected." In essence, David realized he had to protect himself from himself! Management scholars refer to this knowledge of self—this insight into one's strengths and weaknesses—as self-awareness. In the words of management teacher Stephen Covey "Through . . . self - awareness . . . we become conscious of areas of weakness, areas for improvement, areas of talent that could be developed; areas that need to be changed or eliminated from our lives." The Writer of Proverbs shows us just how we can become more self-aware, saying,

> "A hot-tempered man must pay the penalty; if you rescue him, you will have to do it again." (Prov 19:19, NIV)

His words mean that . . .

Looking for Repetitive Patterns of Behavior is the Best Way to Detect Weaknesses, Strengths, and Blindspots

" . . . *if you rescue him, you will have to do it again.*" Those words hit the nail on the head: although a man may deny that he is hot-tempered, his egregious repetition of that particular behavior is what confirms him as hot-tempered. I mean, if you rescue him today from the consequences of his hot-tempered behavior, you would also have to do the same tomorrow. Why? Easy. Because he's a hot-tempered man and hot-tempered persons display those patterns of behavior! To become more self-aware, you must be on the lookout for repetitive behavior—the telltale signs of a personal blindspot. To paraphrase James Bond "The first time, it's an accident; the second time, it's happenstance, but the third time, it's enemy action!" If Mr. Woods had taken the time to reflect on his extramarital escapades, and if he'd invited feedback from trusted persons, he would certainly have noticed the pattern—the uncanny similarity in physique in all the women he pursued! In fact, the job of external counsel in the development of self-awareness is to simply bring an unbiased eye to the question of looking for repetitive patterns of behavior. It's only the self-aware that, like David, can take the necessary steps to protect themselves from their own weaknesses or exploit their own strengths. All this means that . . .

Evaluated Experience—Arising from Reflection— is the Key to Self-Awareness

By definition, to be self-aware is to become conscious of some quality you possess or lack, but the problem with these 'qualities' is that they are only revealed in action. Therefore, the more experience you have under your belt, and the more you can correctly evaluate those experiences, the more self-aware you'll become. Notice carefully that it is not experience per se, but *evaluated* experience that's key to self-awareness. But, here's the rub, evaluated experience is itself the product of reflection—the ability to dispassionately examine past experience. The question becomes, how exactly does reflection work? The writer of Second Corinthians shows us just how reflection works, saying,

> "Examine yourselves as to whether you are in the faith. Test yourselves. Do you not know yourselves, that Jesus Christ is in you? - unless, indeed you are disqualified."(2Cor 13:5, NIV)

Reflection is Personal—Something Only You Can Do

"*Examine yourselves . . .* " There it is in black and white: if you want to "know yourself," you have to begin examining yourself. Reflection is personal. It's something leaders must do for and to themselves. Certainly, persons close to you can provide feedback and serve as sounding boards, but ultimately, you do your own reflecting.

Reflection is Pointed—It Demands that You Keep a Diary or Journal

"Examine yourselves *as to whether you are in the faith.*" These words show that the writer of Second Corinthians wanted the Corinthian Christians to examine a very specific area of their lives—their faith walk. Effective reflection begins by zeroing in on a specific area. It demands that you go over specific areas (work, marriage, personal finances etc)—a thing which best happens if you've kept a personal journal or record of past actions, thoughts and decisions. Taking time to review your diary can help you spot patterns of behavior that would otherwise have escaped your attention.

Reflection is Probing—It Demands that You Ask Yourself Questions

"*Examine yourselves . . .Test yourselves.*" Like a doctor tests a patient by asking probing questions, so reflection requires that you bring some questions to the table. For example, asking, why are my personal finances so fragile?—can help you see otherwise hidden patterns of wasteful spending or ineffective business practices. Becoming self-aware is no cake work, the reason philosopher John Locke famously said that "There are three things extremely hard; steel, a diamond, and to know oneself." But, although the journey to self-awareness is difficult, the rewards—insight into your most valuable asset (you)—are worth the effort. Take some time to reflect on an early-career job loss you experienced. If you keep a diary, look again at your decisions with that employer; do you see any patterns? Is there something about that experience that points to your strengths, values, and weaknesses? If your answers to any of those questions provide you any kind of insight, then you've taken a small step on the road to becoming a more self-aware leader—one who is able to benefit from early-career failures.

Having seen that self-awareness is the tool for managing early-career job loss, we can now turn our attention to . . .

Managing Mid-Career Job loss

Stanford professors James Kouzes and Barry Posner, in their book, *Credibility: How Leaders Gain and Lose It.*, said that,

> "Studies from the Center for Creative Leadership . . . reveal that *successful executives derail in their careers most often because of insensitivity and inability to understand the perspectives of other people.* They undervalue the contributions of others, making them feel inadequate. They listen poorly, act dictatorially, play favorites and fail to give credit to others when it is due . . . The net result is that, over time, these traits and attitudes catch up with them. When these *managers* really need the help of those around them, they are left to fend for themselves, ignored, isolated, and on occasion even purposely sabotaged." (Emphases mine)

The key words in this insightful passage are *"successful executives . . . insensitivity and inability to understand the perspectives of others . . . managers . . . "* These words show that the workers in question are successful executives or managers—people who are probably in midcareer. More importantly, these words show that the major reasons for mid-career derailment are insensitivity and an inability to understand the perspectives of others.

Insensitivity to others often reveals itself as an inability or unwillingness to 'read' the *nonverbal* communications with which co-workers give feedback on our actions. In contrast, an inability to understand the perspectives of others is often the result of an inability to receive feedback in the form of *verbal* or explicit communications. The former is old-fashioned insensitivity, while the latter is often the result of a manager's isolation from reality.

DEVELOPING SENSITIVITY TO OTHERS

Harvard pyschologist Howard Gardner, who was famous for his theory of multiple intelligences, said that "The core of interpersonal intelligence includes the capacities to discern and respond appropriately to the moods, temperaments, motivations and desires of other people." Notice carefully that the individual words "*moods,*" "*temperaments,*" "*motivations,*" and "*desires*" are, not only associated with peoples' feelings, they also tend to be communicated *nonverbally*. In other words, the core of interpersonal intelligence is really all about cultivating sensitivity to the unarticulated and unspoken feelings of others around you! That said, if anyone in the record of Scripture should receive the Silver Cup for insensitivity to others, it must be Esau, twin brother of Jacob. Listen as the writer of Genesis narrates the story of Esau's monumental interpersonal incompetence . . .

> "When Esau was forty years old, he married Judith daughter of Beeri the Hittite, and also Basemath daughter of Elon the Hittite. They were a source of grief to Isaac and Rebekah [their parents in law]." (Gen 26:34, NIV)
>
> "Then Rebekah said to Isaac, "I'm disgusted with living because of these Hittite women. If Jacob takes a wife from among the women of this land, from Hittite women like these, my life will not be worth living." (Gen 27:46, NIV)
>
> With these words, the writer of Genesis shows us that . . .

"Reading" Nonverbal Communications is at the Heart of Sensitivity to Others

"*They were a source of grief to Isaac and Rebekah . . .* '" "*I am disgusted with living because of these Hittite women . . .* " Grief and disgust are emotions so strong that, even when unspoken, are difficult to hide or disguise for long. And when your actions cause grief and disgust to the people closest to you, you certainly should know. Except, as this passage reveals, your name is

Esau! Imagine, Esau marries Hittite wife number one; causing grief to his parents Isaac and Rebekah; yet he doesn't see this and goes ahead to marry another Hittite wife, causing even more grief and disgust to them. Still, Esau doesn't see or know that he is deeply wounding his parents! Howard Gardner, the famous Harvard psychologist, said that "The core of interpersonal intelligence includes the capacities to discern and respond appropriately to the moods, temperaments, motivations and desires of other people." People like Esau who can't, for any reason, discern how significant others feel about them or their actions aren't going to fulfill their potential in group settings. But, the writer of Genesis isn't done yet, he continues his narrative, saying,

> "Esau heard that his father had blessed Jacob and sent him to Paddan-aram to find a wife, and that he had warned Jacob not to marry a Canaanite woman. He also knew that Jacob had obeyed his parents and gone to Paddan-aram. It was now very clear to Esau that his father despised the local Canaanite women." (Gen 28:6–8, NLT)

Esau Finally Gets It!

It took many years and many quarrels, but Esau finally realized that his parents didn't merely disapprove of his actions, they were grieved and disgusted by them! People who are emotionally unintelligent are typically insensitive to the feelings of significant others (bosses, suppliers, spouses, etc.) in their lives and are blind to their nonverbal cues and communications. Such people eventually come to know firsthand the truth of the saying of leadership experts James Kouzes and Barry Posner "Insensitivity to others is the most frequent cause of career derailment." But there's something else I want you to see: By saying "Esau *heard* that his father . . . had warned Jacob not to marry a Canaanite woman . . . *It was now very clear to Esau that his father despised the local Canaanite women*," the writer of Genesis hits a home run, helping us see that,

The Best Leaders Discern How Others Feel, Not from their Verbal Communications, but from their Nonverbal Communications

Esau's people skills were atrocious. Imagine living with people all your life and causing them grief and disgust, and not even even knowing it until you hear them say it in a roundabout way to another person! The core of sensitivity to others is this ability to discern how people feel from their nonverbal (body language etc.) communications. If people have to shout, cry out, raise hell, and tell others about it, before you know how they feel, you are insensitive and your people skills need an upgrade—and your relationship/job/business might just be in jeopardy! Learn to listen not just to what's being said, but to what's *not* being said and, even more importantly, to *how* it's being said. Whenever you sense a discrepancy between what a person says and her body language, go with the latter because, in the words of pioneer psychiatrist George Graham "The body [language] doesnot lie." People may be able to hide behind false words, but body language is more difficult to mask or control.

To become more sensitive to the nonverbal cues that others are constantly sending, you must . . .

- Get Over Yourself: drop your own agenda and learn to listen for what others are saying without words. I may not always tell you how I feel, but I certainly will always show how I feel. To know how I feel you may need to listen to what is not being said, look at my body language, or watch out for how I am saying what I say. Don't be like Esau who couldn't even see the disgust and grief in the countenance of others!

- Get Off Your High Horse: As people become more successful and move up the corporate ladder, they tend to feel less need to listen or pay attention to others. In an interesting experiment, psychologists asked people to take a marker pen and draw, with their dominant hand, the letter E on their foreheads. Leaders who were most powerful or highest up the corporate ladder tended to draw the 'E' in a manner that only they could read. People with less power tended to draw the 'E' in a way that others could read! The take home? Power tends to make leaders insensitive to others' feelings. And it is to the subject of how power can serve as a filter for the feedback that managers receive, that we now turn . . .

LOW GATES VS HIGH GATES: AVOIDING A MID-CAREER DERAILMENT

Power often serves as a filter or sieve of information—allowing some feedback through and blocking out others. Why? Because as people become more powerful, their success can 'shut out' or significantly reduce the range of viewpoints they receive, therefore, the success which accompanies a mid-career executive can influence the nature and sources of feedback she receives. The writer of Proverbs drives the point home, saying,

> "Whoever loves a quarrel loves sin; whoever builds a high gate invites destruction." (Prov 17:19, NIV)

Notice carefully that this Scripture says "... whoever builds a *high* gate invites destruction." The implication is that, if you want to avoid destruction, you should build a *low* gate! Since, gates symbolize entry, this passage is really talking about access. That said, while gates may symbolize access, *high* gates go one step farther—they also symbolize power. Just take a look at "gated communities" and "military compounds"—the ultimate symbols of wealth and power—with their imposing (high) gates which grant access only to insiders and authorized persons. In effect, the words of the writer of Proverbs are a parable about how power and success, because they limit the number and type of persons who get to see a leader, can produce failure and destruction! Since midcareer leaders are the ones most likely to have tasted the career success associated with "high gates," these words of the writer of Proverbs mean that...

Mid-Career Leaders who are Isolated are Setting themselves Up for Destruction!

It bears repeating, by saying "... whoever builds a high gate invites destruction," the writer of Proverbs is really only warning that leaders who unnecessarily isolate themselves from others are on the path to failure and destruction. The question becomes: what exactly do people carry that makes them so valuable to a leader's success? Easy. People carry the information, advice and feedback you need to succeed, manage a crisis, make a decision, stave off failure etc. After all is said and done, the writer of Proverbs is really talking about how leaders who aren't linked to the right persons, who isolate themselves from relevant information, and who aren't properly managing their personal social networks are inviting destruction. He is saying that leaders—especially those in midcareer—who want to avoid failure must take the initiative and get all the information they need.

Further reflection on the phrase "... whoever builds a high gate invites destruction," has helped me see the following truths...

SECTION 1 | MANAGING 'UP'

1. My Gate is High: only the wealthy and successful can speak to me or give me feedback. This mindset listens only to peers, the more accomplished, and the similar. It thinks, "If you aren't well known or similar to me, I won't listen to you!"

2. My Gate is Low: this signifies openness and a willingness to receive information and feedback from any credible source. It thinks, "I'm willing to overlook "who" you are and listen to "what" you know," and reveals itself as a willingness to listen to the younger, the less accomplished and the different.

Putting it Into Practice

Israel's third king, Rehoboam, is an example of a leader who didn't properly manage his personal network—and paid dearly for it. The writer of Second Chronicles gives an account of King Rehoboam's troubles, saying,

> "Rehoboam went to Shechem, where all Israel had gathered to make him king. "Your father was a hard master," they said. "Lighten the harsh labor demands and heavy taxes that your father imposed on us. Then we will be your loyal subjects." Rehoboam replied, "Come back in three days for my answer." So the people went away." (2Chr 10:1–5, NLT)

"Your father [Solomon] was a hard master . . . Lighten the harsh labor demands and heavy taxes that your father imposed on us" The people of Israel delivered a damning verdict on Solomon's leadership—they were impoverished by his reign! Solomon's economic misrule produced plenty of pent up resentment—the reason the people demanded that the new king do something to relieve them economically. It was crunch time, and Rehoboam needed to make a decision—a thing which required that he consult his advisers. The writer of Second Chronicles continues his narrative, saying,

> "Then King Rehoboam went to discuss the matter with the older men who had counseled his father, Solomon. "What is your advice?" he asked. "How should I answer these people?" The older counselors replied, "If you are good to the people and show them kindness and do your best to please them, they will always be your loyal subjects." But Rehoboam rejected the advice of the elders and

instead asked the opinion of the young men who had grown up with him and who were now his advisers." (2Chr 10:6–8, NLT)

Rehoboam Builds a 'High Gate' and Pays Dearly for It!

It's amazing, but the information Rehoboam needed to wisely administer the kingdom was always at his beck and call in the form of advice from the old men who were his father's counselors! His failure to listen to these men—and his crass willingness to give ear only to men demographically similar to him—can only mean one thing: he had built a high gate that prevented him from receiving insight from those who were different from him! I mean, age was the only ostensible reason he rejected advice from his father's advisors and listened to the young men who'd grown up with him! Because a gate is simply a tool for regulating the information we receive, 'high gates'—because they automatically block out information not to our taste or liking—act like unconscious biases in the decision-making process. The nature, variety, and sources of information you've consumed or received over the last few years are pointers to the kind of 'gate' you've built. To manage, or even avoid, mid-career job loss, you must first "out" your biases. Take some time to answer the following questions . . .

- Do I read books, listen to, or attend conferences led, by people who are just like me? (Similarity bias).
- Does all or the majority of the information I think important come from people "above" me? (Success bias).
- Do I allow people or leaders 'below' me supply me information and wisdom? (Position bias).
- Do people different from me give me advice? (Similarity bias).

Your answers to these questions can help you notice whether you're on the road to a mid-career derailment!

Chapter 7

Managing Career Transitions (3)

MANAGING LATE-CAREER JOB LOSS

THE LATE-CAREER STAGE IS the level of top-management—the highest echelon of managers in any group. If you've reached this level, then you must count yourself fortunate to be part of an elite group of senior leaders who run the show in your company. Your logical next step is to make CEO—a tantalizing prize—the step that, more often than not, leads to job loss at this rarified level. Donald Hambrick and co., in their excellent book, *Strategic Leadership*, said that,

> "The replacement of one leader by another has been a matter of fascination and drama through the ages. Executive succession evokes a political picture, with the continuity or disruption of regimes at stake and the creation of clear winners and losers. Turnover at the top instills hope, fear, or simply anxiety in organizational members . . ."

"Executive succession evokes a political picture . . . the creation of clear winners and losers." There it is in black and white: when it comes to late-career transitions, there are no draws, only winners and losers—winners become CEOs and losers get sidelined, put out to pasture, or forced to exit the group. Because, in any well run organization, most top-managers have the requisite technical skills to carry out the duties of CEO, political factors tend to assume outsized importance in CEO selection—the very reason every top-manager must become adept at the politics of executive succession.

Managing Career Transitions (3)

Interestingly, the writer of First Samuel, in his narrative of the events surrounding the last days of Israel's first king, helps leaders put their fingers on the key political factors they must keep track of, if they want to successfully manage late-career transitions, saying,

> "Listen here, you men of Benjamin!" Saul shouted when he heard the news [that David his rival had fled to a stronghold in Judah]. "Has David promised you fields and vineyards? Has he promised to make you commanders in his army? Is that why you have conspired against me? For not one of you has ever told me that my own son is on David's side. You're not even sorry for me. Think of it! My own son—encouraging David to try and kill me!'" (1Sam 22:7-8, NLT)

A King Loses his Cool!

By saying "Saul *shouted* when he heard the news [that David his rival had fled to a stronghold in Judah]," the writer of First Samuel helps us see that the king raised his voice, lost his cool, and was in extremis! The question becomes; what could have made the king lose his cool? The answer is; Saul knew that . . .

Becoming—and Remaining—King is Impossible Without the Support of a Power Base

"Listen here, *you men of Benjamin* . . . " These words reveal a king—the ultimate CEO—surrounded by his 'power base'—men from his own tribe of Benjamin who, when push came to shove, were responsible for sustaining his grip on power. The best leaders today aren't fooled by pretensions of 'modernity'; they know that every CEO, or aspiring CEO, must have a power base. Like King Saul, they also know that . . .

Leaders Begin to Lose or Gain Power When they Lose or Gain the Support of Key Constituents

"*You're not even sorry for* [concerned about] *me* . . . " One of the first signs that a top-leader is losing grip, or is on the way out, is when his power base stops lending him support. King Saul's power base consisted of his kinsmen—men from the tribe of Benjamin: and it seems that, by not informing him of the secret agreement between Jonathan (Saul's son) and David (Saul's rival), they had lost faith in him. Since no member of his power base bothered to tell him about this secret covenant (1Samuel 18:23), the only way Saul could have known about it was through a network of informants from outside the tribe of Benjamin. Saul's kinsmen, normally his eyes and ears, were now against him! This passage is, in effect, Saul's swan song. His power base was no longer supportive and ominously, his rival David, by winning the support of the men of tribe of Judah, had built his own power base. As everyone knows, David went on to make a successful late-career transition (becoming king of Israel), while Saul lost his job. But, and this is crucial, for Saul, it all began with losing the support of key consitutuents. For David, it all began with winning the support of his own power base.

All this has helped me see that managing late-career transitions is easy for leaders who always remember that . . .

1. Late-career transitions are inherently "political."
2. Successfully making the transition from top-management to CEO requires the support of key stakeholders.
3. Not succeeding in the transition from top-management to CEO is often because enough support wasn't garnered from key stakeholders.

Late-career transitions, as the term suggests, occur late in a person's career and are often the last step before retirement. And, it is to the latter that we now turn our attention . . .

MANAGING RETIREMENT

Retirement always comes. No matter how good you are, and no matter how well you take care of yourself physically and professionally, retirement, in one of its many forms, will catch up with you. You may dodge the career transitions of demotion, being passed over, and the wilderness, but no one can dodge retirement. Since the late-nineteenth century, the idea of retirement has gained ground in many countries of the world—and has come to be defined as the time when one chooses (or is mandated) to permanently withdraw from one's occupation or position in the workforce. Because that "time" often coincides with a deterioration in health, retirement is often associated with aging or the onset of old age. Although, some professional sportspersons retire while still relatively young, the truth is that the physical demands of sport often make their relative youth look like "old age"! Which is why retirement can be defined as an age-induced career transition that causes a person to permanently exit the workforce. If, as we've seen, retirement is basically age-induced, then the peculiar psychosocial problems associated with aging should be at the center of that career transition. The words of the writer of Hebrews introduce us to those peculiar psychosocial problems, saying,

> "When God speaks of a new [covenant or agreement], He makes the first one obsolete (out of use). And what is obsolete (out of use and annulled because of age) is ripe for disappearance and to be dispensed with altogether." (Heb 8:13, AMP)

Loss of Place, Position, and Prominence—the 'Three Losses'—is the Principal Effect of Retirement

"*What is obsolete (out of use and annulled because of age), is ripe for disappearance . . .* " These words not only associate the old with obsolescence, they also show that the principal social effect of aging is the consignment of the old to history, oblivion, and disuse. In effect, what I refer to as the 'three losses'—loss of place, position, and prominence—is the principal social effect of retirement. Apart from the obvious decrements in physical health and earnings which often accompany retirement, these three losses can also deal huge blows to the pysche of any retired person—especially if that person was once an accomplished professional or master of the game. Therefore, we can say that a key to managing retirement revolves around managing the three losses. We see that truth writ large in the the Old Testament story of the 'Old Prophet' and the "Young Prophet". The writer of First Kings begins his gripping account of that story, saying,

> "At the LORD's command, a man of God from Judah went to Bethel, and he arrived there just as Jeroboam was approaching the altar to offer a sacrifice. Then at the LORD's command, he shouted, "O altar, altar! This is what the LORD says: A child named Josiah will be born into the dynasty of David. On you he will sacrifice the priests from the pagan shrines who come here to burn incense, and human bones will be burned on you." That same day the man of God gave a sign to prove his message, and he said, "The LORD

has promised to give this sign: This altar will split apart, and its ashes will be poured out on the ground." King Jeroboam was very angry with the man of God for speaking against the altar. So he pointed at the man and shouted, "Seize that man!" But instantly the king's hand became paralyzed in that position, and he couldn't pull it back. At the same time a wide crack appeared in the altar, and the ashes poured out, just as the man of God had predicted in his message from the LORD. The king cried out to the man of God, "Please ask the LORD your God to restore my hand again!" So the man of God prayed to the LORD, and the king's hand became normal again." (1 Kgs 13:1–6, NLT)

From Zero to Hero: a Young Prophet Begins Public Ministry!

Imagine, an unknown young prophet comes to the southern Kingdom of Israel from the northern Kingdom of Judah and prophesies against the altar. On hearing the prophet, an enraged King Jeroboam orders his servants to seize him. Then, surprise, surprise, the hand which the king pointed at the prophet shrivels! A contrite king begs the prophet to pray that his hand be restored, and miracle number two—the king's hand is restored—happens as the prophet prays! As if two miracles aren't enough to announce this unknown prophet, a third takes place; the bronze altar splits apart and its ashes spill on the floor as the prophet had predicted minutes before! Three miraculous signs in one day! The young prophet's work receives so much acclaim and recognition that the king even invites him to lunch at the palace!

While the young prophet was making waves in the city of Bethel, there was, unbeknown to him, another prophet in that same city. The writer of First Kings continues his narrative, saying,

> "As it happened, there was an *old prophet* living in Bethel, and his sons came home and told him what the man of God had done in Bethel that day . . . The *old prophet* asked them, "Which way did he go?" So they told their father which road the man of God had taken . . . .And . . . he rode after the man of God and found him sitting under an oak tree. The old prophet asked him, "Are you the man of God who came from Judah? Yes," he replied, "I am." Then he said to the man of God, "Come home with me and eat some food." "No, I cannot," he replied. "I am not allowed to eat any food or drink any water here in this place. For the LORD gave me this

command: 'You must not eat any food or drink any water while you are there, and do not return to Judah by the same way you came.'" But the old prophet answered, "I am a prophet too, just as you are. And an angel gave me this message from the LORD: 'Bring him home with you, and give him food to eat and water to drink.'" But the old man was lying to him. So they went back together, and the man of God ate some food and drank some water at the prophet's home." (Emphases mine) (1Kgs 13:11-19, NLT)

The Young Prophet is Deceived by Another Prophet!

"*But the old man was lying to him . . .* " Those words are the 'long and short' of this story. The young prophet, after his powerful ministry at Bethel, was on his way home when another prophet deceived him and caused him to return to Bethel and share a meal. If you go on to read the rest of the story, you'll see that the young prophet was later killed by a lion because he had disobeyed the word of the Lord which expressly commanded him not to eat in Bethel. In this sense, the death of the young prophet was the result of the lie told him by the other prophet. The big question becomes; why did the other prophet lie to the young prophet? Or, simply put, what did the other prophet stand to gain by lying to the young prophet? The answers to those questions are revealed only as we better understand the social circumstances of the "other prophet." A close study of the words of the writer of First Kings has helped me see that . . .

The "Other Prophet" was an Old and Retired Prophet!

The interesting thing about the nine verses which make up the above passage is this: not only is the term, *old prophet,* used four times to describe the "other prophet," he is also outrightly described—once—as an *old man*! Indeed, by saying "and his sons came home and told him what the man of God had done in Bethel that day," the writer of First Kings drives home the point: this "other prophet" had grown sons and a house—signs of a financially comfortable person! All this helps us see that the "other prophet" was not only an old man, he was also an old prophet who was probably comfortably retired. By also saying "As it happened, there was an old prophet living *in Bethel,*" the writer of First Kings buttresses the point: the old prophet was living in Bethel, *but wasn't used by God to deliver the message*! Since, as we've seen, loss of place, position, and preeminence, is a major challenge associated with managing retirement; and since those three losses signal a loss of relevance, might it be that it was a desire to remain relevant that pushed the old prophet to deceive the young prophet? The words of the old prophet—after he went to retrieve the corpse of the young prophet—seem to confirm this! Listen once more to the writer of First Kings . . .

> "So the prophet laid the body of the man of God on the donkey and took it back to the city to mourn over him and bury him. He laid the body in his own grave, crying out in grief, "Oh, my brother!" Afterward the prophet said to his sons, "When I die, bury me in the grave where the man of God is buried. Lay my bones beside his bones." (1Kgs 13:29–31, NLT)

These intriguing words show that,

It was a Desire to Remain Relevant that Made the Old Prophet Deceive the Young Prophet!

"He laid the body [of the young prophet] in his own grave . . . *When I die, bury me in the grave where the man of God* [the young prophet] *is. Lay my bones beside his bones.*" There it is in black and white: even in death, the old prophet wanted to be identified with the young prophet. In effect, he had lied to the young prophet and caused him to come to his own house because he wanted to be identified with the success of the latter. He wanted some of the relevance associated with being "in active service"! It was a hunger for recognition, acclaim, and relevance—the things that a worker loses at retirement—that led to his egregious behavior. The old prophet's time had passed, but like some retirees, he still craved the acclaim and recognition which active ministry brings. To get this acclaim, he was willing to do anything—lie and deceive—as long as it allowed him to be associated with the young prophet.

The tragic story of 'The Old Prophet and the Young Prophet' has helped me see that the effective management of the social challenges associated with retirement requires that you . . .

1. Be Realistic and Manage Your Expectations: nothing lasts forever—and that includes your career! If, like I said before, a career denotes movement—milestones, choice points, goals and endpoints—then the endpoint of any career must be retirement. When your time is over, or

when it's time to call it a day, then the healthy thing to do is to adjust your expectations—to accept that someone else would now be in the limelight and receive all the acclaim. Acceptance is the recognition of reality. Anything less than that is setting yourself up for depression, jealousy and resentment—things that are not only harmful to your health, but that may also sabotage your relationships with others. In this sense, managing retirement is an inside job!

2. Seek Significance and Status in Other Ways: we tend to receive much of our sense of worth from the work we do, which is one reason retirement hits us so hard. But the truth is that we can also get some sense of worth from other activities that being retired can bring—"give back" opportunities like mentoring younger persons, community and charitable work etc.

In conclusion, one should always remember that the Latin word, *carraria*, from which we get the English word "career," signifies a journey, and since all journeys have endpoints, the logical endpoint of careers is retirement. The latter, unlike other career transitions, always requires a person to *permanently* leave the workforce. It's this permanent exit from the workforce—and the accompanying loss of a sense of self worth—that makes retirement so traumatic for many. Most retirement management literature deal with the financial aspects for retirement—which is good—but the story of "The Old Prophet and the Young Prophet" forces us to go one step farther. It forces us to deal with the *social* aspects of retirement.

Chapter 8

Problems and Pitfalls of Managing 'Up'

THE PROBLEMS AT THE BOTTOM OF THE PYRAMID

"Wherever we are in the hierarchy, our health is likely to be better than those below us and worse than those above us."—MICHAEL MARMOT

PROMOTIONS, LIKE I SAID in Chapter 5, are the most coveted type of career transition, and the reasons aren't difficult to fathom—promotion is always associated with...

1. Increased salary and benefits.
2. Increased responsibility for work done in the group. Since hierarchies are vertical divisions of labor where progressively smaller numbers of higher-ups oversee the work of progressively greater numbers of subordinates, promotion is synonymous with increased responsibility.
3. Increased discretion and self-expression: the higher you go, the more control you have over calendars and schedules—both yours and others'—and the more you can inject your personal preferences into your work.

Although, much had been written about the impact of increased salaries and benefits on the health of promoted workers, little was known about the impact of #2 and #3 above until the groundbreaking work of British epidemiologist Michael Marmot.

Problems and Pitfalls of Managing 'Up'

In his book, *Power: Why Some People Have It, And Others Don't*, Stanford professor Jeffrey Pfeffer said that,

> "Michael Marmot's study of 18,000 British civil servants—all people working in office jobs in the same society—uncovered that *people at the bottom of the hierarchy had four times the risk of death from heart disease as did those at the top.* Controlling for risk factors such as smoking or obesity did not make the social gradient in health disappear, nor did statistically controlling for the longevity of one's parents. As Marmot concludes, "*Social circumstances in adult life predict health.*" *So seek power as if your life depends on it. Because it does.*" (Emphases mine)

These amazing words reveal the connection between being in power—at the top of the hierarchy or 'food chain'—and a person's health! More importantly, they helped me better understand Jesus' Parable of the Talents . . .

> "His master said to him, Well done, you upright (honorable, admirable) and faithful servant! You have been faithful and trustworthy over a little; I will put you in charge of much. Enter into and share the joy (the delight, the blessedness) which your master enjoys." (Matt 25:23, AMP)

Jesus' words mean that . . .

Being in Power is Good for Your Health!

This story—the Parable of the Talents—is always used to show how faithfulness in using our talents will lead to our promotion. And rightly so. But there's another, I dare say, under-appreciated, aspect of this parable. By saying *"Enter into and share the joy (the delight, the blessedness) which your master enjoys,"* Jesus shows us that, apart from the well-known material blessing, promotion also comes with nonmaterial or psychological blessing—delight and blessedness. In other words, being in power over others—the faithful steward was promoted to a position of power—has a positive impact on a person's psychological wellbeing! Since, psychological and emotional factors are major contributors to the "social circumstances in adult life [which] predict health," one isn't surprised at Dr. Marmot's research finding that being in power is good for your health!

The question becomes "How exactly does being in power impact a person's health?" The answer is in 2 parts—functional and structural. The

SECTION 1 | MANAGING 'UP'

former has to do with the functions (work) of higher-ups, while the latter is directly connected to the structure (design) of organizations. Obviously, both factors are interrelated. Let's begin with the functional reasons . . .

Being in Power Gives You Control Over Schedules and Calendars

What, in your opinion, distinguishes a boss from her subordinates? Most people would immediately say "Control over agendas, schedules, people, and resources." And they are correct. In effect, being in power means that you have greater control over your life. The company president normally has power to schedule meetings, and rare is the president who would schedule a meeting for a time or place that inconveniences her! In contrast, lower-level operatives have to attend scheduled meetings even when those meetings are inconvenient. Therefore, being lower in the hierarchy means you have less control over your life and work, and higher stress levels—things which negatively impact your health in the long-term. It's this difference in perceived or actual control over life and work that's a key reason for the disparities in health between people at the top and people at the bottom.

Being in Power Gives You Discretion—Allowing You Inject Your Personal Preferences into Your Work

Researchers Donald Hambrick and Gregory Fukutomi, in their 1991 Academy of Management Review article, *The Seasons of a CEO's Tenure*, said that " . . . the highest level officer is the one most likely to possess discretion . . . with least restrictive oversight and, hence, (relative to lower level managers) has the ability to manifest personal preferences and energies into organizational outcomes." Their words mean that the higher up the hierarchy you climb, the less restrictive the oversight becomes, and the more you can inject your personal preferences into your work. The worker on the assembly line has almost no discretion—he simply must install the machine part required by the process. In contrast, the production manager may have leeway to choose which of two or more machine parts are to be used in the assembly line. The former cannot inject his personal preferences into the work done, but the latter can—another reason for the social gradients in health that's so prevalent in organizations. But long before Professors Hambrick and Fukutomi's research findings, the writer of Proverbs had this to say about discretion,

Problems and Pitfalls of Managing 'Up'

"Like a gold ring in a pig's snout is a beautiful woman who shows no discretion." (Prov 11:22, NIV)

His words drive the point home...

Discretion is the Exercise of Personal Preference or Choice

As everyone knows, a pig has no preferences when it comes to where to search for food. That animal will poke its snout into the mud, a garbage can, or just about anywhere if that is what will bring it some food—even if it wears an expensive gold ring on its snout! By comparing a beautiful woman without discretion to a gold ring on a pig's snout, the writer of Proverbs wants us to see that that beautiful woman will not be choosy about the quality of men with whom she has romantic relationships. Donald Hambrick and Greg Fukutomi were correct after all; discretion is simply this: infusing your style, choices and personal preferences into the situation or the work at hand.

Discretion is Easiest for People at the Top of their Game

"... is a *beautiful woman* who shows no discretion." In the "market" for suitors, only the most beautiful women get to pick and choose, and the not-so-beautiful women have little choice but to make do with the men that show up! The moral of all this? Discretion—the exhibition of personal preference is possible only for those at the top of their game—the best in the business. Success brings options. The more successful you are, the more options are available to you, and the more your personal preferences can come into play. For those players just coming up, the proverb "Half bread is better than none," suffices. But those at the top can choose between bread and cake! On a more serious note, it's this discretion or autonomy at the higher levels of the organization that furthers the health status of the people in power. How? Because discretion is an important aspect of the "Social circumstances in adult life [which] predict health." No wonder, after the master in the Parable of Talents said "You have been faithful and trustworthy over a little; I will put you in charge of much," he followed it up with "Enter into and share the joy (the delight, the blessedness) *which your master enjoys.*" There's an especial enjoyment that being in power brings—an enjoyment arising from an ability to inject your personal preferences into the work you do—a thing that's good for your long-term health.

Being in Power Helps You See the Big Picture—Which Can Positively Impact Your Health

Imagine that you live on the tenth floor of an apartment building that is besieged by insurgents. As the battle rages in and around the vicinity of your building, the occupants of the ground floor apartment, seeing no hope of relief, might be tempted to throw in the towel and surrender to the insurgents. But things look a little different from your perch on the tenth floor; you refuse to surrender because you are able to see—afar off—a convoy of police vehicles snaking its way through the debris-strewn road to your apartment block. This ability to see the big picture was the difference-maker between you and the occupants of the ground floor apartment. Being too low in the hierarchy is a lot like living in that ground floor apartment—producing what management scholar Robert H. Thomas refers to as " . . . limited visions of the relationship between one's work and the overall organizational products or goals." Not being able to see the big picture makes lower-level operatives more prone to bouts of depression and feelings of alienation—things which produce poor health in the long-term.

Promotion is all about increase—an increase in pay, an increase in responsibility (which increases a person's ability to see the big picture), and increase in control over agendas and calendars. But, and this is crucial, the last two factors play key roles in creating the social circumstances that so decisively affect peoples' health. Most people, seeing only the increase in financial remuneration, are blind to the "social gradient"—to the impact of their position in the hierarchy on their own health.

Having seen the *functional* reasons for the health disparities in organizations, we now turn our attention to the *structural* reasons. The words of the writer of Ecclesiastes are our jumping-off point . . .

> "If you see the poor oppressed in a district, and justice and rights denied, do not be surprised at such things; for [because] one official is eyed by a higher one, and over them both are others higher still." (Eccl 5:8, NIV)

These intriguing words reveal . . .

Problems and Pitfalls of Managing 'Up'

The Operations of a Classical Hierarchy

Political scientist Steven Lukes defines hierachies as "The organization of persons in graded ranks, each of which controls others below it. Hierarchies are vertical divisions of labor." The key terms in that definition are *"graded ranks,"* and *"each of which controls others below it."* Those terms show that hierarchies have people overseeing and supervising others below them. In this light, the words of the writer of Ecclesiastes " . . . one official is eyed [controlled or supervised] by a higher one, and over them both are others higher still," are a dead giveaway; they describe the operations of a classical hierarchy!

Hierarchical Organizations are Inherently Unjust to People at the Bottom of the Pile!

"If you see the poor oppressed in a district and justice and rights denied, *do not be surprised, because one official is eyed by a higher one, and over them both are others higher still."* There it is in black and white: oppression, the denial of rights, and the abuse of power—the pitfalls and problems of managing 'up'—are par for the course in hierarchically structured groups! In other words, it's the structure (design) of the organization—not so much as the persons who run the organization—that's responsible for many of the pitfalls and problems workers at the bottom of the pyramid encounter in hierarchical careers. But the writer of Ecclesiastes isn't done yet; he goes ahead to show us just why hierarchies can do so much damage to the welfare—and, by division, the health—of people at the bottom . . .

Hierarchies are 'Bad' for People at the Bottom Because Supervision and Coordination are Cumbersome

Effective supervision and coordination require the timely and unbiased flow of information. For hierarchies, the many layers of authority (" . . . one official is eyed by another, and over them both are others . . . ") through which information must pass before it reaches the top, makes this easier said than done. Indeed, conniving officials in middle management often exploit this structural weakness and withhold information or worse, give outrightly inaccurate or biased information to higher-ups. In essence, the distance between center and periphery, the many layers of authority, and the presence of only one channel for transmitting information mean that the larger an organization becomes, the less effective the supervision from headquarters.

Hierarchies are Bad for People at the Bottom Because Power is Centralized

While it's true that the many layers in a hierarchy make the transmission of information cumbersome, one might even ask "Why do you even need to transmit information upward?" The answer is this: decision-making power lies mostly with higher-ups! That is, approvals for most initiatives or course corrections must first be received from higher-ups before any action is taken. Since, as we've seen, power is good for a person's health, this centralization of power is also responsible for creating the social gradient and the "social circumstances in adult life which predict health."

Wrap Around

The pitfalls of managing 'up', because they involve peoples' health, are pretty scary. But the increasing prevalence of "flat organizations" offers hope that some of those pitfalls can be remedied. Flat organizations decentralize power and make coordination less cumbesome. Social scientist Francis Fukuyama, in his lecture series, *Social Capital*, said that "Authority does not disappear in a flat or networked organization; rather, it is internalized in a way that permits self-organization and self-management." Hopefully, the increased levels of self-management in today's flat organizations can protect lower-level operatives from the deleterious effects of hierarchy. In contrast, remedying the pitfalls arising from the functions (behaviors) of managers begins with acknowledging this fact: a key difference between managers and leaders is that the former work within systems, while the latter can change the systems within which they work. Therefore, one way to remedy the functional reasons that produce these pitfalls is to supply managers (especially senior managers) the information to better lead their people.

SECTION 2

Managing 'Across'

PREAMBLE

"The social network in which we find ourselves defines our prospects. It does so by defining whom we meet."—NICHOLAS CHRISTAKIS AND JAMES FOWLER

WHAT REALLY ARE YOUR career prospects? How far can you advance in your chosen vocation or profession? These questions have agitated the minds of many career persons down the ages. And, until recently, the answers to those questions were anchored in individualist explanations that said "My career success is wholly the result of my own actions." This individualist perspective is beginning to give way to one that acknowledges the impact of others. Nicholas Christakis and James Fowler in their illuminating book, *Connected: The Surprising Power of Our Social Networks and How They Shape Our Lives*, drive home the point, saying "The social network in which we find ourselves defines our prospects. It does so by defining whom we meet." Unlike most authors who hem and haw, and qualify their words with provisos, the definitive and matter-of-fact nature of the words of Christakis and Fowler pushed me to take a closer look at the role of social networks in workplace success. Although the duo, by saying "The social networks in which we find ourselves," seem to promote a passive view that sees a person's social network as set in stone, the fact is that your social network can grow. Author Dan Schawbel, in his book, *Promote Yourself: New Rules for Career Success*, makes that point clear, saying "Expanding your social network will eventually help you in your career by putting you in touch with people who know what you can do and are in a position to help you get ahead." The key word in that sentence is "Expanding." Social networks can grow, expand, and become more vibrant.

Closely related to, and just as important as, social networks are the subjects of interdependence, reciprocal behavior, and sensitivity to the feelings of others. Daniel Brass and co., in their Academy of Management Journal article, *Taking Stock of Networks and Organizations,* said that "As is the case with interdependent tasks in organizations, relationships with others affect performance, especially if those relationships involve the ability to acquire necessary information and expertise." In effect, there's more to career success than talent and hard work. To succeed, you must carefully manage reciprocity (the give and take that comes with being part of a group), strive to improve your sensitivity to others, and learn to work interdependently. Singly, each member of this 'troika' is important, but together, all three determine your ability to successfully carry out the second mission-critical 'relationship' of careers—managing 'across'.

In this section, I take a deep dive into the subject of social networks, helping you better understand and apply that concept to your own career. After that, I deal with reciprocal behavior, interdependence and sensitivity to others—what I refer to as the stumbling blocks on the road to career success.

Chapter 9

Social Networks 101
(Why Who You Know is Crucial to Workplace Success.)

THE *POWER* OF SOCIAL NETWORKS: AN IDEA SPREADS AND BECOMES VIRAL—PRECIPITATING A RIOT IN THE CITY OF EPHESUS!

SOCIAL NETWORKS—THE UBIQUITOUS WEB of signals and interactions through which the influence, ideas, opinions, and even diseases of one person pass to another—are best understood by first comprehending their power. If you've ever been the victim of rumormongers and peddlers of fake news, then you've wittingly or unwittingly experienced the power of social networks—their ability to rapidly and informally transmit information from one person to another. In modern terminology, we'd say that social networks are powerful tools for social mobilization. But, and this is crucial, although the study of social networks is a relatively recent phenomenon, the effects of those networks go way back in time. Indeed, the now-famous 'Riot in Ephesus'—where Paul the apostle was almost lynched by a mob—was really only the result of the operation of social networks. The writer of Acts of the Apostles narrates that fateful incident, saying,

"About that time there arose a great disturbance about the Way. A silversmith named Demetrius, who made silver shrines of Artemis, brought in a lot of business for the craftsmen there. He called them together, along with the workers in related trades, and said: "You know, my friends, that we receive a good income from this business. And you see and hear how this fellow Paul has convinced and led astray large numbers of people here in Ephesus and in practically the whole province of Asia. He says that gods made by human hands are no gods at all. There is danger not only that our trade will lose its good name, but also that the temple of the great goddess Artemis will be discredited; and the goddess herself, who is worshiped throughout the province of Asia and the world, will be robbed of her divine majesty." When they heard this, they were furious and began shouting: "Great is Artemis of the Ephesians!" Soon the whole city was in an uproar." (Acts 19:23–29, NIV)

An Idea Goes Viral—And Provokes a Riot!

"Soon the whole city was in an uproar." There it is in black and white: Ephesus, one of Imperial Rome's most sophisticated cities, was engulfed in commotion. Why was this normally sedate city engulfed in riot and anti-christian behavior? The answer becomes clear only when we conduct a social network analysis—which lets us see that the city itself was made up of many interconnected networks . . .

The Network of Silversmiths

"A silversmith named Demetrius, who made silver shrines of Artemis, brought in a lot of business for the craftsmen there . . . " Here we see a network of silversmiths—men involved in the same trade, who were similar because of their skills and their trade.

The Network of Allied Tradesmen

"He [Demetrius] called them [the silversmiths] together, along with the workers in related trades . . . " Again we see another network—a network of workmen in fields related to that of the silversmiths. This network was probably made up of other metalworkers (goldsmiths etc.).

Social Networks 101

Ideas that Crossover into Other Networks are More Likely to Go 'Viral'

"Demetrius... called them [silversmiths] together, along with the workers in related trades... When they heard this [from Demetrius], they were furious and began shouting: "Great is Artemis of the Ephesians!" Soon the whole city was in an uproar." When the members of the networks of silversmiths and allied tradesmen heard the words of Demetrius, they became furious and soon the whole city was in an uproar. In effect, it was the members of the 2 key networks of silversmiths and allied craftsmen who spread the word to their friends and acquaintances across the city—and birthed a city-wide riot! This shows us that, before an idea can become 'viral', it must first be accepted by members of important networks, then it must gain critical mass by crossing over into many other social networks. Ideas that are able to fulfill these conditions are likely to more quickly shape the thinking of the wider society.

Ideas that 'Crossover' Must "Resonate" with the Members of the Receiving Network

The riot at Ephesus, as we've seen, had its roots in an idea that was first accepted by the network of silversmiths before spreading to the network of allied tradesmen, and finally berthing ship in the wider society of Ephesus. The question becomes: why did the idea spread so easily through these ostensibly different networks? The answer is this: the idea—or, more correctly, *the way the idea was presented*—resonated with each succeeding network. By saying *"You know, my friends, that we receive a good income from this business,"* the writer of Acts shows us that it was the prospect of financial loss that made the idea "resonate" with the networks of sundry tradesmen. But, by also saying "When they [the tradesmen] heard this, they were furious and began shouting: *"Great is Artemis of the Ephesians! Soon the whole city was in an uproar,"* the writer of Acts shows us that it was the prospect of the goddess Artemis being discredited that stirred devout townsfolk to fever pitch—and tipped the city into riot. What 'resonated' with the tradesmen—commerce—was clearly not going to 'move' the townsfolk, so the idea had to be consciously tweaked, modified, and presented in a different light—a religious light—before it could be accepted by townsfolk.

Section 2 | Managing 'Across'

Ideas that Crossover' from One Network to Another Require the Services of a "Convener"

"*He* [Demetrius] *called them* [the silversmiths] *together, along with the workers in related trades, and said . . .* " Conveners are persons whose central positions allow them bring disparate groups together—giving them the unique opportunity to coordinate the actions of others. Writer Marissa King, in her book, *Social Chemistry*, aptly describes their behavior, saying "By simply creating social events in which friends have the opportunity to become friends, one can become more of a convener. Part of what makes a convener is the depth and strength of their ties." Conveners serve as bridges for sharing ideas and resources among otherwise disparate groups of persons. And they are able to do this because they belong to these different groups. If conveners are influential persons with membership or links to multiple social networks, then Demetrius was the ultimate convener. His power arose not only from his belonging to, or having links with, more than one network, but also from his influence (he brought in a lot of business for all the craftsmen). A network analysis shows us that Demetrius belonged to at least 3 networks—silversmiths, sundry groups of allied tradesmen, and a network of customers (from which he brought plenty of business to the silversmiths). Conveners are like bridges through which ideas and information can spread, but their most important action—as the example of Demetrius reveals—is their ability to coordinate the actions of people in otherwise disparate networks.

Although the riot at Ephesus was solely the result of word-of-mouth, much reflection has helped me see the following truths . . .

- The Strongest Networks are Homogeneous—Made Up of Persons with Similar Backgrounds: the silversmiths formed a cohesive network precisely because they were all silversmiths. It would have been difficult for a person without a background in that craft to become a member. Homogeneous networks are like nurseries—the best places for ideas to germinate and take root before spreading.

- Conveners are Individuals Who Belong to More than One Network: Demetrius belonged to at least 3 networks—silversmiths, allied tradesmen and customers. This means that conveners are central precisely because they are also versatile and able to fit into more than one social network. Conveners do more than just belong to more than one network; they are persons who also add value to other members of their networks. They are vital "bridges" between different social groups through which information, ideas, resources, and influence flow.

- **The More Conveners in a System, the Greater the Likelihood that Ideas Can Go Viral:** All things being equal, the greater the number of conveners there are in a system, the greater the chance that an idea will crossover into other networks and become accepted and widespread.
- **The Idea or Message to be Spread May have to be Tweaked and Modified at Each Stage:** Demetrius sold the idea as the prospect of business loss to the tradesmen; the latter sold it to the townsfolk of Ephesus as the prospect of their beloved goddess Artemis being discredited.

Having seen the power of social networks, we now turn our attention to the component *parts* or *people* inside networks . . .

THE *PEOPLE* INSIDE SOCIAL NETWORKS: INSIDERS, OUTSIDERS, STRANGERS, STRONG TIES, AND WEAK TIES

" . . . all relationships are costly, and there is a limit to the number of relationships one can maintain."—CHARLES KADUSHIN

Like I said before, social networks are the ubiquitous set of relationships through which intangibles like influence, information, and even disease, flow from one person to another. Brandeis professor Charles Kadushin, in his book, *Understanding Social Networks,* said that "All relationships are costly, and there is a limit to the number of relationships one can maintain." By division, his words mean that, because of their high 'maintenance costs', we humans can't possibly have too many intense or strong relationships. To drive home the point, I often half-jokingly say that having one wife is easy, but pity the man (e.g., King Solomon) who has seven hundred! This means that the relationships in your social network will necessarily be of more than one kind. Some will be 'strong' and intense, and others 'weak' and less intense. Some will be close (insiders), and others more distant (outsiders). The writer of Proverbs drives home the point, saying . . .

> "Take the garment of one who puts up security for a stranger; hold it in pledge if it is done for an outsider." (Prov 27:13, NIV)

Section 2 | Managing 'Across'

These words show us that social networks are basically made up of 3 kinds of 'ties' or persons . . .

Insiders (Strong Ties), Outsiders (Weak Ties), and Strangers (No Ties)

Although by saying "Take the garment of one who puts up security for a stranger; hold it in pledge if it is done for an outsider," the writer of Proverbs is actually giving advice on credit management to creditors and financial analysts, his words also throw some light on the nature social networks, helping us see that . . .

1. People have a natural aversion to doing business with *outsiders*—persons outside their social circle. With the total *stranger*—someone you don't even know—the garment put up as collateral for the transaction should be 'taken' or counted as lost because that kind of person shouldn't be trusted. With an outsider—someone with whom you are only faintly acquainted, you should adopt a wait-and-see attitude and hold the garment in pledge. The only other kind of person left is the *insider*—a person you know, and with whom you have strong ties and,

2. Social networks are made up of—you guessed right—3 kinds of persons; insiders, outsiders and strangers.

But the writer of Proverbs isn't through with teaching on the nature of social networks. By going on to say,

> "A friend loves at all times, and a brother is born for a time of adversity," (Prov 17:17, NIV),

he shows us that,

Strong Ties (Insiders) Provide Unconditional Support, Solidarity and Social Identity

".A friend loves *at all times* . . . " There it is in black and white: a friend is someone close to you—who you know very well—the epitome of a strong tie. Therefore strong ties, the ties we have with people who are 'insiders' in our social networks, exist to provide unconditional support and solidarity. By comparing "A friend," with "a brother"—the epitome of family and identity—the writer of Proverbs drives the point home: strong ties are also sources of identity. Whether they are the result of an acquired identity (e.g., professional association) or an ascribed identity (e.g., national or ethnic groupings), strong ties provide the links between a relatively small or exclusive group of close-knit persons.

You Normally Have to Win the Respect of Outsiders

Crucially, since support from insiders is unconditional, you normally don't have to prove yourself to belong to these groups. Not so for outsiders! The writer of First Thessalonians makes the point clear, saying,

> "Make it your ambition to lead a quiet life: You should mind your own business and work with your hands, just as we told you, so that your daily life may win the respect of outsiders . . . " (1 The 4:11–12, NIV)

" . . . so that your daily life may *win the respect of outsiders* . . . " How do you know you are dealing with 'outsiders'? Easy. With people who are "outsiders," you must prove yourself or conduct yourself in ways that win their respect! To do this, you must exhibit competence, character, etc.

Having seen the defining qualities of 'strong ties' (insiders) and, because the qualities of 'no ties' (strangers) are self evident, the question becomes: what are the defining qualities of 'weak ties' (acquaintances)? The writer of Genesis, in his narrative of the story of Joseph, proffers an answer . . .

> "Now a certain man found him [Joseph], and there he was, wandering in the field. And the man asked him, saying, "What are you seeking?" So he said, "I am seeking my brothers. Please tell me where they are feeding their flocks." And the man said, "They have departed from here, for I heard them say, 'Let us go to Dothan.' " So Joseph went after his brothers and found them in Dothan." (Gen 37:15–17, NKJV)

Weak Ties Provide Access to Information that's Not Available in Your Own Network

"A certain man found him . . . wandering in the field. And the man asked him, "What are you seeking?" So he said, "I am seeking my brothers. *Please tell me where they are feeding their flocks.*" And the man said, "They have *departed from here, for I heard them say, 'Let us go to Dothan.'"* This unnamed man was certainly not part of Joseph's family, but he knew who Joseph was and was close enough to Joseph's brothers to have " . . . heard them say, "Let us go to Dothan."'" This man was an acquaintance—a 'weak tie'—who provided Joseph with crucial information about the whereabouts of his brothers. Weak ties are persons you see infrequently (Joseph had to travel sixty miles before he could meet this unnamed man) and who, because they move in networks different from yours, are privy to information you do not possess. Wharton professor Adam Grant, in his book, *Give and Take: A Revolutionary Approach to Success,* puts it beautifully, saying,

> "Strong ties provide bonds, but weak ties serve as bridges: they provide more efficient access to new information. Strong ties are our close friends and colleagues, the people we really trust. Weak ties are our acquaintances, the people we know casually. Our strong ties tend to travel in the same social circles and know about the same opportunities as we do. Weak ties are more likely to open up access to a different network, facilitating the discovery of original leads."

But the Writer of Proverbs still isn't done yet with teaching on social networks. By saying,

> "Many curry favor with the ruler, and everyone is a friend [acquaintance] of a man who gives gifts." (Prov 19:6, NIV),

he shows us that . . .

The Rich Have More Weak Ties than the Poor!

" . . . *everyone is a friend* [acquaintance] *of a man who gives gifts."* There it is in black and white; as a rule, the rich and successful (who have the resources to give) tend to have more 'friends'—casual acquaintances and weak ties—than the poor. The result? The rich are better able to access information about jobs and opportunities from networks other than theirs (I speak more about this in Chapter 10)—partly contributing to the differences in incomes between both groups. Some might say that this is really a chicken and egg situation—insisting that it is the rich person's wealth which allows him make plenty of casual acquaintances in the first place. Whatever, being rich is associated with having plenty of weak ties. In contrast, the poor tend to be associated only with those with whom they have strong ties.

SOCIAL NETWORKS 101

In this introduction to social networks, we first looked at the *power* of social networks (how they aid the spread of information, ideas and influence), before examining the *people* in our networks (strong ties, weak ties, outsiders etc). We now turn our attention to the *predictive value* of social networks...

WHAT ARE YOUR CAREER PROSPECTS?
(THE *PREDICTIVE* VALUE OF SOCIAL NETWORKS)

"... the social network in which we find ourselves defines our prospects. It does so by defining whom we meet."—NICHOLAS CHRISTAKIS & JAMES FOWLER

What are your prospects? What does the future hold in stock for you? Some people would give a top-of-mind answer and, paraphrasing wisdom teacher Mike Murdock, say "The secret of [my] future is hidden in [my] daily routine." While that may be true (I write more on the Power of Routine in Chapter 20), being derived from the individualist perspective that attributes success to what I, and I alone, do, it is only partially true. The big picture is that, since careers occur in the context of interdependence, the input of others is critical to whether I experience success or not. Therefore, a more accurate prediction of my career prospects must take into account the inputs of others.

Nicholas Christakis and Paul Fowler, in their illuminating book, *Connected: The Surprising Power of Our Social Networks and How they Shape Our Lives*, said that "... the social network in which we find ourselves defines our prospects. It does so by defining whom we meet." Not only do these intriguing words help us see the vital role of social networks in a person's career, they also helped me better understand the career path of a humble shepherd boy who rose to high office. Listen to the writer of First Samuel, as he tells the story of David...

> "All right," Saul said. "Find me someone who plays well and bring him here." One of the servants said to Saul, "The son of Jesse is a talented harp player. Not only that; he is brave and strong and has good judgment. He is also a fine-looking young man, and the LORD is with him." So Saul sent messengers to Jesse to say, "Send me your son David, the shepherd."" (1Sam 16:17–19, NLT)

Section 2 | Managing 'Across'

David's Social Network Predicted His Future!

King Saul, troubled by debilitating depression, needed music to soothe his nerves. So he ordered his men to find him a skillful musician. By saying "One of the servants said to Saul, "The son of Jesse is a talented harp player," the writer of First Samuel helps us see that, although David was a skillful musician, in the final analysis, what brought him to the palace was his being in the same social network as a key servant of Saul! Christakis and Fowler were correct after all " . . . the social network in which we find ourselves defines our prospects. It does so by defining whom we meet."

Ultimately, your social network plays a predictive role in determining your career prospects. Therefore, my question for you is this: who are the people in your network, and how do you plan to grow your social network? Whatever your answers, by now you'd agree with me that managing your personal network is crucial to career success. And that topic is the subject of the next chapter . . .

Chapter 10

Managing Your Personal Network

YOUR PERSONAL SOCIAL NETWORK, or rather, how you manage your personal social network is crucial to your success. Why? Because your personal network determines the variety and volume of information and feedback you receive, and the kind of information others receive about you—key factors in workplace progress. In an illuminating Harvard Business Review article, *The People Who Make Organizations Go — Or Stop,* researchers Rob Cross and Lawrence Prusak said that "Through social network analysis, people can identify when to build more or better relationships . . . Is all the manager's information coming from people above him rather than below him? . . . Is he missing feedback from people with different perspectives?" These words show how social network analysis—the more practical side of social network theory—can help you identify the sources of information and advice you receive and, just as important; help you trace the persons who give out information to others about you and your work. In this sense, social network analysis is really only personal contact analysis. All this calls to mind the words of the writer of Proverbs,

> "Whoever loves a quarrel loves sin; whoever builds a high gate invites destruction." (Prov 17:19, NIV)

For years, the phrase " . . . whoever builds a high gate invites destruction," spooked me. Why? Notice carefully that the passage says " . . . whoever builds a high *gate* invites destruction." It doesn't say " . . . whoever builds a high *wall* invites destruction." This must be because . . .

SECTION 2 | MANAGING 'ACROSS'

1. Walls keep out intruders, unwanted guests and enemies, while gates regulate the access of friends and associates,
2. A low gate is a more welcoming sign, but a high gate is a "keep off" sign and,
3. A gate is a metaphor for the work of managing your personal network of friends, colleagues and confidantes.

In effect, these words of the writer of Proverbs mean that,

Leaders Who Don't Manage their Personal Networks are Setting themselves Up for a Fall!

By saying " . . . whoever builds a high gate invites destruction," the writer of Proverbs is shouting out the warning that leaders who unnecessarily isolate themselves from others are on the path to failure and destruction. The question becomes: what exactly do other people carry that makes them so valuable to your success? Easy answer. People carry the information, advice, and feedback you need to succeed, manage a crisis, or stave off failure. Therefore, this passage of Scripture is really talking about how leaders who aren't linked to the right persons, who insulate themselves from relevant information, and who aren't properly managing their personal social networks are inviting failure. In a nutshell, if you want to experience workplace success, you must take the initiative and manage your personal network. As you do that, always keep in mind the following fact . . .

Personal Contacts are the Engines of Workplace Success

Personal contacts provide timely information that can help you do your work and navigate the cultural minefield that's the hallmark of the modern workplace. Like the "high gates" of the words of the writer of Proverbs which both let in people (signifying information *for* you), and let out others (signifying information *about* you), personal contacts bring information to you, and carry information about you to others outside your circle of influence. Sociologist Ronald Burt, in his book, *Structural Holes: The Social Structure of Competition*, puts it beautifully, saying,

> "Personal contacts get your name mentioned at the right time in the right place so that opportunities are presented to you. Their

referrals are a positive force for future opportunities. They are the motor expanding the third category of people in your network, the players you don't know who are aware of you."

A major quirk of organizational life is that anyone blowing her own trumpet or saying that she is the right person for a job is always treated with suspicion. But this doesn't apply to personal contacts. The latter are given leeway and possess the legitimacy to make recommendations about people they think should get a particular job opportunity—the very reason opportunities tend to fall kindly at the feet of workers with plenty of personal contacts. Again, Professor Burt drives the point home, saying,

> "Beyond logistics, there is the issue of legitimacy. Even if you know about an opportunity and can present a solid case for why you should get it, you are a suspect source of information. The same information has more legitimacy when it comes from someone inside the decision-making process who can speak to your virtues."

While it is given that you must work hard and smart, it is also true that the more people you have in your network who would go out of their way to help you succeed, the likelier it is that you will succeed.

Since we have seen the importance of personal networks and since, we have also seen how to manage one's personal network, we can now turn our attention to . . .

GROWING YOUR PERSONAL NETWORK

As I read former Microsoft executive Tim Sanders's excellent book, *Love is the Killer App*, I came across these words,

> "Think about business that you've lost or promotions someone else grabbed, or competitive one-on-one situations where a rival triumphed. Calculate the size of the winner's network versus yours. For the most part, the winners are those with the largest networks, the most powerful connections, and the ability to call in their reserves at the moment of truth."

" . . . *the size of the winner's network . . . winners are those with the largest networks.*" These words helped me see that, if personal networks are like a fisherman's net, then the larger the net, the more fish the fisherman can catch. In other words, your personal network is a "working net" which helps spread your influence in the workplace. The question becomes, what exactly does it take to grow your current personal network? The writer of Proverbs proffers an answer saying,

> "The world of the generous gets larger and larger, the world of the stingy gets smaller and smaller." (Prov 11:25, MSG)

Sharing Your Resources Expands Your Network!

"The world of the generous gets larger and larger . . ." There it is in black and white: the personal network ("world") of the generous is ever expanding. That is, if you want to grow your personal network or increase the number of persons who would be willing to go the extra mile to help you, then you must be willing to share—not hoard—what you have. Wharton professor Jonah Berger, in his excellent book, *Contagious: Why Things Catch On,* puts it beautifully, saying,

> "Passing along useful things also strengthens social bonds. If we know our friends are into cooking, sending them a new recipe we found brings us closer together. Our friends see we know and care about them, we feel good for being helpful, and the sharing cements our friendship."

As I reflected on this little appreciated truth, I came to see that the times when my career really took off have been times when someone somewhere was willing to recommend me to a decision-maker somewhere else. But, and this is the clincher, those recommenders were always people with whom I had, you guessed right, first shared something.

The question on your mind at this point must be "What exactly must I share in order to grow my network?" The answer, to paraphrase Tim Sanders, is that you should . . .

Share What You Know

Don't hoard what you know. If someone—a colleague or associate—is hard-pressed about getting a job done and you know how to get the job done, by all means tell the person what you know. But before you can even begin to share what you know, you must first 'know'. Therefore, growing your influence network is an inside job—a thing which begins with personal development, with taking some time to improve yourself. Read books and attend conferences so that you can have something to share. As you do this, remember these words of the writer of Proverbs,

> "Many beg favors from a prince; everyone is the friend of a person who gives gifts!" (Prov 19:6, NLT)

Because "... everyone is the friend of a person who gives gifts," people are, wittingly or unwittingly, more likely to be part of your personal network when you give freely to them of your wisdom.

Share "Who" You Know

To grow your network of contacts, you must do something counterintuitive; you must be willing to share your current "contacts"—the people you think can be helpful to others—with others. Sharing 'contacts' is one reason the growth of a person's network is often exponential—beginning slowly from a small base, and then accelerating as the number of contacts in your kitty crosses a threshold. Sharing "who" you know always begins with asking yourself this question "Is there someone I know that I think this person should know?"

Share What You Have

This is the classic way to grow a network. Everyone—politicians, dictators and Wall Street CEOs—utilizes this tactic whenever they invite their associates to join the proverbial gravy train! Sharing material resources—like all other kinds of sharing—kick-starts the operation of the principle of reciprocity. Simply put, that principle states that "People are more likely, or even duty bound, to help others who have previously helped them." (I take a really deep dive into this principle in Chapter 12). David, long before he became king, deliberately grew his influence network by sharing war booty with the elders of his native tribe of Judah (1Samuel 30:26–31). Interestingly, it was these same elders who rallied and anointed him king of Judah some time later!

Is your "world" getting larger or smaller? Is your network—the number of people ready and willing to help you—growing or contracting? Whatever your answers to these weighty questions, always bear in mind that growing your influence network is like cultivating a garden—it takes time and deliberate effort, and requires skill and resources. Therefore, the real question that you must answer is this: when last did you share something? Like I said before, sharing is an 'ongoing thing' for the best leaders, a 'yesterday thing' for average leaders and a 'never-done-it-before' thing for the 'also rans'. Crucially, the assumption undergirding the concept of 'sharing' is that you grow your network by sharing resources only, or mostly, with persons with whom you have close or strong ties. But personal networks can also grow by sharing resources with persons with whom you have weak ties. And it is to that topic that we now turn our attention . . .

GROWING YOUR PERSONAL NETWORK BY CULTIVATING "WEAK TIES'

Two things happen whenever a leader says or thinks "He that is not with me is against me." First, he fries the uncommitted, causing only the people committed to his mission to remain on his team—which is all well and good. Second, and this isn't so good, he drives away the fence-sitters—people who, while not totally committed to his cause, are still not against it. From a social network perspective, this second group of persons are acquaintances—people with whom the leader has "weak ties," and who belong to other networks. To be clear, losing people who are against you does little harm to your work, but losing 'weak ties' does you great harm. Why? Because weak ties are your connections or bridges to other social networks—people who can help spread your influence and give you access to resources available in other networks. In effect, leaders who want to grow their personal network should also share some of their resources with people with whom they have weak ties.

Interestingly, Jesus highlights this same principle. Listen to the writer of Luke's Gospel . . .

> "John said to Jesus, "Master, we saw someone using your name to cast out demons. We tried to stop him because he isn't in our group." But Jesus said, "Don't stop him! Anyone who is not against you is for you." " (Luke 9:49–50, NLT)

Growing Your Personal Network Requires that You Also Share Some of Your Resources with People Outside Your Own Network

"... we tried to stop him, *because he isn't in our group* [we don't have strong ties with him]." Although, this unknown man who was casting out demons in the name of Jesus was clearly not one of the disciples (he must have been part of another social network), Jesus surprisingly gave him a thumbs up! The disciples were antagonistic because the man was not one of them: *they assumed that anyone who is not one of them must be against them.* But, by saying "... *Don't stop him! Anyone who is not against you is for you,*" Jesus lays down a new criterion for dealing with people—and, by division, for growing our personal networks. He helps us see that there are people who are not with you (not inside your network), who can still be for you. From a social network perspective forming alliances with this group of persons grants you access to the resources available in other networks and helps spread your influence.

Leaders who throw down the gauntlet and share resources *only* with those with whom they have strong ties are invariably unable to corral support from those with whom they have weak ties. In effect, the natural tendency to relate, or share resources, exclusively with persons with whom you have strong ties can short-circuit your ability to grow your network. *For too long we've held the view that a person not with us—not belonging inside our social network—is automatically of little value to us. In this passage, Jesus takes a hammer to that kind of binary thinking.* He reveals a new criterion for growing your network: sharing some of your resources with persons outside your own social network—people who are *both* not with you and not against you. In a nutshell, most of us concentrate our networking efforts on building strong ties(insiders), but because these insiders are already in our social network, what they know is probably known to us or will, in due time, be known to us. To obtain new job and business information and opportunities, it may be necessary to cast our nets farther afield and cultivate weak ties.

Chapter 11

How Mentoring Can Advance Your Career

German researcher August Kekulé was probably the leading organic chemist of his day (in his time, there was no Nobel Prize), yet his greatness shone like a million stars when that prize was later instituted. How do I mean? Kekulé's doctoral students won three of the first five Nobels awarded in Chemistry (van't Hoff in 1901, Fischer in 1902, and Baeyer in 1905)! Kekulé's relationships with his protégés best illustrate the phenomenon of mentoring—a relationship between a father-figure and his protégé that furthers the career of the latter. The word "mentor" has its roots in classical Greek mythology where Ulysses, before departing to fight in the Trojan Wars, committed his son Telemachus to the care of an older man called Mentor. I have decided to include mentoring in this section on "Managing Across" because, although mentoring is often a relationship with a more experienced person, it doesn't have to be with a person within your own organization. And even if you have a mentor within your organization, since the relationship is entirely voluntary, it isn't encumbered by the authority issues that normally crop up when you manage 'up'. Notwithstanding, the key question is "In what ways can mentors boost a person's career?" The answer is: three ways . . .

1. By providing information,
2. By acting as 'sponsors' and,

3. By acting as models...

Mentors as Providers of Information—of *Tacit* Knowledge

Information is the currency of work. Whoever you are and whatever the nature of your job, you need knowledge both to get your job done and to navigate the cultural minefield that's the hallmark of organizations, groups or teams. You need to know what to do, who to ask (and who not to ask), and where to go, if you want to get your job done. But, as it turns out, all knowledge is not the same. Management researcher W. Richard Scott, in his book, *Organizations and Organizing*, makes this clear, saying

> "We know more than we can tell... Tacit knowledge is "sticky," "slippery," elusive, less observable, and less teachable than is explicit knowledge. Tacit knowledge is embedded in the skills of workers and in work routines..."

Professor Scott's words show that the knowledge you require to do a job is of two broad kinds—*tacit* and *explicit*. The latter, being codified and available in books, is easy to teach and grasp; the former, being embedded in the skills and experience of workers, is less easy to transfer from person to person—the reason it's also known as the 'tricks of the trade'.

The writer of First Kings, in his narrative of the conflict between Kings Ahab of Israel and Ben Hadad of Syria, opens a window into the subject, saying,

> "Then Ben-Hadad sent another message to Ahab: "May the gods deal with me, be it ever so severely, if enough dust remains in Samaria to give each of my men a handful." The king of Israel answered, "Tell him: '*One who puts on his armor should not boast like him who takes it off.*'" (Emphasis mine) (1Kgs 20:10-11, NIV)

In this incident, Ahab king of Israel, calls the bluff of an over-confident Ben-Hadad of Syria by reminding the latter of his inexperience in battle. Ahab's words mean that,

SECTION 2 | MANAGING 'ACROSS'

Training (Explicit Knowledge) is No Substitute for Experience (Tacit Knowledge)

"One who puts on his armor should not boast like one who takes it off." Figuratively speaking, a soldier puts *on* his armor only after undergoing a period of training and formal instruction in a military academy—the epitome of explicit or codified knowledge. But, as these wise words of King Ahab reveal, training alone cannot provide a soldier with all the knowledge he needs to defeat the enemy in battle. The 'extra' insight comes from the actual doing of the act—from battlefield experience—from figuratively "putting *off* the armor" after having first put it on. In other words, tacit knowledge comes primarily from experience, from learning by doing, and not from learning about something. Therefore . . .

Effective Task Performance Requires Both Tacit and Explicit Knowledge

"One who puts on his armor should not boast like him who takes it off.'" Ahab's wise words mean that, although formal training is necessary, it is not sufficient for effective battlefield performance. In effect, getting your job done requires more than just formal training (explicit knowledge); it also requires that you learn the tricks of the trade (tacit knowledge). If, as we've seen, both tacit and explicit knowledge are needed to get your job done, and if explicit knowledge is received via formal classroom-type environments, the question becomes, how exactly—apart from the actual doing of the task—can one obtain tacit knowledge? The answer comes through reflection on the words of the writer of Jeremiah . . .

> "This is what the Lord says, "Behold I will lay stumbling blocks before this people and the fathers and sons together shall fall on them. The neighbor and his friend shall perish." (Jer 6:21, NIV)

Mentoring is the Intergenerational Transfer of Knowledge

" . . . fathers and sons together shall fall on them." Whenever I read this passage of Scripture I often say "God forbid"! Why? Because the thought of a father and his son falling *together* (simultaneously, and at the same time) on the same stumbling block is unnerving. I mean, shouldn't the more experienced father—who possibly had passed that road before—have pointed out the stumbling block to his son? When fathers and sons stumble on the same block, it may just be that the more experienced father didn't or couldn't tell his son about the stumbling block—which, in reality, is a failure to transfer information and insight from one generation to another. Therefore mentoring, because it involves persons in two generations (one more experienced than the other) is the intergenerational transfer of knowledge and insight.

Mentoring answers the question posed by Gary Keller and Jay Papasan in their book, *The One Thing* "If you could go back in time and talk with the 18-year old you or leap forward and visit with the 80-year old you, whose advice would you be willing to take?" The answer is a no-brainer; I would choose to visit with the 80-year old me! But someone might now ask "What type of knowledge does mentoring transfer?" The answer is only revealed by taking a closer look at the words of the writer of Jeremiah, a thing which shows us that . . .

Mentoring Transfers Tacit Knowledge

Notice carefully that the writer of Jeremiah does *not* say "I will lay stumbling blocks before this people, and *teacher and student* shall together fall on them." On the contrary, he says "I will lay stumbling blocks before this people, and *father and son* together shall fall upon them" In this way, he takes us away from the formal classroom setting of teacher and student—the zone of explicit or codified knowledge—to the informal setting of mentoring (fathers and sons)—the zone of tacit, hard-to-explain-and-teach knowledge. Indeed, by saying "I will lay stumbling blocks before this people and . . . *The neighbor and his friend* shall *perish*," the writer of Jeremiah shows us that, when it comes to the transfer of tacit knowledge, even close friendships between neighbors don't do as well as father-son relationships. Why? Because, while fathers and sons who stumble together on the stumbling blocks only *fall*, neighbors and friends who undergo the same experience *perish*! The moral of all this is that a mentoring (father-son) relationship is the primary way to transfer tacit knowledge.

Section 2 | Managing 'Across'

Tacit Knowledge is More than Just Knowing the Way; It's Knowing the Pitfalls and Problems Along the Way—and How to Handle Them

"I will lay *stumbling blocks* before this people and fathers and sons shall stumble upon them." The highlighted words reveal the fine distinction between explicit knowledge and tacit knowledge. The former shows the way or general path to be taken, while the latter is more nuanced—showing the stumbling blocks or pitfalls and problems along that same path, and how they can be sidestepped. In this sense, tacit knowledge prepares you for the peculiar problems along the way—helping you sidestep, or even exploit, those problems. *Knowing the way—the purview of explicit knowledge—imparts a sense of direction, but knowing the locations of the stumbling blocks along the way—the realm of tacit knowledge—increases your speed, decreases the time taken to reach your destination, and allows you accomplish more in less time.*

Having seen that mentoring boosts careers by transferring tacit knowledge, the question becomes "How exactly does mentoring transfer tacit knowledge?" The writer of Matthew's Gospel, in his account of a series of amazing healings which occurred in Jesus' ministry in the region of Gennesaret, proffers an answer . . .

> "And when they [Jesus and his disciples] had crossed over, they landed at Gennesaret. And when the men of that place recognized Jesus, they sent word to all the surrounding country. People brought all their sick to him and begged him to let the sick just touch the edge of his cloak, and all who touched it were healed." (Matt 14:34–36, NIV)

" . . . *the men of that place recognized Jesus.*" "That place," was Gennesaret and "the men of that place," were the same men who had previously witnessed the now-famous healing of the woman with the issue of blood in that very locale (Matthew 9:19–21). Seeing Jesus again helped them connect the dots: they realized that their sick folk could be healed in the same way the woman with the issue of blood was healed. In other words, the men remembered how, by simply touching Jesus' garment, a woman was healed—causing them to instruct the sick to simply touch the hem of Jesus' garment! These men obtained *tacit* knowledge by simply observing Jesus at work. Their example shows that . . .

How Mentoring Can Advance Your Career

Mentoring Transfers Tacit Knowledge via "Shadowing"

The men of Gennesaret, by "shadowing"—closely observing Jesus at work—had learned exactly how the healing anointing worked in Jesus' ministry—informaton that Jesus never explicitly taught. The *Gartner Human Resources Glossary* says that,

> "Job shadowing is a type of on-the-job training that allows an interested employee to follow and closely observe another employee performing the role. This type of learning is usually used to onboard new employees into an organization or into a new role. Job shadowing may also be used as a learning opportunity for interns or students to gain an understanding of the role requirements and the job tasks."

Those words say it all: the major way tacit knowledge is transferred during mentoring is when the protégé closely 'shadows' the mentor at work. In this sense . . .

Shadowing' Involves Learning from Another as He Performs a Task

"And when the men of *that place* recognized Jesus . . . " Like I said before, those men had observed how Jesus' healing anointing operated because they had 'shadowed' or closely watched him as he healed the woman with the issue of blood. Which brings me to an important point: because mentoring requires 'shadowing'—something which demands that mentor and protégé be co-located or in close proximity when the former performs a task—it is difficult to mentor many persons at once or from afar! Shadowing involves a conscious decision by a more experienced person to allow a less experienced person stay close to her as she goes about her work. Shadowing is location sensitive and location specific, and requires that mentors go out of their way to create or orchestrate situations that can help protégés learn.

Interestingly, Luke's account of the same incident reveals another aspect of shadowing . . .

> "And there was a woman in the crowd who had had a hemorrhage for twelve years. She had spent everything she had on doctors and still could find no cure. She came up behind Jesus and touched the fringe of his robe. Immediately, the bleeding stopped. "Who touched me?" Jesus asked. Everyone denied it, and Peter said,

"Master, this whole crowd is pressing up against you." But Jesus told him, "No, someone deliberately touched me, for I felt healing power go out from me." When the woman realized that Jesus knew, she began to tremble and fell to her knees before him. The whole crowd heard her explain why she had touched him and that she had been immediately healed." (Luke 8:43–47, NLT)

'Shadowing' Works Best When the Mentor Helps the Protégé Make Sense of What's Happening

"*No, someone deliberately touched me, for I felt healing power go out from me.*" Come to think of it, although the men of Gennesaret were at the right location, the experience with the woman with the issue of blood would have been of little benefit to them if Jesus had not put it in perspective. It was Jesus who explained why and how the woman with the issue of blood obtained her healing. In effect, shadowing works best when the mentor can help the protégé make sense of what's happening.

Mentors as 'Sponsors'

It is difficult to advance in a profession or taste the grapes of career success without the input of a mentor. The key word in that sentence is "advance." After all is said and done, mentors help advance the careers of protégés. And, as we've seen, one way they do that is by providing tacit knowledge. As I reviewed Brandeis professor Charles Kadushin's excellent book, *Understanding Social Networks*, I came across the following passage,

> "There are . . . two kinds of effective mentors who help persons advance through organizations. The first is described as a source of social resources and information and . . . The other kind of mentor is embedded in a more dense support network shared by the protégé that allows for acceptance..[by other members of].. the organization . . . "

"*. . . two kinds of . . . mentors . . . The first is . . . a source of social resources and information.*" Clearly, these words paint a picture of a mentor as a person who provides information, especially information of the tacit variety. But things get really interesting as Professor Kadushin goes on to say that "*The other kind of mentor is embedded in a more dense support* *network shared by the protégé that allows for acceptance... [by other members of] ... the organization."* These words hit the nail on the head: mentors are also "sponsors"—persons who help protégés gain the acceptance and approval of key persons in the organization or network. Sooner or later, your career will require that a powerful and exclusive group of persons give you the nod of approval. Mentors introduce you to these persons and help you obtain their approval. To do this effectively, mentors themselves must belong to those exclusive groups. Being part of the small core of persons whose nods of approval is a passport for moving ahead is the relationship that mentors leverage to the benefit of protégés. In this sense, mentors are brokers—brokers of influence.

Paul the apostle—the writer of two-thirds of the New Testament—is widely acknowledged as Christianity's greatest evangelist. In his early days, notwithstanding his qualifications as lawyer and Pharisee, Paul was like any other person just starting out in a career—unknown, unsung, unaccepted, and in need of sponsorship. The writer of Acts narrates Paul's predicament, and his subsequent sponsorship by Barnabas, saying,

> "When Saul [Paul] arrived in Jerusalem, he tried to meet with the believers, but they were all afraid of him. They thought he was only pretending to be a believer! Then Barnabas brought him to the apostles and told them how Saul had seen the Lord on the way to Damascus. Barnabas also told them what the Lord had said to Saul and how he boldly preached in the name of Jesus in Damascus. Then the apostles accepted Saul, and after that he was constantly with them in Jerusalem, preaching boldly in the name of the Lord." (Acts 9:26–28, NLT)

A New Kid on the Block Seeks Acceptance!

"When Saul [Paul] arrived in Jerusalem, he tried to meet with the believers, but they were all afraid of him ... " Paul, in his previous life, was a notorious persecutor of Christians and, immediately after his conversion on the road to Damascus, attempted to associate with the Christians in Jerusalem. The latter, to a man, were having none of that because they thought he was pretending. Paul was in a quandary about how to gain approval and acceptance until ...

Section 2 | Managing 'Across'

A Mentor Stepped in and 'Sponsored' Him

"*Then Barnabas brought him* [Paul] *to the apostles . . . Then the apostles accepted* [Paul], *and after that he was constantly with them in Jerusalem.*" Those words say it all: the leaders of the Church at Jerusalem—a small close-knit group of apostles—acting as gatekeepers, determined who was accepted or not. Barnabas, a member of that same group, used his influence with the group to get them to accept Paul. The rest, as they say, is history—Paul went on to become Christianity's greatest evangelist. But it all began with being sponsored by his mentor Barnabas. Mentors are like Barnabas, advancing the careers of protégés by introducing them to influential persons in their networks. In essence, your workplace transition from "outsider'"—with little or no influence—to "insider" will probably require the services of a mentor. Which is why the best mentors are persons with deep connections to the most influential persons in your industry. If, as writer Dan Schawbel argues "Expanding your social network will eventually help you in your career by putting you in touch with people who know what you can do and are in a position to help you get ahead," then the sponsorship provided by mentors is the ultimate way to expand your social network.

Mentors as Models

In his book, *Leadership BS: Fixing Workplaces and Careers, One Truth At a Time,* Stanford professor Jeffrey Pfeffer said that "People are profoundly influenced by those with whom they have contact, as these others provide information and also models for behavior." Mentors are the classic "models for behavior," or living examples—showing protégés how the task should be performed, and how they should conduct themselves. The writer of Luke's gospel stresses this point, saying,

> "The disciple is not above his master, but everyone who is perfectly trained shall be like his master." (Luke 6:40, NKJV)

Mentors are Living Examples

" . . . [Every protégé] who is perfectly trained *shall be like his master* [mentor]." There it is in black and white: show me your mentor and, I can without fail, predict most of your operations and behavior. That mentors are models is connected with the "shadowing" protégés must do to obtain tacit knowledge. Indeed, it is because mentors are models that protégés have to "shadow" them as they work.

Having seen the three ways mentoring can advance your career, we necessarily end the discussion by turning out attention to the subject of . . .

Selecting a Mentor

Since a mentor-protégé relationship is almost always voluntarily entered into, the key factors that should guide you when you select a mentor are . . .

1. The expertise of the mentor: since mentoring involves the transfer of tacit knowledge, and since tacit knowledge is associated with high levels of know-how, look out for the persons who are reasonably competent at what you want to do. People who are competent and willing to allow you "shadow" them, make the most effective mentors.

2. The "connectedness" of the mentor: mentoring is sponsorship. Mentors help protégés gain acceptance and approval from 'insiders'—the people who call the shots—in a profession or organization. Therefore, the best mentors must themselves belong to the group of insiders or, at least, have vital links to them.

3. Your "fit" with the proposed mentor: a mentor shouldn't just be competent or expert, he should be competent and expert at the tasks that are relevant to your work. In other words, there should be a high degree of "fit" between what you do and what your proposed mentor does. "Fit" can even be expanded to include character and value questions—whether your values are in tandem with those of your proposed mentor or not. Since mentoring involves the development of close relationships, it would be uncomfortable if the values of mentor and protégé are very different or even at loggerheads. 'Fit' can also include career phase questions. If you are just starting out in a career (say, politics or business), then you don't yet need to be mentored by the top-leaders in that field (say, the president of your country, the governor of your state or the CEO of the corporation). The most effective mentors are those who are just ahead by one or two rungs on the corporate ladder (e.g., Army Majors, not Generals, are the best mentors for Lieutenants).

Section 2 | Managing 'Across'

Because #1, #2, and #3 above are often difficult to find in one person, it might be necessary to have more than one mentor. For example, Mentor A might be good for you because her deep connections with the people that matter in your organization make her an excellent sponsor etc.

Chapter 12

Give and Take

Understanding Reciprocal Behavior in the Workplace

"Reciprocity is the almost universal belief that people should be paid back for what they do—that one good (or bad) turn deserves another."
—Alvin Gouldner

THERE'S MORE TO CAREER success than individual hard work and talent. To succeed in the workplace, you also need to carefully manage reciprocal behavior—the give and take that comes with being part of teams and organizations. If you work hard for an organization all through the month, then you expect them to reciprocate and give you a paycheck. If your analysis and advice helped get a project off the ground, then you expect the project manager to reciprocate and put in a good word for you with higher-ups. If you supported a colleague's proposal at a major conference, then it's natural to expect her to reciprocate and support yours at the upcoming board meeting. The key word in the examples cited above is "expect." People everywhere—in all climes and cultures—expect that what they give to, or do for, you will be repaid to them. If not by you, then by others; and if not to them, then to others. Researchers Michael Arthur and Kathy Kram, in *Handbook of Career Theory,* drive the point home, saying "Reciprocity . . . is . . . what individuals and organizations give back in return for what they draw from each other."

Section 2 | Managing 'Across'

In this chapter, I take a deep dive into reciprocity and altruistic behavior—the behaviors that power the cooperation that characterizes managing 'across'. I also help you see that there's more to reciprocity than just giving and receiving. Indeed, the effective management of reciprocal behavior demands that you understand that there are givers, takers, fakers and matchers. Not fully grasping that fact can negatively impact your career and health.

GIVERS, TAKERS, FAKERS AND MATCHERS (WHY SOME GIVERS END UP AS LOSERS IN THE WORKPLACE)

It bears repeating: there's more to success than individual hard work and talent. Workplace success requires that you carefully manage reciprocity—the give and take that comes with being part of relational networks. In practice, this means that you must first answer questions like "How much of my time, talent and resources should I give to my organization?" Or "What should I legitimately expect to receive for all that I give to my group?" I was once part of an organization where just a few persons were getting fabulously rich while the majority of staff got poorer by the day. With my own eyes, I saw altruistic givers—men who sacrificed all for the 'cause'—leave the organization poor and broken. That experience made me ask myself some hard questions: "Is it possible to be a giver and still end up with the short end of the stick?" And "Is there more to giving than what we already know?" Only after reviewing Wharton professor Adam Grant's excellent book, *Give and Take: A Revolutionary Approach to Success*, and stumbling on the following words, was I able to find answers to those perplexing questions "Success involves more than just capitalizing on the strengths of giving; it also requires avoiding the pitfalls. If people give too much time, they end up making sacrifices for their collaborators and network ties, at the expense of their own energy." Nothing could be clearer: giving has both strengths and pitfalls. My altruistic associates received the short end of the stick because they weren't able to avoid its pitfalls! The pitfalls of giving are best appreciated if you understand that there are approximately four categories of persons in your social network. Listen again to Professor Grant . . .

> ""Whereas *takers* view success as attaining results that are superior to others' and *matchers* see success in terms of balancing individual accomplishments with fairness to others, *givers* are inclined

to ... characterizing success as individual achievements that have a positive impact on others." (Emphases mine)

Did you notice that Professor Grant places people in three broad categories—givers, takers, and matchers? Incidentally, a fourth category, 'fakers', is my own creation (I'll come to this category later). Did you also notice that each category is differentiated from others by the way it sees success? Givers tend to see success as having a net positive impact on others, while takers view success from the prism of receiving or getting more from others. Meanwhile, matchers see success as getting or giving only as much as others. Interestingly, the record of Scripture is chock-full of descriptions of these categories of people ...

> "Give, and it will be given to you: good measure, pressed down, shaken together, and running over will be put into your bosom. For with the same measure that you give shall it be measured to you." (Luke 6:38, NKJV)

Givers

"*Give*. . . . For with the same measure that you give shall it be measured to you." Notice carefully that while this scripture promises that what you give will be given to you in the future, it doesn't exactly say who it is that will give back to you! Therefore givers—the persons who ostensibly subscribe to the tenets of this scripture—are people who add value to others without expecting those particular persons to repay them. Their attitude is best described by Harvard political scientist Robert Putnam "I'll do this for you without expecting anything specific back from you, in the confident expectation that someone else will do something for me down the road." Since givers don't expect to receive from the specific persons they give to, they tend to put others' interests ahead of their own—making them, as we shall soon see, particularly vulnerable to takers and fakers. Why? Because their willingness to help others often places them at risk of being duped.

Takers

> "Now David came to the two hundred men who had been so weary that they could not follow David, whom they also had made to stay

at the Brook Besor. So they went out to meet David and to meet the people who were with him. And when David came near the people, he greeted them. Then all the wicked and worthless men of those who went with David answered and said, "Because they did not go with us, we will not give them any of the spoil that we have recovered, except for every man's wife and children, that they may lead them away and depart." But David said, "My brethren, you shall not do so with what the Lord has given us, who has preserved us and delivered into our hand the troop that came against us. For who will heed you in this matter? But as his part is who goes down to the battle, so shall his part be who stays by the supplies; they shall share alike . . . " (1Sam 30:21–25, NKJV)

The story in brief is this: while on one of his usual raids, David's base camp was attacked by the enemy. Since the wives and belongings of all team members were carried away by the raiders, David and his men pursued the raiders and recovered everything that had been lost (plus plenty of war booty). During the chase, 200 teammates became fatigued but nevertheless elected to remain at a temporary base camp, while the remaining 400 continued with the pursuit. On returning to base camp, the 400 'strong' men—insisting that "Because they [the 200 fatigued men] did not go with us, we will not give them any of the spoil that we have recovered, except for every man's wife and children, that they may lead them away and depart"—didn't want to fully reward the 200 men!

Notice carefully that the '200' were givers who had given their all to the team and were so exhausted that they couldn't go on to battle, electing to continue giving by remaining behind to guard base camp. Yet the '400' wanted to deny the '200' their just rewards. The '400' were takers. Takers not only don't like to give, they—you guessed right—also regularly discount the contributions of teammates and want to take what rightfully belongs to others. Professor Grant's words best describe them "If you're a taker, your driving motivation is to to make sure you get more than you give, which means you're carefully counting every contribution that you make. It's all too easy to believe that you've done the lion's share of the work, overlooking what your colleagues contribute." The '400' deliberately overlooked the contributions of the '200'. If not for David's just leadership, the '200' would have gone home unrewarded. Being a "giver" in a team of takers can leave you at the bottom of the pile—the reason the altruistic givers in my former organization got their fingers burnt!

Matchers

> "But when all goes well with you, remember me and show me kindness; mention me to Pharaoh and get me out of this prison." (Gen. 40:14, NIV)

Matchers are majorly motivated by the theme of tit-for-tat, and by the doctrine of scratch-my-back-and-I'll-scratch-yours. They give or add value to others and expect to receive from them. And, this is what differentiates them from givers, when you receive from them without giving back, they reduce or stop their giving, and recalibrate their relationship with you. Because matchers want to receive after giving, they tend to give strategically—only to those they believe can be of help to them in the future. Joseph the prisoner, as we see from the words of the writer of Genesis above, was a matcher who expected Pharaoh's official—whose dream he'd interpreted in prison—to repay him by putting in a favorable word to Pharaoh king of Egypt on his behalf.

Fakers

> "Do not eat the food of a begrudging host, do not crave his delicacies; for he is the kind of person who is always thinking about the cost. "Eat and drink," he says to you, but his heart is not with you. You will vomit up the little you have eaten and will have wasted your compliments." (Prov 23:6–8, NIV)

"... for he is the kind of person who is *always thinking about the cost*..." Fakers are agreeable takers. They, like amiable hosts, go to great lengths to prepare a feast to charm you, but their sole concern is what they can get from you. Because fakers must take more than they give, they are constantly calculating the cost of what they give. Since people are alert to takers, the latter often tend to be fakers, masking their greed with polite and amiable demeanors. Fakers are also greatly concerned with how people see them; because they value public recognition more than helping others, their giving is often done in the public. Professor Grant drives the point home, saying "Research shows that givers usually contribute regardless of whether it's public or private, but takers are more likely to contribute when it's public."

SECTION 2 | MANAGING 'ACROSS'

PRACTICAL STEPS TO MANAGING RECIPROCAL BEHAVIOR IN THE WORKPLACE

For most people, the gold standard on reciprocal behavior are Jesus' famous words—"Give, and it shall be given to you." For that reason, many, seeing only the benefits of giving, are enthusiastic givers who think they should *always* give to others—wittingly or unwittingly becoming like the proverbial workman whose only tool is a hammer, and to whom every problem is a nail! But the writer of Matthew's Gospel records some additional teachings of Jesus on giving that give cause for pause and show the pitfalls of giving . . .

> "Do not give what is holy to the dogs; nor cast your pearls before swine, lest they trample them under their feet, and turn and tear you in pieces." (Matt 7:6, NKJV)

With these weighty—and oft-ignored—words, Jesus introduces us to the pitfalls of giving and helps us see that . . .

The Idea that You're to be a Giver At All Times and to Everyone is Naive and Unscriptural!

"Do not give. . . . " Nothing can be clearer than this short phrase. We are not to give at all times and to everyone. Why? Because giving has pitfalls! When you give to the wrong persons (figuratively speaking "dogs. [and] . . . swine"), not only are your resources (time, money, etc) wasted, but your very life (career, family, etc) may also be jeopardized. Professor Grant was correct after all "Success involves more than just capitalizing on the strengths of giving; it also requires avoiding the pitfalls." Most givers end up with the short end of the stick because they are unable to avoid a prime pitfall of giving—giving to the wrong persons. This kind of altruistic, albeit naive, givers need to know that . . .

Engaging in Reciprocal Behavior With the Wrong Persons Can Harm You and Hinder Your Career

"Do not give . . . your pearls to swine, lest they trample them under their feet, and turn and tear you in pieces." Giving your precious time, energy and effort ("pearls") to the wrong set of persons ("swine") will not only see the latter devalue your offerings, it might also lead to harmful effects on your life and career. Therefore, we can say that...

Effective Reciprocal Behavior ('Giving') Always Begins with 'Sincerity Screening'

In his book, *Give And Take,* Professor Grant goes on to say that "When dealing with individuals, it's sensible for givers to protect themselves by engaging in sincerity screening and [act] primarily like matchers in exchanges with takers." He might just as well have taken his bearings from the words of Jesus! How do I mean? Easy. By saying " *Do not give . . . to dogs; nor cast your pearls before swine,*" Jesus is really saying that effective giving begins with first discerning the true nature and intent of the receiver—what Professor Grant refers to as "sincerity screening." The question becomes: what are the biblical ways through which givers can practice 'sincerity screening'? The answer is: by always bearing in mind the words of the Psalmist...

> "With the merciful, You will show Yourself merciful; With a blameless man, You will show Yourself blameless; With the pure You will show Yourself pure; And with the devious You will show Yourself shrewd." (Ps 18:25–26, NIV)

These amazing words help us see that,

Not Only is God a Giver, He Can Also Switch Mode And Become a Matcher!

God is not only a giver; he is also, unbeknown to many, a matcher! How do I mean? By saying " . . . With the pure, [God] will show himself pure. And with the devious, he shows himself shrewd!" the Psalmist shows us that God's behavior is always entirely appropriate to the person he is dealing with! He firsts tests the person on the other side of the table, and then adapts his own behavior to match that person. If the person is open-handed, then God continues to give. If not, he begins to match that person's behavior. As leaders, this means that . . .

Section 2 | Managing 'Across'

The Best Way to Manage Your Relationships With Takers and Fakers is to Become a Matcher

When you sense that you're dealing with takers or fakers, you need to switch mode and become a matcher—you need to demand greater accountability and transparency from beneficiaries of your time, talent and money. You need to demand that they show good faith and visible fruit for all they've received from you before you continue to give. Why? Because continuing to give to takers and fakers wastes your resources and puts your welfare in jeopardy. This kind of matching behavior does three things . . .

1. It protects your resources from wastage,
2. It protects you from donor fatigue, and emotional and psychological burnout (more on this in Chapter 15 when I write about the pitfalls of managing 'across') and,
3. It holds receivers accountable by prodding them to be of good behavior.

Since success in the workplace depends on your skill at managing 'across', and since skill at managing 'across' is dependent on your ability to manage the give and take associated with reciprocal behavior, I have created the following diagnostic grid . . .

1. Giver in the Midst of Takers = Sheep Among Wolves (You'll suffer lack and privation as colleagues take advantage of you).
2. Giver in the Midst of Fakers = Sheep Among Wolves-in-Sheep's Clothing (You'll suffer lack and privation as colleagues take advantage of you).
3. Giver in the Midst of Matchers = Sheep Among Goats (You'll get only what you deserve).
4. Giver in the Midst of Givers = Sheep Among Sheep (You'll flourish and prosper).

Wrap Around

Career success always requires the careful management of reciprocity—the give and take that comes with being part of work groups. To effectively manage reciprocity, always keep in mind the following facts . . .

- Givers, Takers, Fakers and Matchers are all differentiated by the way they see success.
- Givers are altruistic—willing to give to others even at the expense of their own wellbeing.
- Takers are driven by the desire to get more than they give.
- Fakers are agreeable takers, masking their desires under a cloak of pleasantness, religiosity etc.
- Matchers give and expect to get back from those they give to.
- A Giver in the midst of Takers and Fakers always gets the short end of the stick.
- Giving has pitfalls.
- Leaders protect themselves from the pitfalls of giving by engaging in 'sincerity Screening'.
- If you sense you're dealing with takers and fakers, then you need to become a Matcher.

Chapter 13

How Insensitivity to Others Can Negatively Impact Your Career

"Sensitivity to others requires an almost clinical interest in the observation of behavior. It requires not only self-awareness, but more important, awareness of others. These skills are not taught in school or in management education courses, except in a few rare instances." —Jeffrey Pfeffer

IF ANY WORD BEST describes what happens when people manage 'across', it must be "interdependence." Because you are a colleague with whom I have to work, we are mutually dependent—what you do affects the results I obtain and vice versa. In this sense, managing 'across' refers to relationships where workers are colleagues who have equal or almost equal jurisdiction and authority. If interdependence defines the landscape when people 'manage across', insensitivity to the feelings and statuses of others best explains why many people can't seem to manage 'across' successfully. Insensitivity to the feelings of others means that I am unwilling or unable to sense the unspoken desires of others, while insensitivity to their statuses means that I don't take their education and training into account in my dealings with them. Either way, I am setting the stage for ineffective work relationships.

How Insensitivity to Others Can Negatively Impact Your Career

READING PEOPLE LIKE A BOOK: THE STORY OF ESAU

"If you step into a room and you don't immediately know who is for you, and who is against you, you don't belong in politics."—LYNDON BAINES JOHNSON

In the Scripture record, probably no one is cast more in the role of the "other" than Esau. I mean, who can forget the famous words,

> "... I loved Jacob. And I hated Esau ... " (Mal 1:2–3, KJV).

To worsen matters, Esau's personal behavior does little to stop his 'otherization'. Witness the casual disregard he displayed for his own inheritance—an inheritance he sold to his twin brother Jacob for a mere plate of porridge! But that 'otherization' comes to its fullness in Esau's troubling inability to sense the true feelings of close family members, a thing which made him a virtual outsider (the 'other') in his own family. Although, I first dipped my toes into the story of Esau in Chapter 6, that story is such a treasure trove of insights, that it can, with some modification, bear repetition. The writer of Genesis, narrates Esau's troubling story, saying,

> "When Esau was forty years old, he married Judith daughter of Beeri the Hittite, and also Basemath daughter of Elon the Hittite. They were a source of grief to Isaac and Rebekah." (Gen 26:34–35, NIV)

> "Then Rebekah said to Isaac, "I'm disgusted with living because of these Hittite women. If Jacob takes a wife from among the women of this land, from Hittite women like these, my life will not be worth living." (Gen 27:46, NIV)

These pungent words help us see that ...

"Reading" Nonverbal Communications is Key to Developing Sensitivity to Others

"They [the wives Esau took] were a source of *grief* ... I'm *disgusted* with living with these women [Esau's wives ... " Like I said before, grief and disgust are such strong emotions that, even when not verbally communicated, they are almost impossible to hide or disguise for long. And when your actions cause grief and disgust to the people closest to you—family members who live with you on a daily basis—you certainly should know. Except, as this passage reveals, your name is Esau! Imagine, Esau marries wife number one; causing grief to his parents Isaac and Rebekah. He doesn't notice this and goes ahead to marry another Hittite wife, causing even more grief and disgust. Still, Esau doesn't see or know that he is deeply wounding his parents! Howard Gardner, the famous Harvard psychologist, said that "The core of interpersonal intelligence includes the capacities to discern and respond appropriately to the moods, temperaments, motivations and desires of other people." People like Esau who can't, for any reason, discern how significant others feel about them or their actions aren't going to fulfill their potential in group settings.

The writer of Genesis continues his sobering narrative, saying,

> "So Isaac called for Jacob and blessed him and commanded him: "Do not marry a Canaanite woman . . . " Now Esau learned that Isaac had blessed Jacob and had sent him to Padan Aram to take a wife from there . . . Esau then realized how displeasing the Canaanite women were to his father Isaac . . . " (Gen 28:6–8, NIV)

Esau Finally Gets It!

"*Esau then realized how displeasing the Canaanite women were to his father Isaac.*" It took many years, many missteps and many quarrels, but Esau finally got it. He finally realized that his parents didn't merely disapprove of his actions, they were grieved and disgusted! People who are insensitive to the feelings of significant others (bosses, suppliers, spouses etc.) in their lives are often blind to nonverbal cues and communications. Such people eventually come to know firsthand the truth of the saying of leadership experts James Kouzes and Barry Posner "Insensitivity to others is the most frequent cause of career derailment." But there's something else I want you to see: by saying "Esau then realized how displeasing the Canaanite women were to his father Isaac," the writer of Genesis helps us see that . . .

The Best Leaders Discern How Others Feel from their Nonverbal Communications

Esau's people skills were atrocious. Imagine living with people all your life and causing them grief and disgust, and not even even knowing it until you *hear* them say it in a roundabout way to another person! The core of sensitivity to others is the ability to discern how people feel from their body language or nonverbal communications. If people have to shout, cry out, raise hell or tell others about it before you know how they feel, your people skills need an update (and your relationship/job/business might just be in jeopardy). Learn to listen not just to what's being said, but to what's not being said and, even more importantly, to how it's being said. Whenever you sense a discrepancy between what a person says and his body language, choose the latter because, in the words of pioneer psychiatrist George Graham "The body [language] doesnot lie." People may be able to hide behind the mask of false words, but body language is more difficult to mask or control.

Interestingly,, the writer of Proverbs has much to say about body language and nonverbal communication . . .

> "Whoever winks with their eye is plotting perversity; whoever purses their lips is bent on evil." (Prov 16:30, NIV)

This intriguing passage highlights what many already instinctively know: you can decipher the thoughts of another by carefully observing their face or posture! The man who purses his lips is a man whose mind is made up, and who is bent on doing evil. The point of all this is that people are like books that must first be "read" to understand their meaning. Reflection on these words of the writer of Proverbs has helped me see two ways to 'read' people . . .

Carefully Observe the Face: Facial Expression Offers a Rich Source of Meaning and Communication

"Whoever winks with the *eye* . . . whoever purses their *lips* . . . " Did you notice that the lips and eyes mentioned in the passage are both located on the face? When it comes to communication, facial expression offers probably the richest source of meaning. Why? Easy. Because the muscles of that region are directly attached to the skin, and their every twitch, contraction or relaxation opens a window into a person's soul. If you really want to know what a person thinks or feels, look carefully at her face. Whoever first said that "There is no art to find the mind's construction on the face," is either a poor judge of people or hasn't yet read the book of Proverbs! Agreed that coaching and deception can help people mask their facial expressions, but sooner or later those masks will fall off and their true feelings will be revealed.

Carefully Observe Posture and Gesture: Posture and Gesture Offer Another Rich Source of Meaning and Communication

"Whoever winks . . . whoever purses their lips . . . " Apart from speaking, people also communicate with their bodies—or more correctly, with their gestures and postures (winking and pursing the lip are gestures). Effective leaders take the time and make the effort to "hear" and "listen" to 'body language'—to what others are saying with their bodies. Psychologist Robert Bolton drives this point home, saying,

> "A person cannot not communicate. Though she may decide to stop talking, it is impossible for her to stop behaving, The behavior of a person—her facial expressions, posture, gestures, and other actions—provide an uninterrupted stream of information and a constant source of clues to the feelings she is experiencing. The reading of body language, therefore, is one of the most significant skills of good listening."

Whenever there's a Disconnect Between the Verbal and the Nonverbal, Go With the Latter!

Body language is the richest source of communication because it is often involuntary or automatic and involves the use of multiple muscles. A frown involves the use of many specific facial muscles and is therefore more difficult to hide or control than mere speech. All this means that whenever you observe a disconnect between what a person says and her body language, your best bet is to go with her body language. Remember "The body language never lies!"

Wrap Around

To become more sensitive to the unarticulated feelings of others, and to become a leader who is not like Esau, you must . . .

- Get Over Yourself: drop your own agenda and learn to listen to what others are saying without words. I may not always tell you how I feel, but I certainly will always show how I feel. To know how I feel you may need to listen to what is not being said, to look at my body language, and to listen to how I am saying what I say. Don't be like Esau who couldn't even see the disgust and grief in the countenance of others!

- Get Off Your High Horse: As people become more successful and move up the corporate ladder, they tend to feel less need to listen or pay attention to others.

The writer of Proverbs drives the point home, showing us that the two factors listed above are often precursors to loss of both crown and riches, saying,

> "Be sure you know the condition of your flocks, give careful attention to your needs, for riches do not endure forever, and a crown is not secure for all generations . . . " (Prov 27:23-24, NIV)

Did you notice what factors hinder leaders from paying careful attention to the conditions of the people they lead? You guessed right. It is the wealth ("riches") and power ("crown") of the leaders themselves. Like I said before, in an interesting experiment, psychologists asked people to take a marker pen and draw, with their dominant hand, the letter E on their foreheads. Leaders who were most powerful or highest up the corporate ladder tended to draw the 'E' in a manner that only they could read. People with less power tended to draw the 'E' in a way that others could read! The take home? Power tends to make leaders insensitive to others—the more reason, as you climb the corporate ladder, you should get off your high horse!

Chapter 14

Pitfalls and Problems of Managing 'Across'

INTERPERSONAL CONFLICT, PROFESSIONAL JEALOUSIES & BURNOUT

" . . .the available slots become fewer and fewer as one nears the top of an organization or a profession."—EDGAR SCHEIN

MANAGEMENT TEACHER EDGAR SCHEIN, in his excellent book, *Career Dynamics*, said that " . . . the available slots become fewer and fewer as one nears the top of an organization or profession." Those insightful words mean that, because there are increasingly fewer openings than qualified personnel as you move up the corporate ladder, the most prevalent types of conflict in organizations are rooted in the struggle for access to, and control of, resources, recognition and rewards—what I refer to as the 3Rs. In other words, organizations, by design, promote interpersonal conflict! That is, it is the structure of organizations, and not necessarily the character of the people who work in them, that's responsible for most of the conflict in organizations. When the friction occurs between two persons with essentially *similar* backgrounds who are vying for resources, recognition or rewards, the resulting conflict is a professional rivalry or jealousy that can be deadly. And, when the friction is between persons or groups with *different* backgrounds, it's a more simple interpersonal conflict. And, it is to one of

Pitfalls and Problems of Managing 'Across'

the latter—an interpersonal conflict between two very different leaders in Roman-administered Palestine—that we now turn our attention . . .

PONTIUS PILATE VS. KING HEROD (MANAGING WORKPLACE CONFLICT)

"Next to physical survival, the greatest need of any human being is psychological survival—to be understood, to be affirmed, to be validated, to be appreciated."
—Stephen Covey

Management teacher Stephen Covey, in his co-authored book, *First Things First*, describes the 3 kinds of competencies needed to survive in the modern workplace . . .

- Technical Competence: the knowledge and skill to achieve agreed-upon results, or the ability to think through problems and look for new alternatives,

- Conceptual Competence: the ability to see the big picture, to examine assumptions and shift perspectives and,

- Interdependent Competence: the ability to interact effectively with others, including the ability to listen, communicate, get to third alternatives, create win-win agreements, and work towards synergistic solutions; the ability to see and operate effectively and cooperatively in complex organizations and systems.

In my days as an emerging leader, I was totally dedicated to improving my technical and conceptual competencies, and that's how it should be for emerging leaders. These days, I realize that reaching and operating at the highest echelons of my vocation takes more than just technical and conceptual competence: it also requires a huge dose of interdependent competence. This fact is vividly illustrated by the account of the breakdown in the relationship between the two key leaders of government business in Roman-administered Palestine. The writer of Luke's Gospel, as part of his gripping account of the arrest, trial, and crucifixion of Jesus, narrates that incident, saying,

> "When Pilate heard of Galilee, he asked if the man [Jesus] was a Galilean. As soon as he knew that [Jesus] belonged to Herod's jurisdiction, he sent him to Herod, who was also in Jerusalem at

Section 2 | Managing 'Across'

that time... Then Herod questioned [Jesus]... And the chief priests and scribes stood and vehemently accused him. Then Herod... sent him back to Pilate. That very day Pilate and Herod became friends with each other, for previously they had been at enmity with each other." (Luke 23:6–12, NIV)

A Key Working Relationship Breaks Down!

"That very day Pilate and Herod became friends...for previously they had been at enmity with each other." There it is in black and white: what should have been a cooperative working relationship between two key government officials had at some point degenerated into enmity and antagonism. But the writer of Luke's Gospel doesn't leave us in the dark as to the reasons for this enmity, saying (in two separate passages),

> "In the time of *Herod king of Judea* there was a priest named Zechariah..." (Emphasis mine) (Luke 1:5, NIV)

> "In the fifteenth year of the reign of Tiberius Ceasar—when Pontius Pilate was governor of Judea, *Herod was tetrach of Galilee,* his brother Philip tetrach of Iturea... " (Emphasis mine) (Luke 3:1, NIV)

Taken together, these two verses of Scripture reveal the probable reason Herod was at daggers drawn with Pilate. The story begins with a first "Herod"—Herod the Great; the "Herod" who ordered the massacre of all Jewish baby boys below the age of two years when he heard that Christ had been born in Israel (Matthew 2.1–16). This Herod was king over all of Judea. The story continues with a second "Herod"—Herod Antipas, son of Herod the Great—who is tetrach (ruler of a fourth part of a kingdom) of a smaller entity called Galilee. After the death of Herod the Great, it seems that the Roman emperor, by appointing Pontius Pilate as governor of Judea, began to severely limit the power and authority of the Herod family. The latter, who once had unlimited jurisdiction over the whole of Judea, now had authority over a smaller area. These events—a classic 3R conflict over resources, recognition and rewards—were the probable cause of the enmity between Herod and Pontius Pilate.

To worsen matters, Pilate went ahead to "infringe" on Herod's jurisdiction. The writer of Luke's Gospel makes this last point crystal clear, saying,

Pitfalls and Problems of Managing 'Across'

> "Now there where at that time some present who told Jesus about the Galileans whose blood Pilate had mixed with their sacrifices." (Luke. 13:1, NIV)

Imagine that you are Herod, *ruler of Galilee,* and you hear that Pilate, Roman governor of Judea, leaving his own jurisdiction over people in Jerusalem, has proceeded to try, sentence, and execute Galileans (people over whom you have legitimate authority). Pilate's very public show of disrespect would probably make you his antagonist—another reason Herod became Pilate's enemy. Pontius Pilate didn't seem to appreciate Stephen Covey's words "Next to physical survival, the greatest need of any human being is psychological survival—to be understood, to be affirmed, to be validated, to be appreciated." Fortunately, Pilate—ever the skilled people person— made amends for his mistakes. Listen again to the writer of Luke's Gospel,

> "On hearing this, Pilate asked if the man [Jesus] was a Galilean. *When he learned that Jesus was under Herod's jurisdiction, he sent him to Herod . . . When Herod saw Jesus, he was greatly pleased . . . That day Herod and Pilate became friends—before this they had been enemies."* (Emphases mine) (Luke 23:6–12, NIV)

Reflection on the above words has helped me see that getting along with others within the competitive-by-design structure of organizations begins with . . .

Publicly Recognizing the Authority, Person, and Contribution of Third Parties

The chief priests bypassed Herod and brought Jesus directly to Pilate, but when the latter found out that Jesus was indeed a Galilean who ought to have first been tried by Herod, he sent him back to Herod. By doing this, Pilate sent out a powerful, public, and pointed message to everyone that he recognized and respected the office and person of Herod. The need to be recognized, appreciated, affirmed, and respected supplies the hidden driver for most human interactions—and the fuel for many a workplace conflict. The best leaders, like Pilate, know that meeting that need is key to managing 'across'—to winning over estranged third parties and working cooperatively with people of coequal authority. When Pilate took the initiative and publicly acknowledged the authority of his old enemy Herod, he broke down the dividing wall that separated both of them. One way to redeem broken relationships is to publicly and genuinely esteem the other person, because people naturally gravitate to those who value them and their contributions. The long and short of managing 'across' is to use humankind's great need "to be understood . . . to be appreciated," as the touchstone for dealing with people.

You Hold the Keys: If You Want to Win Someone Over, You Must Take the First Step

Pilate was proactive; he did not sit around waiting for Herod to make the first move, rather he initiated the action which won over his old enemy. Leadership by definition is proactive, so anytime you find yourself waiting for another to make the first move, it might just mean that you are reacting, not leading. As we've seen from the conflict between Pilate and Herod, the most common type of conflict in managing 'across' is one arising from the struggle for resources, recognition and rewards. But, there is another dimension to this type of conflict that is so peculiar to managing 'across' that it demands special treatment. And it is to that dimension that we now turn our attention . . .

HANDLNG PROFESSIONAL JEALOUSY (LESSONS FROM THE LIFE OF JEREMIAH)

"Your most dangerous competitors are those that are most like you."
—Bruce Henderson

Beware the green-eyed monster! Envy and jealousy can make people so implacably opposed to you that they will actively try to hinder your progress or seek your downfall. Because managing 'across' involves working with peers and co-workers who are roughly at par with you in the hierarchy—people who can openly answer back or push back—it is particularly prone to conflicts rooted in professional jealousy. Quick, stop and think; envy has little or no room to play when people manage 'up' or 'down'. And the reason isn't far-fetched: army Privates don't ordinarily compare themselves with Generals! Brandeis professor Charles Kadushin drives the point home, saying,

Pitfalls and Problems of Managing 'Across'

> "... there is no motivation to associate with or be envious of those who "won't return your phone calls." There is no point for me to envy Bill Gate's or George Soros's fortunes. They are entirely out of reach. One is more likely to compare oneself and to try to associate with those others who are not too far removed from one's own rank."

"*One is more likely to compare oneself . . . with those others who are not too far removed from one's own rank.*" Those wise words hit the nail on the head: professional jealousy is more likely to arise between persons of roughly similar ranks, qualifications, and social standing—conditions aptly fulfilled when you manage 'across'.

Anyone familiar with the Bible probably knows that most of biblical Israel's prophets were murdered by kings and people in authority. But, in an interesting exception to that rule, Jeremiah the prophet was almost killed by, believe it or not, his professional rivals—other prophets and priests! The writer of Jeremiah narrates that incident, saying . . .

> "But when Jeremiah had finished his message, saying everything the LORD had told him to say, the priests and prophets and all the people at the Temple mobbed him. "Kill him!" they shouted. "What right do you have to prophesy in the LORD's name that this Temple will be destroyed like Shiloh? What do you mean, saying that Jerusalem will be destroyed?" And all the people threatened him as he stood in front of the Temple." (Jer 26:8–9, NLT)

A Prophet Comes Under Attack—from His Rivals!

"... the *priests*, the *prophets* and all the *people* mobbed him. 'Kill him!' they shouted." This passage shows us the prophet Jeremiah—who, by the way, was also a priest (Jeremiah 1:1)—under attack. After speaking God's word to the people of Judah, a motley group of priests, prophets and ordinary people seized him and wanted him put to death. Notice carefully that it was Jeremiah's professional colleagues—priests and prophets—that were at the head of that lynch mob! But Jeremiah was wise to what was happening . . .

> "Then Jeremiah spoke in his own defense. "The LORD sent me to prophesy against this Temple and this city," he said. "The LORD gave me every word that I have spoken. *Then the officials and the people said to the priests and prophets,* "This man does not deserve the death

sentence, for he has spoken to us in the name of the LORD our God." " (Emphasis mine) (Jer 26:12,16, NLT)

Jeremiah Makes His Defense

Under pressure, Jeremiah turned to the officials and the people (notice that he didn't even bother to address his rivals, the priests and prophets) and opened his defense: God had sent him to say the things he said. The result? *"Then the officials and people said to the priests and the prophets* [who were still hellbent on killing Jeremiah], *"this man should not be sentenced to death . . . "* Again, notice carefully that while Jeremiah's defense swayed the officials and people of Judah, it did not sway his professional rivals—the priests and prophets. The latter group was still hellbent on putting him to death! Professional jealousy is implacable—the very reason Jeremiah didn't even attempt to sway or influence it. It's the same reason, when dealing with professional jealousy, you should spend little or no time trying to win over jealous rivals. Instead, focus your efforts on key decision-makers whose eyes haven't yet turned green with envy!

The moral of Jeremiah's travails is that . . .

1. Professional jealousy is a fact of life in the workplace: Jeremiah was aware of the intense jealousy that professional rivalry can bring. You too need to wise up to this bitter reality of the workplace—your greatest opposition will probably arise from people in the same trade as you.

2. Professional rivals are, in the main, not easily influenced or swayed: because they ostensibly stand to gain when you fall or fail, no amount of convincing can make them 'love' you. It's best if, like Jeremiah, you address your words to other audiences.

3. Professional jealousy increases as you become more successful. It was Jeremiah receiving a clear word from God—the ultimate proof of success in ministry—that got his rivals all worked up!

We now turn our attention to the third pitfall associated with managing across . . .

Pitfalls and Problems of Managing 'Across'

BURNOUT: SYMPTOMS, CAUSES & HOW TO COPE (LESSONS FROM THE LIFE OF ELIJAH)

"Burnout: a state of emotional, physical, and mental exhaustion caused by excessive and prolonged work-related stress. It occurs when you feel overwhelmed, emotionally drained, and unable to meet the constant demands of work and life."—Wikipedia

Managing 'across' involves handling the give-and-take or the multiple demands that are par for the course when dealing with colleagues and customers—which often requires you to put the interests of others first if you want to experience career progress. But, putting others' interests first, as we've seen, has its drawbacks. Wharton professor Adam Grant, in his book, *Give and Take: A Revolutionary Approach to Success,* describes these drawbacks, saying "Since givers tend to put others' interests ahead of their own, they often help others at the expense of their own well-being, placing themselves at risk for burnout." In effect, managing 'across' can significantly increase your risk of suffering a burnout. "So, what," you might ask, "are the symptoms of a burnout?" Again, Professor Grant provides an answer, saying "For many years, experts believed that the stress response involved a choice: fight or flight. Since burnout means we lack the energy to fight, it's natural to choose flight, coping by avoiding the source of stress." These eye-opening words helped me see that "flight"—a desire to get away from it all—is a principal symptom of burnout. They also helped me better understand the phenomenon of burnout from probably the most famous burnout in the record of Scripture—the burnout of Elijah the prophet. Listen to the writer of First Kings,

> "Then Jezebel sent a messenger to Elijah, saying, "So let the gods do to me, and more also, if I do not make your life as the life of one of them by tomorrow about this time." And when he saw that, he arose and ran for his life, and went to Beersheba, which belongs to Judah, and left his servant there. But he himself went a day's journey into the wilderness, and came and sat down under a broom tree. And he prayed that he might die, and said, "It is enough! Now, Lord, take my life, for I am no better than my fathers!" (1 Kgs 19:2-5, NKJV)

SECTION 2 | MANAGING 'ACROSS'

Elijah Suffers a Burnout!

In this passage, we see all the classical symptoms of burnout in the life of the prophet—fatigue ("I have had enough, Lord . . . "), fear ("Elijah was afraid and ran for his life."), suicidal thoughts ("Lord, take my life . . . "), and clinical depression ("When he came to Beersheba, he left his servant there, while he himself went a day's journey into the desert."). Above all, we see the flight response as an obviously fatigued Elijah fled from a looming 'fight' with Queen Jezebel. But, as one follows the narrative of the writer of First Kings, one notices another interesting fact: Elijah displayed other symptoms of burnout! Listen once more to the writer of First Kings,

> "There he went into a cave and spent the night. And the word of the LORD came to him: "What are you doing here, Elijah?" He replied, "I have been very zealous for the LORD God Almighty. The Israelites have rejected your covenant, broken down your altars, and put your prophets to death with the sword. I am the only one left, and now they are trying to kill me too."" (1Kgs 19:9–10, NKJV)

Elijah's Burnout Coincides With the Development of an Alternate Reality

Notice carefully that only one of the six assertions that Elijah makes in the passage above (" I have been very zealous for the LORD,"), is true! Five— ". . . the Israelites have rejected your covenant, broken your altars, and put your prophets to death . . . I am the only one left, and now they are trying to kill me too," are either outrightly incorrect or out-of-date statements! It does seem that the prophet's burnout coincided with his living in an alternate reality! In simple terms, his burnout led to a skewed interpretation of the facts or an incorrect way of framing reality. For example, by saying " . . . the Israelites have rejected your covenant," Elijah refused to acknowledge that the same Israelites had come to Jehovah after the Contest at Carmel. Indeed, they had helped him kill all 450 prophets of Baal—a thing he alone couldn't have accomplished! To worsen matters, Elijah goes on to say that " . . . now they [the Israelites] are trying to kill me too"—a blatant misinterpretation of events, as it was Queen Jezebel (not the Israelites) who was after his life! Indeed, the most glaring evidence that Elijah had lost touch with reality was his outlandish claim that "I am the only one left." A

Pitfalls and Problems of Managing 'Across'

claim which God quickly dispelled by reminding him that there were 7000 other persons in Israel who had not bent the knee to Baal! It does seem that an inability to correctly interpret the facts correlates with burnouts—the classic 'Glass-is-half full' vs. 'Glass-is-half empty' phenomenon.

Having seen the classic symptoms of a burnout, a careful reading of the passage has also helped me see the following predisposing factors . . .

Burnouts Occur, Not Necessarily because You Work too Hard, but because You Think All Your Hard Work Doesn't Make a Difference!

"I have had enough . . . I am no better than my fathers." Those words say it all: Elijah felt that his efforts to influence Israel for God didn't make a dent on the problem because things were no better than in the days of his predecessors. At the root of a burnout is this inability to see a connection between the weight of effort you put in, and the results you obtain. When you consistently, like Elijah, put in so much into work and give to others, but can't see your work making a dent on things, you just might be on the road to a burnout. Again, another predisposing factor for burnouts can be gleaned from the words of the writer of First Kings,

> "And the word of the Lord came to him: "What are you doing here, Elijah?" He replied, "I have been very zealous for the Lord God Almighty. The Israelites have rejected your covenant, torn down your altars, and put your prophets to death with the sword. I am the only one left, and now they are trying to kill me too." (1 Kgs 19:9–10, NKJV)

Loners—Persons Without Social Support Networks—are Prime Candidates for Burnouts

When asked "Elijah, what are you doing here?," the burnt-out prophet essentially answered "I am the only one left to do this job and I don't think my efforts are making a dent on Israel's idolatrous culture." Elijah, a highly altruistic person who believed in going it alone, was always a prime candidate for a burnout. Professor Grant confirms this, saying "As burnout expert Christina Maslach and colleagues conclude, "there is now a consistent and strong body of evidence that a lack of social support is linked to burnout."

Section 2 | Managing 'Across'

But the writer of First Kings isn't done yet, he goes ahead to show us just how God helped Elijah overcome his burnout . . .

> "The Lord said to him, "Go back the way you came, and go to the Desert of Damascus. When you get there, anoint Hazael king over Aram. Also, anoint Jehu son of Nimshi king over Israel, and anoint Elisha son of Shaphat from Abel Meholah to succeed you as prophet." (1Kgs 19:15–17, NIV)

Combating Burnout Begins With Rest and Positive Feedback

Apart from the required rest which Elijah got by reason of his long trip into the desert away from the madding crowd, God, by increasing the scope of Elijah's ministry and sending him to anoint a new king in faraway Syria, showed Elijah that he was pleased with his (Elijah's) work in Israel. I mean, why increase the man's ministry if he wasn't already doing well? This means that when leaders *see* that their work makes a difference—when they receive positive feedback—they become emotionally reenergized. Positive feedback helps combat the discouragement, and depression that's at the root of job burnout. Thus, positive feedback can serve as a buffer against the work-related stress that's at the root of burnouts.

Combating Burnout Continues With Seeking Social Support

" . . . anoint Elisha..to succeed you as prophet." God appointed a person—Elisha—to help give some social support to Elijah. In fact, God had to remind Elijah that there were 7000 other persons who had not bowed the knees to Baal. Elijah was not alone: he simply needed to connect with others!

Combating Burnout Concludes With Learning to Re-frame the Facts

Facts are sacred and they cannot be denied, but the way you interpret the facts is just as important as the facts themselves. Although the water remaining in the 50ml glass is actually 25ml, the experience of Elijah offers conclusive proof that thinking the glass is half-empty is a lot more depressing than thinking it is half-full. Same glass, same contents, but different interpretations. So the next time you hear someone say "Look on the bright

Pitfalls and Problems of Managing 'Across'

side of things," or "Count your blessings; name them one by one," just take a deep breath and do exactly as the person says. Why? Because it might just be the 'pill' you need to reframe the happenings in your life and stave off a burnout!

In conclusion, because a burnout has its roots in two things: a feeling that all your hard work is in vain, and a sense of social isolation, it can be combated by keeping a record of the fruit of your work (the persons healed, helped and delivered through your hands, the number of widgets sold, etc), and by being part of a strong social support network.

SECTION 3

Managing 'Down'
Managing Your Relationships With Subordinates and Associates

PREAMBLE: WHAT EXACTLY IS MANAGING 'DOWN'?

"I describe managers as being able to control insiders, but having to convince outsiders. Employees, after all, are paid to accept managerial authority."
—HENRY MINTZBERG.

IN HIS BOOK, *MANAGING*, management teacher Henry Mintzberg said that "I describe managers as being able to control insiders but having to convince outsiders. Employees, after all, are paid to accept managerial authority." In other words, control—the direction of the behavior of others in ways that produce compliance—which helps accomplish an organization's objective, is at the heart of managing 'down'. The key phrase in the last sentence is "the direction of the behavior of others in ways that . . . help accomplish an organization's objectives." That phrase shows that managing 'down' is where the proverbial rubber meets the road—where you work with the people who actually get the work done. It is doing the work of execution, of getting things done, and working with the people at the frontline. Indeed, some would even argue that the words "managing" and "management" are merely synonyms for managing 'down'!

Managing down is impossible without authority and power. But, while almost everyone knows that power corrupts, few realize that it also reveals. Power reveals the character of its holder. Therefore, nothing reveals your character and default leadership style like managing 'down'—an essentially 'asymmetric' work relationship in which you hold most of the power. Although managing 'up' also takes place in the context of asymmetric relationships, the difference is that, in managing 'up', power lies with another—another has power to reward or punish you—causing you to behave strategically so that the real you is hidden from public view. Not so for managing 'down'—where, because power lies with you—you can afford to let it all hang out! Which is why managing 'down: is the best place to know a person's true character and default leadership style.

Chapter 15

Carrot or Stick
What's Your Default Leadership Style?

"Ultimately the leadership style one adopts springs from one's core ideas about the nature of man."—STEPHEN COVEY

POWER AND AUTHORITY ARE at the center of any discussion on leadership styles. The latter is mainly about how you use the power of your position to achieve the goals of your organization or group—which, as we've seen, happens best when you manage 'down'. Since, power is simply the ability to do work, and since it is impossible to do any work in a group context without the input of others, your leadership style is best revealed in the nature of your relationships with direct reports and in your attitude to work. For example, although two persons may be appointed—in rapid succession—as coach of a professional basketball team, the first person may be highly authoritarian, while his successor (the second person) may have a more participatory approach. *What* both individuals do—coach basketball and manage players—is the same, but *how* they do what they do is distinctly different. *What* they do is the job, *how* they do what they do is their leadership style.

The writer of Isaiah, in his prophecy about the nature of the ministry of the soon-coming Messiah, reveals the two world views that drive the styles people display when they manage 'down', saying,

Carrot or Stick

> "The Spirit of the Sovereign LORD is on me, because the LORD has anointed me to preach good news to the poor. He has sent me to bind up the brokenhearted, to proclaim freedom for the captives and release from darkness for the prisoners, to proclaim the year of the LORD's favor and the day of vengeance of our God, to comfort all who mourn," (Isa 61:1-2, NIV)

Reward ('Carrot') and Punishment ('Stick') are the 2 Themes that Drive Leadership Styles

Since God is the only person in the universe who always manages 'down' when dealing with others, by saying "... the *year* of the Lord's favor and the *day* of his vengeance," the writer of Isaiah helps us see that,

1. Leadership styles are driven basically by either the carrot (using the prospect of favor or reward as the tool for managing 'down') or the stick (using the prospect vengeance and punishment as the tool for managing 'down') and,

2. God, by figuratively choosing to spend a whole *year* on favor, and just one *day* on vengeance in his dealings with the people he leads, prefers the carrot to the stick!

No matter who you are or what industry you operate in, your leadership style is founded on one, or a mixture, of these two great themes of 'prospect of reward' or 'prospect of punishment'. Crucially also, leadership styles founded on the 'prospect of punishment' tend to use fear as a tool to get people to do what they should or must do.

Speaking about fear, psychologist Daniel Goleman, in his illuminating book, *Social Intelligence*, said that "'Banish fear' was the slogan of the late quality control guru, W. Edwards Deming. He saw that fear froze a workplace: workers were reluctant to speak up, to share new ideas, or to coordinate well, let alone to improve the quality of their output." Incidentally, the writer of First John thinks the same way too, saying,

> "There is no fear in love. But perfect love drives out fear, because fear has to do with punishment ... " (1John 4:18, NIV)

This short, but illuminating, verse of Scripture drives the point home ...

Section 3 | Managing 'Down'

A Person's Leadership Style is Rooted Either in Fear or Love

After all is said and done, leading people comes down to one or, at best, a hybrid of these two forces—fear or love. The chief characteristic of fear is that " . . . fear has to do with punishment." When fear of punishment—fear that I would lose my job, lose my status, etc—is the principal shaper of your leadership style, then intimidation is widespread, and cover-ups and the 'blame game' multiply on your team. I mean, who wants to take the rap for a failed project when the punishment is career threatening? Organizations, even the so-called Christian organizations, where fear is the principal tool for getting people to do their jobs often develop an atmosphere of deadly competition and damaging rivalries. Leaders who 'move' others primarily with the tool of punishment, of what would happen if their people fail or don't get the job done, tend to discourage creativity and risk taking, and virtually ensure that their teams never fulfill their potential.

The question becomes "What exactly are the behaviors associated with a person whose style is founded on fear of punishment?" Paul the apostle, in his Second Letter to the Corinthians (where he defends his leadership style), proffers an answer, saying,

> "I call God as my witness that it was in order to spare you that I did not return to Corinth. Not that we Lord it over your faith, but we work with you for your joy . . . So I made up my mind that I would not make another painful visit to you." (2Cor 1:23–24—2Cor 2:1, NIV)

Close inspection of this passage reveals not only Paul's leadership style, but also the particular behaviors exhibited by people who operate the two broad kinds of leadership styles . . ..

Style 1 Leader: I Am the Boss Here!

"Not that we *lord it over* . . . *you* . . . " There it is in black and white: some leaders lord it over followers. This style is authoritarian—seeing itself as boss, brooking no nonsense from associates, and revelling in the use and display of positional power and authority. It is also the bodily expression of Whistler's law "You may not always know who is right, but you will always know who is in charge!" People operating in Style 1 mode are ever ready to confront, intimidate, and punish wrongdoing—the very reason fear of punishment is the guiding ethos for getting things done in the groups they lead.

CARROT OR STICK

People Work for a Style 1 Leader

"Not that we Lord it over . . . you, but we work *with* you . . . " The leader who operates a Style 1 mindset sees the staff as people who work *for*—not *with*—him. That distinction is crucial because how we see others determines what value we attach to them. To see people as working for you is to basically see them as people to be directed; people without initiative of their own who must be told what to do. Style 1 leaders tell people what to do (no matter how competent those people are). That kind of thinking buys the backs of people, but never buys their greatest resource—their hearts and minds. This leadership style tends to keep all the credit and most of the fruit for itself.

Style 2 Leader

This leader uses her positional power and authority only as a tool of last resort. She sees people as associates who work with her ("but we work *with* you"). This style builds healthy alliances and partnerships, and taps into peoples' greatest resource—their hearts and minds. By saying "I call God as my witness that it was in order to spare you that I did not return to Corinth," Paul the apostle surfaces a key component of Style 2 leaders—confrontations and shows of force are seen as necessary evils and rarely engaged in! This style takes to heart the words of leadership teacher John Maxwell "When it is painful for you to criticize others, you're probably safe doing it. If you get the slightest bit of pleasure out of doing it, you should hold your tongue." Style 2 leadership uses positional power only as a last resort when other methods of influence have failed.

In real life, few leaders fall squarely into either one of these two styles. Most tend to display a mix of both mindsets. Indeed, depending on the external conditions (emergencies, challenges to their authority, etc.), leaders tend to display more of a particular mindset. Even so, all leaders have a default mode—a mindset that prevails at ordinary conditions. Like I said before, your leadership style is revealed in the nature of your relationships with direct reports and in your attitude to the work being done in your group. Since we've seen how your style impacts relationships with subordinates and associates, we can now turn our attention to how it impacts the work being done in your team . . .

SECTION 3 | MANAGING 'DOWN'

HANDS-ON (DOING) OR HANDS-OFF (DIRECTING): WHAT LEADERSHIP STYLE SHOULD I ADOPT?

For many leaders the question of whether to adopt a hands-on style (being more of a "doer" who keeps a close eye on things and operates at the frontline), or a hands-off style (that's more "director" than "doer") is determined by their individual temperaments. But as I studied the leadership of Joseph, I began to see that the issue should actually be determined by the nature of the task at hand. Listen to the writer of Genesis,

> "And the keeper of the prison committed to Joseph's hand all the prisoners that were in the prison; and whatsoever they [all the prisoners] did there, he was the doer of it." (Gen 39:22, KJV)

A Hands-on Style is Needed to Handle Organization-wide Tasks or Projects

By saying "And the keeper of the prison committed to Joseph's hand all the prisoners," the writer of Genesis shows us that Joseph was responsible for the conduct and administration of all the prisoners. By also saying " . . . and whatsoever they [all the prisoners] did there, he was the doer of it," he helps us see that Joseph became a doer or hands-on manager—directly involved with the task—only under certain conditions; only when all the prisoners worked together on a task. Ordinarily, leaders are once removed from the action, and tend to manage people in a hands-off style that encourages, motivates or provides the resources or information they need to get the job done. But, as we see from the leadership of Joseph, leaders become "doers"—hands-on and directly responsible for getting things done—when organization-wide responses to change and unforeseen events, or group-wide projects are to be carried out. These organization-wide projects tend fall between the cracks because they span more than one division and so require leaders to fold their sleeves and directly coordinate the actions of multiple units.

A Hands-on Style Works Side-by-side With Associates

" . . . and whatsoever they [all the prisoners] did there, he was the doer of it." Any project or task that requires the simultaneous deployment of personnel from multiple units of the group will probably require hands-on management. And hands-on management is any task where leaders—who are normally are not on the front line—have to step out with the people to serve customers, interface with third parties or otherwise get the job done. In essence, it is the task that should determine the style that leaders display. As a rule, and because of the finite time and energy leaders have, such organization-wide projects should be few and far between. Management writer Henry Mintzberg, in his book, *Managing*, drives the point home, saying,

> "When the time came some years ago to redesign Pampers, Proctor & Gamble's most important product, the chief executive of the whole company headed up the task force. When Johnson & Johnson faced a crisis after someone tampered with a few of its Tylenol packages, it was the CEO who headed up the response effort . . . These examples suggest that there are two aspects of the doing role: managing projects proactively and handling disturbances reactively."

Notice carefully when the top-leaders of Procter and Gamble, and Johnson and Johnson took on more hands-on styles: it was when they faced major organization-wide projects—redesigning Pampers and handling a major crisis that threatened the whole organization.

Being responsible for a group or unit doesn't automatically mean that you should be directly involved in 'frontline' work. It requires that you always keep in mind the following words of the writer of Hosea,

> "The Israelites are stubborn, like a stubborn heifer. How then can the Lord pasture them like lambs in a meadow?" (Hos 4:16, NIV)

Situational Leadership Tailors its Style to Suit the Persons it Leads

These words of the writer of Hosea reveal a profound leadership truth: God tailors his leadership style to suit the nature and character of the persons he leads! He uses one style to lead stubborn heifers and another style to lead more docile sheep. In effect, God uses situational leadership. Why? Because attempting to lead a stubborn heifer with the methods for leading docile lambs is foolhardy. Researchers Paul Hersey, Ken Blanchard, and Dewey Johnson, in their landmark book, *Management of Organizational Behavior*, first introduced the Situational Leadership Model, which basically states that,

"The fundamental principle of the situational leadership model is that there is no single "best" style of leadership. Effective leadership is task-relevant, and the most successful leaders are those who adapt their leadership style to the . . . ability and willingness . . . of the individual or group they are attempting to lead or influence. Effective leadership varies, not only with the person or group that is being influenced, but it also depends on the task, job, or function that needs to be accomplished."

All this means that . . .

1. When it comes to leading people, one size doesn't fit all and there is no one 'best' way to manage 'down',
2. Effective leaders first discern the conditions of the people they want to lead, and then lead them appropriately,
3. Effective leaders adapt themselves to their associates. Expecting followers to adjust to your style may be unwise and,
4. The best leaders have a repertoire of leadership styles.

To drive home the point about leadership styles and situational leadership, listen to the words of the writer of Exodus,

"When Pharaoh let the people go, God did not lead them on the road through the Philistine country, though that was shorter. For God said, "If they face war, they might change their minds and return to Egypt." So God led the people around by the desert road toward the Red Sea. The Israelites went up out of Egypt ready for battle." (Exod 13:17–18, NIV)

This amazing passage helps us see that . . .

God Practices Situational Leadership!

"God did not lead them on the road through the Philistine country, though that was shorter . . . " There was a shortcut through the country of the Philistines to the Promised Land. So why didn't God lead the Israelites through that route? Easy. Because he had checked out the condition of the Israelites and discerned that they were not yet ready for war with the Philistines ("For God said, "If they face war, they might change their minds and return to Egypt."). So, to avoid a rebellion, he prudently led the people along the much longer route that skirted the territory of the war-like Philistines. In effect, God adapted his leadership to the people he led! This is conclusive proof that the best leaders adapt their styles to the needs and conditions of the led and not the other way around. When their people are discouraged, they encourage. When associates are confused, they provide a more directing style etc.

Wrap Around

Your default leadership style is a window into your soul—a reflection of your character, upbringing, and personality—that reveals, not only your own world-view, but also the world views of the people who have influenced you in the past. In his book, *Principle-Centered Leadership,* management teacher Stephen Covey said that "Ultimately the leadership style one adopts springs from one's core ideas about the nature of man." If you believe that people need to be pushed and monitored before they do their jobs, then your default style will be Style 1—authoritarian and founded on using the "stick." If, on the other hand, you think that most people really want to get the job done and don't need to be cajoled or pushed before they do so, then your default style will be Style 2—founded on the "carrot." If your beliefs about the nature of people lie somewhere between these two extremes, then your default leadership style will lie on a continuum between Style 1 and Style 2.

Chapter 16

Getting Results Through Others

LIKE I DISCUSSED IN the preamble to this section, managing 'down' is where the proverbial rubber meets the road, where you work with the people at the frontlines—people who actually get the work done. Therefore, managing 'down' is the realm of productivity and results, and of getting things done. Which is why this chapter will deal mainly with productivity issues—getting results through others, providing feedback performance to subordinates, motivating the latter to go the extra mile, and the art of delegation.

PYGMALION IN MANAGEMENT (LESSONS FROM THE LEADERSHIP OF POTIPHAR)

The Pygmalion Effect: a phenomenon where a subordinate's behavior is shaped and influenced by her leader's positive expectations. Because I expect the best behavior from my associate, she in turn strives to live up to my expectations—a kind of self-fulfilling prophecy.

Anyone who has taken time to study the leadership of Joseph—the Hebrew slave-boy who rose to become Governor of Egypt—will be struck by the quality of his leadership. Not only was Joseph's management of his master's business excellent and without any trace of financial corruption, his refusal to sleep with his master's wife (even when she serially threw herself at him) is also noteworthy. The question becomes: what exactly was the "force" that motivated Joseph to display such scrupulously honest and upstanding behavior? As I read Stanford professors Jeffrey Pfeffer and Robert Sutton's illuminating book, *Hard Facts: Dangerous Half-Truths & Total Nonsense,* the faint outlines of an answer began to form from the following words,

> "[A] randomized field experiment with Israeli soldiers confirmed the Pygmalion Effect, that high or low performance expectations can become self-fulfilling. When drill instructors were tricked into believing that certain randomly selected individuals would achieve superior performance, those soldiers subsequently performed better on tests like firing weapons and reading maps than soldiers in control conditions who did not have higher performance expectations. This experiment and numerous other studies show that leaders get the performance they expect from subordinates."

The phrase that grabbed my attention was " . . . *leaders get the performance they expect from their subordinates.*" It does seem that one way leaders can influence the performance of subordinates is to set and communicate high expectations for them. This so-called Pygmalion effect, is a powerful tool for developing subordinates and, as a close study of the book of Genesis reveals, was the principal reason for Joseph's superlative performance as Potiphar's manager. Listen to the writer of Genesis,

> "And it came to pass after these things that his master's wife cast longing eyes on Joseph, and she said, "Lie with me." But he refused and said to his master's wife, "Look, my master does not know what is with me in the house, and he has committed all that he has to my hand. There is no one greater in this house than I, nor has he kept back anything from me but you, because you are his wife. How then can I do this great wickedness, and sin against God?" (Gen 39:7–9, NKJV)

Much reflection on this passage has helped me see the following management truths . . .

The Pygmalion Effect was at the Root of Joseph's Superlative Leadership

"But he refused and said to his master's wife, " . . . *my master . . . has committed all that he has to my hand* [i.e., my master trusts me] . . . *How then can I do this great wickedness and sin against God?*"" There it is in black and white: Joseph didn't sleep with his master's wife because his master

(Potiphar) trusted him! Potiphar, by appointing Joseph as overseer of his business, showed not only that he trusted, but that he also expected the best behavior from him. In simple terms, it was Potiphar's high expectations (revealed by his appointment) that motivated Joseph's outstanding moral conduct. Pfeffer and Sutton were correct after all " . . . leaders get the performance they expect from subordinates." But the writer of Genesis, not done yet with showing Pygmalion in the management of Potiphar, goes ahead to say,

> "And his master saw that the Lord was with him and that the Lord made all he did to prosper in his hand. So Joseph found favor in his sight, and served him. Then he made him overseer of his house, and all that he had he put under his authority." (Gen 39:3–4, NKJV)

These words show that,

The Best Leaders Tailor their Expectations to the Abilities of their Subordinates

"And his master *saw* . . . all [Joseph] . . . did . . .*Then he made him* [Joseph] overseer of his house." There it is in black and white: before Potiphar trusted, committed resources to, or communicated his high expectations to, Joseph, he first tested and assessed his performance. When it comes to putting Pygmalion into practice, the wise test before they trust, while the young trust before they test or even trust without testing! Pygmalion certainly doesn't mean that in setting expectations for you, I should overlook your innate abilities or limitations. It bears repeating: leaders who utilize the Pygmalion principle know that they must test before they trust, and that they must tailor the weight of their expectations to the ability and character of the subordinate in question. After all is said and done, your expectations for subordinates must be grounded in reality because ducks seldom take wings and fly like eagles.

In the final analysis, the Pygmalion principle shows us the power of expectations in shaping the conduct of subordinates. Leaders who check the performance of subordinates are certainly on the right track because they are measuring progress, but the Pygmalion principle, because it *promotes* progress, goes one step further. Leadership expert John Maxwell was spot on when he said that "Examinations measure progress, but expectations promote progress." Pygmalion's power lies in its ability to promote progress.

Closely linked to the Pygmalion Effect is the art of delegation—another tool for managing 'down' to which we now turn our attention . . .

THE TRIPOD OF DELEGATION (PRINCIPLES OF DELEGATION)

A tripod is a stool with 3 legs. Remove one of the legs, and the unstable tripod will not be able to safely carry the weight set upon it. The writer of Ezekiel, in his description of how God delegated his original duty—the judgment of Israel—to the Babylonians, Assyrians and other nations, helps us see that effective delegation involves 3 factors or 'legs' . . .

> "Therefore . . . thus says the Lord GOD: "Behold, I will stir up your lovers against you . . . And I will bring them against you from every side: The Babylonians . . . the Assyrians with them . . . And they shall come against you with chariots, wagons, and war-horses, With a horde of people. They shall array against you Buckler, shield, and helmet all around. "I will *delegate* judgment to them, And they shall judge you according to their judgments." (Emphasis mine) (Ezek 23:22–24, NKJV)

This amazing passage is the biblical primer for understanding the managerial principles underlying delegation, and much reflection has helped me see that effective delegation is founded on three interconnected factors . . .

I Own the Job (The Job is Mine)

God is the Judge of Israel—the person with original authority to investigate and punish wrongdoing among the citizens of Israel. In simple terms, the judgment of Israel is God's job. But, by saying *"I will delegate judgment to them,"* the writer of Ezekiel shows us that God delegated a portion—judgment—of his job to others. God's action highlights two things: firstly, you can delegate a job only when it's yours; and secondly, to be effective, you must clearly communicate the portion(s) of the job you want to delegate.

SECTION 3 | MANAGING 'DOWN'

I 'Lend' You the Job (I Grant You Authority to Act on My Behalf)

"I will delegate judgment to them, *and they shall judge you according to their judgments . . .* " Notice carefully that God allowed the Babylonians and Assyrians plenty of freedom to act as they carried out his punishments on the Israelites. The degree of autonomy and authority granted to a delegatee is at the heart of the art of delegation. Because the Babylonians were especially skilled and cruel at warfare, God gave them great liberty to use their judgment in deciding exactly how Israel was going to be punished. Effective delegation, as we shall soon see, is founded on skill in appraisal of the subordinate. Why? Because it is the competence of the subordinate that determines just how much autonomy you can grant her.

I Train You to Do the Job

By saying "I will stir up your lovers [the Babylonians] against you . . . And I will bring them against you on every side," the writer of Ezekiel shows us the third leg of the tripod of delegation—training and providing resources (which prepares people for the job), and ongoing accountability (which helps them keep the main the main thing). God didn't just delegate a job, he first invested some time training, preparing and setting boundaries of acceptable behavior for his delegatees.

Effective delegation—like any tripod—rests on the 3 factors enunciated above. Absent one of those factors, and the whole process becomes unstable and ineffective. Having seen the tripod (principles) of delegation, we now turn again to the leadership of Potiphar to see those principles in practice . . .

THE ART OF DELEGATION (LESSONS FROM THE LEADERSHIP OF POTIPHAR)

What do you do when you have to combine the job of chief security officer to probably the greatest head of state on earth with running your own business on the side? Potiphar, captain of the guard to Pharaoh king of Egypt, faced that difficult situation. The writer of Genesis shows us just how skillfully he solved the problem—and, as a byproduct—developed a slave-boy called Joseph into a first-class leader . . .

"Now Joseph had been taken down to Egypt. Potiphar, an Egyptian who was one of Pharaoh's officials, the captain of the guard, bought him from the Ishmaelites who had taken him there... Potiphar put [Joseph] in charge of his household, and he entrusted to his care everything he owned. From the time he put him in charge of his household... The blessing of the Lord was on everything Potiphar had, both in the house and in the field. So Potiphar left everything he had in Joseph's care; with Joseph in charge, he did not concern himself with anything except the food he ate ... " (Gen 39:1–6, NIV)

To Delegate is to Put Someone in Charge of a Portion or All of Your Original Duties

"*So Potiphar left everything he had* [the business he ran from inside his house] *in Joseph's care; with Joseph in charge* ... " These words corroborate all we've seen so far: to delegate is to put another—usually a subordinate—in charge of a portion, or all, of your own work. Delegation involves the transfer of authority to do a job (or portions of it) from a superior to a subordinate while still leaving the superior with ultimate responsibility for the work. In the case of Portiphar, delegation was total and complete—meaning that he literally entrusted the conduct of the operations of his personal business to Joseph. Suffice to say that not all subordinates are as competent or trustworthy as Joseph, which is why there are varying degrees of delegation (a thing we will be looking at later on). The question becomes: why delegate? Why put someone else in charge of portions of your original job? The answers are ...

Delegation Frees Up a Leader's Time—Time He can then Invest in 'Higher Value' Tasks

By saying,

"So she [Potiphar's wife] kept his [Joseph's] garment with her until his master [Potiphar] came home," (Gen. 39:16, NIV)

the writer of Genesis conclusively shows us that it was only at the close of work from his official duties with the king that Potiphar could hold Joseph accountable. Thus, delegation freed Potiphar to give more of his own time to the king's business. Delegating the work of running his private business to an excellent subordinate like Joseph allowed Potiphar concentrate on his 'high value' day job of protecting Pharaoh king of Egypt without slighting his own personal business. In effect, when properly executed, delegation makes leaders more effective by allowing them concentrate on the most important things—the things only they can do. Motivational speaker Brian Tracy was correct after all "The more of your essential tasks that you can teach and delegate to others, the greater the time you will have to do the things that only you can do."

Delegation Develops Subordinates

No amount of classroom instruction and exhortation can substitute for the growth and development that the actual doing of a task can bring. Delegation, because it gives associates responsibility for jobs to which they are hitherto unaccustomed, is a great way to help associates develop, and gain experience and confidence. *Success* Magazine writer Susan Madsen drives the point home, saying,

> "By delegating, not only do you free yourself up to focus on what is really important, but you also help grow and develop other people. When you delegate correctly, you motivate and stretch the person you are delegating to, and you contribute to his or her professional development needs, confidence, and competence."

Having seen the two broad benefits of delegation—one to the senior leader, and the other to the subordinate—you need to always remember that . . .

Delegation is not Abdication. It Merely Transfers Responsibility for Operations to Another While Still Holding Them Accountable

Apparently, the fact that Potiphar had delegated operations to Joseph didn't mean that he had ceded overall responsibility to the latter. How do I know this? Because Potiphar still came back regularly to the house—the place where the business operated—and was available to receive reports and hold Joseph accountable. If this was not so, the writer of Genesis would not have said that "So she [Potiphar's wife] kept his [Joseph's] garment with her until his master [Potiphar] came home."

But the writer of Genesis isn't done yet. Using the leadership of Potiphar as his jumping off point, he goes ahead to reveal exactly how effective delegation works, saying,

> "But he [Joseph] refused. "With me in charge," he told her, "my master does not concern himself with anything in the house; everything he owns he has entrusted to my care. No one is greater in this house than I am. My master has withheld nothing from me except you, because you are his wife. How then could I do such a wicked thing and sin against God?"" (Gen 39:8–9, NIV)

Effective Delegation Requires Clear Communication

"With me in charge . . . My master has withheld nothing from me except you, because you are his wife." These words spoken by Joseph to Potiphar's wife show that Potiphar—Joseph's master—had clearly communicated Joseph's job description and the limits of his authority. Joseph knew that, although he was in charge of all business operations taking place in Potiphar's house, sexual relations with the man's wife was strictly forbidden! Communication is the currency of work and the best 'delegators' are clear as to the exact nature of the jobs they want to delegate to associates.

After all is said and done, Potiphar was dealing with a Joseph whose prior experience as an overseer in his father—Jacob's—agribusiness made him an experienced subordinate. Since, not all subordinates are like Joseph, the question at the heart of delegation becomes: how much autonomy should I give my associates? The writer of Proverbs throws some light on the matter, saying,

> "Train up a child in the way that he should go, and when he is old, he will not depart from it." (Prov 22:6, NKJV)

To help you better understand the passage, I have paraphrased it like this "Train up a child [inexperienced worker] in the way that he should go, and when he is old [mature and experienced], he will not depart from it." This paraphrase immediately helps leaders see how they ought to behave when delegating portions of their original duties to subordinates . . .

Section 3 | Managing 'Down'

With an Inexperienced Subordinate, You Should Adopt a Directing Style

"*Train up a child* [less-experienced operative] *in the way that he should go* . . . " There it is in black and white: with the less-experienced operative; one who lacks rudimentary knowledge of how things are done, leaders should adopt a more hands-on and directive style that shows operatives the way things are done. This style requires leaders to stay close to inexperienced subordinates, to require shorter times for reporting, to impose stricter limits on spending, to offer more frequent feedback, and to be always available for them. In effect, less-experienced operatives should be given as little autonomy as possible.

With a More Experienced Subordinate, You Should Adopt a Participative Style

"*. . . when he is old* [more mature and experienced], *he will not depart from it.*" The more-experienced subordinate is already reasonably acquainted with the way things are done, so she is best managed by granting her a greater degree of autonomy. She should be given room to make suggestions, freely express her opinions, and inject her discretion into tasks. Micromanagement can backfire here. Crucially, her questions and discretionary inputs shouldn't be seen as challenges to her leader's authority. All this means that . . .

Success in Delegation is Founded on Effectiveness in Appraisal

"Train up a child [a less-experienced operative] . . . when he is old [more-experienced] . . . " The key factor for success in delegation is appraisal—knowing who is a still figuratively "a child," knowing who is "old and mature," and knowing who is making or not making progress on the continuum from "childhood" to "maturity." The best 'delegators' match the right tasks to the right subordinates—a thing which requires great skill at appraising human performance. Not only must you match autonomy with skill at the beginning, you must also be ready to increase or reduce the autonomy granted as the associate matures and succeeds at the task or, as the case may be, regresses or shows signs of task failure. Harvard researcher Linda Hill, in her book, *Becoming a Manager*, was spot on when she said that "Delegation [involves] interpersonal judgment, taking calculated risks on whom to trust . . . Making these determinations require assessing subordinates by three criteria: competence, personal integrity, and motivation to assume greater responsibility." Because "Delegation [involves transferring] . . . responsibility," and because responsibility is like a weight, delegation is akin to giving another weights to lift. Delegate too soon, and the person is unable to carry the weight. Delay to delegate, and the subordinate might remain stunted and underdeveloped because she doesn't get the exercise she needs to grow! The best managers know just when to delegate responsibility—and they also know that since delegation is not abdication, they must provide feedback and accountability at all times. And it is to the subject of providing performance feedback that we now turn our attention . . .

2 KINDS OF FEEDBACK (POSITIVE FEEDBACK AND NEGATIVE FEEDBACK)

Whatever the nature of your work, long-term career success is founded on continuous improvement and adaptation. But, and this is important, you can't improve unless you change or modify a practice, behavior or attitude. And you can't know which modification to make unless you receive feedback—which is why feedback is crucial to career success. By the way, feedback is any communication that paints an accurate picture of the reality in which you operate or work. That said, it is necessary to add that all feedback is not the same. Some feedback—positive feedback—point at things you should basically continue to do, while others—negative feedback—point at things you should basically discontinue or stop doing. The former gives the "green light," while the latter gives the "red light." When it comes to managing 'down', the 2 categories, as we shall soon see, are as different as night and day.

POSITIVE FEEDBACK: CONTINUING WHAT'S WORKING (THE 'GREEN LIGHT')

Feedback is basically any information that links cause and effect. In the case of positive feedback, it is information which, when put into use, can increase the magnitude or size of the original effect or result. In essence, positive feedback is anchored on catching a person doing something right and then supplying them that information in order to help improve their performance. The writer of Proverbs makes this last point clear, saying,

> "The crucible is for silver and the furnace is for gold, but man is tested by the praise he receives." (Prov 27:21, NIV)

To bring out the meaning of this verse of Scripture, I often paraphrase it as "The crucible is for silver and the furnace for gold, [so] a man is tested [refined] by the praise [positive feedback] he receives." This paraphrase helps us see that,

Positive Feedback is a Key to Improvement

Like the furnace and crucible refine gold and silver—making them better and more valuable—so positive feedback ("praise") makes people better. Plainly put, improvement is easiest when you stick with the things for which you now score the highest marks. If you really want your associates to improve, help them locate and work on the areas where they are strongest, the areas where they already receive the highest praise. *Doing more of what they already do best puts them in the 'crucible'—refining and making them more valuable.* The corollary to this rule is also true: doing less of what they already do poorly can also make them better. Why? Because it frees up time and resources which they can invest elsewhere. Please don't get me wrong; if people have character weaknesses, then they should by all means work and spend lots of time to strengthen themselves in that particular area. But, when it comes to improving the ability to produce, they should work in the area of their greatest strength; the area where they currently receive the highest praise (positive feedback).

Positive feedback works via the principle of reinforcement—showing people the areas where they're doing well—causing them to continue, to reinforce, or to improve upon, the actions that, in the first place, led to the initial positive results. The key phrase in that sentence is "showing people the areas where they're doing well." Positive feedback is founded on the communication of information about the positive or good effects (results) of a person's actions. Since people have little or no problems with receiving the good news that they are doing well, giving positive feedback is often uncomplicated and hitch-free. Not so for negative feedback, the other kind of feedback to which we now turn our attention . . .

NEGATIVE FEEDBACK: FIIXING WHAT'S BROKEN (THE 'RED LIGHT')

"Criticism may not be agreeable, but it is necessary; it fulfills the same function as pain in the human body; it calls attention to the development of an unhealthy state of things."—WINSTON CHURCHILL

Akio Morita, the legendary chairman of Sony Corporation USA, had just received a stinker—a letter heavily criticizing the technical performance of one of his company's major products. What to do? Mr. Morita employed the person who wrote the letter! He figured that the sharpness of mind which delivered the stinging criticism could be of great benefit to his company. Interestingly, the critic Mr. Morita employed later rose to become Sony chairman! Criticism is basically information that points out what is going wrong or what's broken and, in a few cases, how to right what's going wrong. Although many of us mentally agree that the road to fixing what's broken passes through the gates of the city called 'Criticism', few of us possess the largeness of heart, the thickness of skin, and the presence of mind of an Akio Morita—the character qualities needed to embrace negative feedback. Nathaniel Branden, the notable American psychologist, said that "The first step towards change is awareness. The second step is acceptance." The negative feedback offered by criticism can make you more aware of the terrible state of things in your life or the group you lead and, crucially also, can help you change things for the better. The writer of Proverbs drives the point home, saying,

> "The tongue that brings healing is a tree of life, but a deceitful tongue crushes the spirit." (Prov 15:4, NIV)

As I reflected on this amazing proverb, I came to see that . . .

Negative Feedback is Crucial to Healing What is "Sick" in Our Lives and Organizations

Things are going horribly wrong; sales targets aren't being met, key clients are deserting, and key relationships are at breaking point. In the words of former British Prime Minister Winston Churchill "an unhealthy state of things" has developed. How then can the healing process be kick-started? The writer of Proverbs proffers a solution, saying *"The tongue* [communication] *that brings healing* is a tree of life, but *a deceitful tongue* crushes the spirit." By contrasting the tongue that brings healing with a deceitful tongue, the writer of Proverbs helps us see that frank, honest, and down-to-earth communication is what kick-starts the healing of 'sick' processes. In other words, the healing process always begins with feedback that is truthful and factual—one that calls attention to the unhealthy state of things. Negative feedback—communication that pulls no punches and that is not deceitful—is always crucial to healing whatever is wounded or 'sick' in our lives. Blessed is the leader that has people in her inner circle to always give her honest feedback, and even more blessed is the leader who is open to such feedback.

Negative Feedback Can Produce Huge Productivity Increases

Notice carefully that the writer of Proverbs said that "The tongue that brings healing is *a tree of life.*" Since, the tree of life (Revelation 22:1–2)—which yields 12 harvests every year—is a metaphor for productivity, and since negative feedback is a tree of life, it follows that negative feedback is key to achieving huge productivity gains! While positive feedback can produce incremental gains in personal and organizational productivity, negative feedback, because it points out what you should stop doing and changes your direction, can produce much larger productivity gains. People, like Akio Morita, who are open to negative feedback are some of the most productive people on earth. The key word in the previous sentence is "open." Because negative feedback delivers information that's often unpalatable, and because people tend to resent those who deliver unpalatable news (think of the dictum "don't shoot the messenger"), negative feedback often genders conflict between providers and receivers of feedback. Therefore, it is to the delicate subject of how to communicate negative feedback that we now turn our attention . . .

COMMUNICATING NEGATIVE FEEDBACK

"*Giving feedback meant being prepared to confront and manage conflict.* Because most wished to avoid conflict, they held news back too long, thereby cheating their subordinates out of a chance to learn and improve their performance."
—LINDA HILL (Emphasis mine)

On the surface, the above words of researcher Linda Hill (culled from her excellent book, *Becoming A Manager*) seem to make sense. But, on second thought, those words leave me scratching my head. Come to think of it, will giving you positive feedback (praise and commendation) bring you and I into conflict? The answer is an emphatic "No!" The only time my feedback to you can gender conflict is when the feedback is negative—criticism or information about something unpalatable that you need to correct. Dr. Hill's words unwittingly reveal a common misconception—people tend to conflate positive feedback with negative feedback. The correct phrase should be "Giving *negative* feedback meant being prepared to . . . manage conflict." Why? Because most people are defensive when it comes to receiving negative feedback. The writer of Proverbs, in a triad of alternating verses, shows leaders how to master the difficult, but essential, art of delivering negative feedback . . .

> "A servant will not be corrected by mere words; For though he understands, he will not respond." (Prov 29:19, NKJV)

Negative Feedback, As a Rule, is Unwelcome—the Reason it Creates the Conditions for Conflict!

By saying "A servant will not be corrected by *mere words*," the writer of Proverbs gives the game away—it takes more than mere words or expert information to cause a change in the behavior of associates. Indeed, depending on mere words often arouses subtle resentment in the persons being corrected. Which is why, leaders who attempt to use positional power ("I am the boss"), or expert power ("I know this stuff more than you") as the basis for delivering negative feedback to their associates will meet subtle resistance. Why? Because people are hardwired to be defensive when receiving negative feedback. Daniel Goleman, in his bestselling book, *Emotional Intelligence*, puts it beautifully, saying "Defensiveness in a listener takes the form of ignoring or immediately rebutting [another's] complaint, reacting as though it were an attack rather than an attempt to change behavior." Interestingly, defensiveness in associates can also take on more subtle forms like foot-dragging and stonewalling. But the writer of Proverbs isn't done yet, he continues his discourse on communicating negative feedback, saying,

> "Correct your son, and he will give you rest; Yes, he will give delight to your soul." (Prov 29:17, NKJV)

Negative Feedback is Only Welcome When Your Relationship With the Receiver of the feedback is Healthy, Caring, and Strong

"Correct your *son* . . . and he will give delight to your soul." Here we see the leader successfully correct an associate. And why did the correction process succeed? You guessed right! It was because the leader was dealing with a "son," not a "servant." This means that when it comes to correcting people, it's always the relationship before the facts. Why? Because people are hardwired to see truth and information through the prism of their relationship with the person correcting them. Inexperienced leaders tend to put the cart before the horse and think that fact is more important than relationship. They forget the words of psychologist Robert Cialdini "People are more favorable to a communication if they're favorable to the communicator." When the leader is seen as distant, disrespectful and uncaring then, even if the associates understand what's being communicated, they will not respond positively. The writer of Proverbs drives home this truth with the third leg of his triad of verses, saying,

> "He who pampers his servant from childhood Will have him as a son in the end." (Prov 29:21, NKJV)

The Communication Process Begins Long Before You Actually Deliver the Feedback!

If "servants" are refractory to correction and, if "sons" are "responsive" to rebukes, then it follows that the way you treat a person long before the person needs correction matters. If you shower a "servant" with care from his 'childhood', you'll have him as a "son" (in his 'adult' years) who will willingly accept correction. If you haven't taken the time and made the effort to develop healthy relationships with people, then your attempts to deliver negative feedback may just meet a brick wall. Why? Because people are hardwired to be defensive when they receive negative feedback. *In effect, delivering negative feedback is a litmus test of the state of a leader's relationships with associates. If the relationships are healthy, all is likely to go well. If they are not, then there's trouble ahead!* The main point is this: before you attempt to correct anyone, first make sure that you have showed that you respect and care for him. Anything less than that is asking for trouble!

It bears repeating: correcting people—the aim of negative feedback—is an art, and knowing who, when, and how, to correct is a litmus test of leadership. Why? Because even when they are clearly in the wrong and in need of correction, people are hardwired to respond to correction in ways that foster strife, disagreement and conflict. Although, as we've seen, a healthy relationship with subordinates is a precondition for delivering negative feedback, there's more to correcting people than healthy relationships. To master the art of correction, we must also master the mechanics—the actual process of delivering correction. For that, we must turn to the leadership of Jesus . . .

THE ART OF CORRECTING PEOPLE (LESSONS FROM THE LEADERSHIP OF JESUS)

"Not everything that is faced can be changed, but nothing can be changed until it is faced."—JAMES BALDWIN

The book of Revelation is commonly perceived as a book of prophecy, a vivid unveiling of the events which will occur at the end of the age, and rightly so. But, "Revelation" is also a book about masterful communication—the kind Jesus deployed as he himself famously corrected the seven Churches of Asia. The writer of Revelation, gives an account of those communications with the Church at Ephesus, saying,

> "To the angel of the church of Ephesus write, "These things says He who holds the *seven stars* in His right hand, who walks in the midst of the seven golden lampstands:" (Emphasis mine) (Rev 2:1, NKJV)

Section 3 | Managing 'Down'

Your Connection: Begin by Emphasizng Your Relationship to the People You Want to Correct

To better understand the above passage, it's necessary to understand the term *"seven stars"*—a thing which requires that we track back to a previous passage . . .

> "The mystery of the *seven stars* which you saw in My right hand, and the seven golden lampstands: *The seven stars are the angels* [pastors] *of the seven churches*, and the seven lampstands which you saw are the seven churches." (Emphasis mine) (Rev 1:20, NKJV)

Here we see that the phrase "seven stars" refers to the pastors ("angels") of the seven churches in Asia Minor (modern day Turkey), while the term "seven lampstands," refers to the seven churches themselves. In effect, by saying "To the angel of the church of Ephesus write, "These things says He who holds the seven stars in His right hand, who walks in the midst of the seven golden lampstands," Jesus is stressing his relationship with the people who are in the Ephesian Church. This means that, before Jesus could even begin to deliver some negative feedback, he had to stress his connections with the pastor and the people who make up the congregation. All this chimes with what we've discussed before: healthy relationships are the foundation for delivering negative feedback. Therefore, the best leaders don't just have healthy relationships with the people they want to correct, they *emphasize* those relationships as they begin the correction process. But the writer of Revelation isn't done yet, he goes ahead to say that,

> "I [Jesus] know your works, your labor, your patience, and that you cannot bear those who are evil. And you have tested those who say they are apostles and are not, and have found them liars; and you have persevered and have patience, and have labored for My name's sake and have not become weary." (Rev 2:2–3, NKJV)

Their Contributions: Continue by Acknowledging their Contributions

"*I* [Jesus] *know your works . . . and* [how] *you have persevered . . .* " These words say it all: Jesus took time to acknowledge the effort and contributions of the people. Speaking about peoples' contributions before delivering the actual correction not only means that a leader has done her homework, it 'humanizes' the process—creating a positive atmosphere that makes people more willing to listen to you. The writer of Revelation reveals the next—and possibly the most critical step—saying,

> "Nevertheless I have this against you, that you have left your first love." (Rev 2:4, NKJV)

The Correction: Gently, but Clearly and Firmly, Point Out Failings, Faults, and Foibles

"Nevertheless, I have this against you, that you have left your first love." Notice carefully that it is only now that Jesus mentions the actual feedback he wants to give. At this point, the best leaders gently, but firmly, point out the specific areas where people are missing it. This is also the point where you allow people respond, make suggestions, etc. If the feedback you receive from them reinforces your initial convictions, then you can proceed to the next step (as adduced from the following words of the writer of Revelation),

> "Remember therefore from where you have fallen; repent and do the first works, or else I will come to you quickly and remove your lampstand from its place—unless you repent." (Rev 2:5, NKJV)

The Consequences: Clearly Layout the Consequences of Continuing Without Correction

" . . . do the first works, or else . . . " While it is true that people learn from the consequences they suffer, it is also true that smart people can learn from the *prospect* of the consequences they would suffer. The delivery of negative feedback rides on the back of this last point. Jesus clearly set out the consequences that would occur if the Ephesian Church continued to do wrong. The best leaders are like him; they don't pull any punches as they let their people know the consequences of not taking correction to heart.

The writer of Revelation ends his discourse of Jesus' masterful delivery of negative feedback with the following words,

> "But this you have, that you hate the deeds of the Nicolaitans, which I also hate. "He who has an ear, let him hear what the Spirit says to the churches. To him who overcomes I will give to eat from the tree of life, which is in the midst of the Paradise of God." (Rev 2:6-7, NKJV)

Section 3 | Managing 'Down'

A Last Word of Comfort: End the Communication Process With Encouragement

"To him who overcomes, I will give to eat from the tree of life . . . " Negative feedback points out problems along the way that people must overcome—a thing which can be demoralizing. Therefore, ending the communication with a word of comfort boosts peoples' morale and helps them make the required behavioral changes.

After all is said and done, the aim of managing 'down' is to improve the productivity of associates, and delegation—which we discussed earlier—is a powerful tool for doing just that. Notwithstanding, delegation's impact is limited by the fact that it is all about ceding portions of your own job to others. Productivity is greatest, as we've seen with the Pygmalion effect, when associates are motivated to do their own jobs well, and it is to the subject of helping associates to do their own jobs well that we again turn our attention . . . .

CONVERTING CAREERS INTO CALLINGS (LESSONS FROM THE LEADERSHIP OF NEHEMIAH)

"Principle-centered leadership suggests that the highest level of human motivation is a sense of personal contribution."—Stephen Covey

In 2015, the satellite news station, *Euronews*, celebrated the bicentennial anniversary of Napoleon's defeat at Waterloo with a documentary highlighting the French Emperor's achievements. Say what you want, one thing is clear: Napoleon was skillful at motivating men and making them give their all—even in the face of defeat and terrible suffering—to a cause. Imagine, military historians estimate that only two percent of the huge army Napoleon led into Russia in 1812 marched back out fit for battle. Yet, that disastrous campaign did not stop men from flocking to his banners! In fact, years later, after his escape from captivity and reappearance on French soil, thousands of his old comrades returned to join him in his renewed battle against the Continental Alliance! The question becomes: what exactly is it that makes people give their all to the cause of an organization? Management writer Stephen Covey, in his book, *Principle-Centered Leadership*, proffers an answer, saying "Principle-centered leadership suggests that the highest level of human motivation is a sense of personal contribution."

Imagine my astonishment when I saw that Dr. Covey's line of thinking was at the root of the rebuilding of the wall of Jerusalem! The writer of Nehemiah tells the story of how a wall that had lain broken down for decades was rebuilt in just fifty-two days . . .

> "So we rebuilt the wall till all of it reached half its height, for the people worked with all their heart." (Neh 4:6, NIV)

The Heart of the Matter!

Nehemiah had achieved the near-impossible. A wall that had lain broken down for about one hundred and twenty years was rebuilt in a record fifty-two days! By saying " . . . the people worked *with all their heart*," the writer of Nehemiah lets the cat out of the bag; the reason the wall was rebuilt in record time was because the people worked with all their heart. Nehemiah didn't just buy their hands or backs, he got them to work with all their hearts—to give their best, and then some! Every time people are so highly motivated that they willingly give their best to a task, everyone wins: the organization operates at its peak, the people produce a quality product and leaders make maximum impact. So why did Nehemiah's people work with all their hearts, and not just their hands and minds? Why didn't they hold back some of their effort or initiative? Again, the words of the writer of Nehemiah throw some light on the matter . . .

> " . . . Shallum . . . repaired the next section with the help of his daughters . . . Benjamin and Hashub made repairs *in front of their house,* and next to them, Azariah . . . made repairs *beside his house* . . . Above the Horse Gate, the priests made repairs, each *in front of his own house.* Next to them, Zadok . . . made repairs *opposite his house* . . . Next to them, Meshullam . . . made repairs *opposite his living quarters* . . . Malkishua, one of the goldsmiths, made repairs *as far as the house of the . . . merchants* . . . " (Emphases mine) (Neh 3:12–32, NIV)

Work That's Meaningful Causes People to Work with All their Heart!

" . . . *made repairs opposite his house* . . . " Repairing the wall of Jerusalem is one thing; repairing the wall of Jerusalem that passes right in front of my house is another thing! The first scenario is general in nature, while

Section 3 | Managing 'Down'

the second is very personal—showing me my own part in the much larger work and the effect of the work on my personal life. Nehemiah was skillful with people, so much so that, as much as possible, he put men to work on portions of the wall in front of their own homes! In one case, he even let a leader work closely with his own daughters ("Shallum... repaired the next section *with the help of his daughters*..."). Imagine building a wall with your own children. You'd be forgiven if you think that you are building your own children! But, and this is crucial, to put people to work on portions of the wall next to their own homes, Nehemiah had to first know their home addresses. To give work that's meaningful to a person, you must first have an idea of what's meaningful to him. Knowing a person's firelighters (like Nehemiah knowing a person's home address) is the first step to designing work that's meaningful to him.

Leaders who bring out the best in others consciously help them see how the 'little' effort they make, or small part they play, meshes into the bigger picture. In this way, they help provide meaning and a sense of contribution to their people. Nehemiah's people worked with all their heart because he aligned their personal goals with those of the organization. When people can fulfill their deepest emotional needs from the work they do, then their careers become transformed into their callings. To help you better understand all this, I have drawn up the following grid...

Table 1 (3 Kinds of Jobs: Jobs that 'Buy My Hand', 'Buy My Mind' or Tap into My Heart)

Leaders who...

Buy my hand	Buy my mind	Tap into my heart
Give me a job that provides for me materially	Give me a job that utilizes my training and talent	Give me work that allows me make a contribution
Give me work that meets my economic needs	Give me work that meets my mental needs	Give me work that meets my deepest psychological needs

Careers are converted into callings when people can see the connection between what they are doing and the bigger picture. The words of writer Lazlo Bock, from his book, *Work Rules!*, are the "last word" for converting careers into callings,

> "We all want our work to matter. Nothing is a more powerful motivator than to know that you are making a difference in the world.

Amy Wrzesniewski of Yale University told me people see their work as just a job ("a necessity that's not a major positive in their lives"), a career (something to "win" or "advance"), or a calling ("a source of enjoyment and fulfillment where you're doing socially useful work").

Chapter 17

Pitfalls & Problems of Managing 'Down'

CONTROL, COMPLIANCE & COMMITMENT: THE LIMITS OF MANAGING 'DOWN'

AFTER ALL IS SAID and done, managing 'down' is basically about how you use the authority of your position to accomplish the goals of your organization or group. If this is so, then it follows that the limits of authority will automatically be the limits of managing 'down'. "So, what," you might ask "are the limits of authority?" Before we go ahead to answer that question, we need to first know what authority is. Henry Mintzberg, in his excellent book, *Managing*, said that "For example, I described managers as being able to control insiders but having to convince outsiders. Employees, after all, are paid to accept managerial authority." These intriguing words mean that,

1. Authority gives a manager the right to control the behavior of subordinates.
2. Control produces compliance. The latter occurs when employees willingly choose to carry out their manager's decisions even if they don't agree with her.
3. Compliance occurs because employees are paid to comply.

Interestingly, the writer of Luke's Gospel, in his narrative of the story of Jesus and the Roman centurion (a soldier heading up a unit of one hundred troops), corroborates this line of thinking, saying,

Pitfalls & Problems of Managing 'Down'

"For I myself am a man under authority, with soldiers under me. I tell this one, 'Go,' and he goes; and that one, 'Come,' and he comes. I say to my servant, 'Do this,' and he does it." (Luke 7:8, NIV)

These words mean that,

Authority—in the Work Setting—is the Right to Control and Direct the Behavior of Others

"I tell this one, 'Go,' and he goes . . . " Only the centurion could legally order his men to 'go" (no other soldier in the same unit could legally do that). Indeed, no centurion overseeing a different band of soldiers could legally give orders to this centurion's men. Therefore, we can say that, authority—in the work setting—is the right to control and direct the behavior of others. Authority vests control of a group (including the persons and resources within the group) in a person—the manager, boss, head, or leader of the unit by whatever name called. The centurion controlled the behavior of his subordinates by means of the information he communicated to them, and in this way, helped them accomplish the overall goals of the Roman Army in Palestine. That said, a closer look at the words of the writer of Luke's Gospel shows us a major limitation of authority, and by extension, a major limitation of managing 'down' . . .

While Control Can Produce Compliance, It Doesn't Necessarily Produce Commitment

"I say to one, 'Go,' and he goes . . . " The soldier who "goes" at the command of the centurion is only expected to comply with the order and no more (even though he may be able to do more). I mean, telling a soldier who ostensibly can march 50 miles to march 40 miles will produce compliance, but the fact is that that soldier can still do more than what was demanded of him. Compliance is getting the soldier to do what you demand. Commitment is getting him to do more than you demand. Why? Because when people are committed to a task, they go the extra mile. Control elicits compliance (a thing of the 'head') but not commitment (a thing of the "heart').

This brings us to the burning question; what management behavior can elicit commitment from associates? Again, Professor Mintzberg comes to our rescue, saying " . . . in the leading role, managers help to bring out the energy that exists naturally within people." The key words in that sentence are "*in the leading role.*" Those wise words show that, it is only as managers become leaders that they can get people to become committed. The writer of Philemon, in his discussion of the relationship between Paul the apostle and Philemon, corroborates that line of thinking, saying,

> "I do wish, brother, that I may have some benefit from you in the Lord; refresh my heart in Christ. Confident of your obedience, I write to you, knowing that you will do even more than I ask." (Phl 1:20–21, NIV)

Authority Produces Compliance, While Influence Elicits Commitmemt

" . . . *you will even do more than I ask.*" These words say it all: Paul was not Philemon's boss (he actually referred to Philemon as "brother"), yet his leadership was so effective that he just knew that Philemon would go the extra mile for him! Why? Because Paul had influence with Philemon! Managing 'down' utilizes authority, while leadership utilizes influence. Authority and influence are tools for controlling and directing the behavior of others: but, while authority gets people to comply, leadership goes one step further—eliciting commitment. Authority connects with peoples' "heads," while influence connects with their "hearts." It is only as managing 'down' transmutes into leading 'down' that you can get people to go the extra mile. In a nutshell, people who operate wholly from the prism of managing 'down' tend to achieve something with people in the workplace, but those who go a step farther and lead, get more out of their people.

Having seen that the limits of managing 'down' are automatically the limits of authority, we now turn our attention to a specific case where authority's effects are also severely limited . . .

MANAGING KNOWLEDGE WORKERS (LEADING WHEN YOU'RE NOT THE EXPERT)

"A very large number of knowledge workers . . . are . . . specialists. Their own field may be quite narrow. But in it they know more than the boss – and they know it. In their field they are superior to their employer, no matter their position in the organization. The knowledge worker is thus a colleague or associate. He is to be managed as such."—PETER DRUCKER

If insensitivity to the *feelings* of others is a key reason for career derailment when people manage 'across', then insensitivity to the *statuses* of others is a key reason for career derailment when they manage 'down'. The first type of insensitivity, as we've seen from the story of Esau (Chapter 13), has to do with being blind to the nonverbal cues that others, regardless of their status, give. The second type is the result of being blind to the statuses of a particular subset of highly educated persons (knowledge workers)—what I refer to as "leading when you are not the expert."

Some time ago, as a leadership instructor in a Bible college, I had to speak to my team leader about a matter involving the teaching of leadership. As we talked, I noticed that, by trying to speak definitively on leadership—a subject about which he knew virtually nothing—my team leader began to come across as disrespectful. Why? Because, by refusing to acknowledge my expertise, and by acting like he knew 'leadership' more than me, he began to treat me like an inferior! He seemed oblivious to the fact that, though he was my organizational superior, yet when it came to the specialty of leadership, I could probably lead him! I left that meeting with the realization that many leaders don't know that there's a whole world of difference between leading a knowledge worker (a specialist) and managing an inferior. "So, who," you might ask, "is an inferior?" The writer of Job, in his account of the argument between Job and his friends, proffers a beautiful answer, saying,

> '[Job continued:] Behold, my eye has seen all this, my ear has heard and understood it. —What you know, I also know; I am not inferior to you." (Job 13:1-2, AMP)

'Inferiors' Are Subordinates Who Are Less Knowledgeable About their Own Jobs than their Managers

"What you know, I also know; I am not inferior to you." These words reveal a little appreciated truth about the relationship between authority and knowledge. Remember that at this time, this greatest of all men in the East had lost all his wealth and was literally penniless; yet Job could still confidently say to his well to do friends, "I am not inferior to you." The reason for this confident assertion? Job knew what they knew! This means that an 'inferior' is a subordinate who knows less about the task at hand than his boss or 'superior'. Indeed, the classical concept of "superior and inferior"—which still dominates the culture of many workplaces today—assumes that the superior knows more about the task than her inferior. Come to think of it, the General is a superior to the Colonel precisely because he, having once being a colonel, presumably knows all about the work of colonels. When it comes to warfare, the General's experience gives him an advantage over the Colonel—the very reason the General can bark orders at the Colonel without expecting any input from the latter! Again, the writer of Luke's Gospel, in his account of Jesus' meeting with the Roman centurion, drives the point home, saying,

> "For I also am a man under authority, with soldiers under me. I tell this one 'Go,' and he goes; and that one 'Come,' and he comes. I say to my servant, 'Do this,' and he does it." (Luke 7:8, NIV)

These words mean that,

Command-and-Control is the Model for Managing 'Inferiors'

With words like " . . . soldiers under me . . . I tell this one, 'Go' . . . that one, 'Come' . . . I say to my servant," the implication is all too clear: the boss (centurion) knew more about the matter at hand than his men! I mean, if you truly know more about the task than me and I am your boss, I would be less authoritarian, more willing to communicate with you, and more willing to listen to your advice and input. When you lead an inferior, you allow little room for initiative, but when you lead an expert or specialist, you should be less authoritarian, and treat the specialist as a colleague or associate. Managing 'down', because it depends majorly on authority, is inherently unable to lead knowledge workers. While the assumption that managers know more about a task than subordinates often holds true in the traditional workplace, that assumption is less applicable to today's knowledge-driven workplace. Even rigid 'command and control' organizations like the US Army know this—and are adapting, as can be seen from this story told to Thomas Friedman by General Stanley McChrystal in the former's co-authored book, *That Used to Be Us*,

> "My grandfather was a soldier. My father was a soldier. From the time my grandfather, at the end of World War I, went from lieutenant to colonel, there was a change in technology. But it was not so fast or so great that his experience did not provide him with a

body of expertise that made him legitimate and credible with his men. The reality today is that when a general officer speaks to a captain, that general officer has almost never used any of the communications systems, intelligence assets, or weapons systems that the captain has. So when the general or colonel goes down there and tries to be the leader and the captain looks at him, [that captain knows] that this guy has never done the job he is doing, nothing close. So the reality is: How does the leader retain his legitimacy in his big organization? What is the basis for his credibility? Is it his good looks? This is a really big deal. Things go so fast now it is very difficult for people to be experts and still be leading."

The armies of today, in the light of General McChrystal's words, must develop generals who see subordinate officers as more than mere inferiors. Subordinate officers must also be seen as knowledge workers who know more about certain specialties than their general officers. The question becomes "If the command-and-control model is of little value in managing knowledge workers, what model of leadership should one use?" The answers to that important question can be gleaned from studying the leadership of one of antiquity's leaders . . .

A Tale of Two "Authorities" (Lessons in the Management of Knowledge Workers from. Pharaoh King of Egypt)

Everyone who has ever attended Church knows the story—the king of Egypt has a dream, and a young Hebrew slave-boy, freshly released from the king's dungeons, interprets the dream. The interpretation is that there will be a famine in seven years time. The Hebrew boy (whose name is Joseph) also provides a plan to save the kingdom from devastation during the upcoming famine. An obviously impressed king does the unthinkable—he appoints Joseph as governor, with responsibility for managing Egypt's agricultural output in order to prepare for the famine. The writer of Genesis tells this inspiring story, saying,

> "And now let Pharaoh look for a discerning and wise man and put him in charge of the land of Egypt. Let Pharaoh appoint commissioners over the land to take a fifth of the harvest of Egypt during the seven years of abundance . . . to be used during the seven years of famine that will come upon Egypt, so that the country may not be ruined by the famine . . . . You [Joseph] shall be in charge of my palace, and all my people are to submit to your orders. Only with

Section 3 | Managing 'Down'

respect to the throne will I be greater than you. " (Gen. 41:33–40, NIV)

Pharaoh, King of Egypt, Hires an Expert!

Although this story is the stuff of many inspirational Sunday School lessons, it's also a treasure trove of insights for managing knowledge workers. By appointing Joseph—a rank outsider and former slave—to the high office of governor, we see this king of Egypt openly hire an expert to head-up a key government agency. The question becomes: how does an absolute monarch with power of life and death over all his subjects work harmoniously with this agricultural expert called Joseph and still remain boss? The writer of Genesis shows us just how Pharaoh managed this delicate balancing act, saying,

> "You shall be in charge of my palace, and all my people are to submit to your orders. Only with respect to the throne will I be greater than you." " (Gen 41:40, NIV)

Pharaoh Manages a Knowledge Worker By Deferring to His Expertise!

"*You* [Joseph] *shall be in charge . . . Only with respect to the throne will I be greater than you.*" There it is in black and white: the king deferred to Joseph's expertise and gave Joseph freedom to act as long as his actions were in line with "the throne." Deferrence, in this case, means that the king allowed Joseph's decisions to stand as long as they didn't significantly detract from the larger interests of the kingdom. Managing 'down', like I said before, is all about using your positional authority to accomplish the aims of your organization. But, here's where things get interesting, the specialist, by reason of his expertise, possesses another kind of authority called 'expert authority'. These two kinds of authority often clash when you manage knowledge workers. The best managers resolve this 'clash' by giving freedom of action to their knowledge workers as long as the actions.of the latter are in line with the policies and general guidelines of the organization.

Since, knowledge workers have freedom to act as long as their actions are, in the words of the writer of Genesis, in line with "the throne," it is important to delve deeper into the meaning of the term, "the throne." The Psalmist shows exactly what that term means, saying,

> "Shall *the throne* of inquity, which devises evil by law, Have fellowship with You?" (Emphasis mine) (Ps 94:20, NKJV)

His words mean that,

Managing Knowledge Workers Turns on Providing them Resources and Accountability

The term "the throne," in the words of the Psalmist, is what "devises" or enacts law and policy that guide the conduct of a group of persons. In other words, the "throne" provides the mechanisms for holding group members accountable and for keeping the main thing the main thing. Therefore, providing resources and accountability is at the heart of managing knowledge workers. While the part about providing resources is easy to do and understand, holding knowledge workers to account is less easy to put into practice. The best managers provide accountability by always holding up the mirror of organizational policies, guidelines for operation, values, and goals. In effect, the experts and specialists who work with, or for, them are free to act as long as their actions are in line with the goals, policy guidelines, and values of the group.

To help you better understand the differences between managing 'down' ('command and control') and managing knowledge workers, I have prepared the following grid,

Table 2 (Comparing 'Command and Control" Methods with Methods for Managing Knowledge Workers)

Command and Control	Managing Knowledge Workers
"Telling": doesn't allow subordinates make inputs or exercise their initiative.	"Selling": allows associates room to exercise initiative.
Works best with 'inferiors."	Works best with knowledge workers and specialists.
Subordinates work 'under' you	Associates are seen as colleagues who work "with" you
People do what they are told. Driven by 'authority'.	People do more than they are told. Driven by 'permission'.

SECTION 3 | MANAGING 'DOWN'

The last pitfall of managing 'down' that we would discuss is . . . .

MANAGING CONFLICT WITH SUBORDINATES (LESSONS FROM THE LEADERSHIP OF JOB)

"Hierarchical behavior avoids an active multilevel dialogue on critical issues and uses power to settle issues rather than broad debate and high-quality analysis."—C. K. PRALAHAD AND GARY HAMEL

I have just finished reading about the disgruntled staff of a notable American airline who disrupted flight operations by deliberately deleting thousands of customer reservations from the airline's database. The reason for that outrageous behavior? The staff felt his grievances were unjustly handled by management and that the latter used their power to cheat him! Hierarchical behavior—the linchpin of managing 'down'—is rooted in the "might is right" paradigm; a perspective that prefers to use power—not dialogue or principles—to resolve disputes. Therefore, hierarchical behavior, not only has the potential to gender conflict with subordinates, it also tends to mismanage those conflicts when they eventually occur. In groups where hierarchical behavior flourishes, subordinates with genuine grievances are subtly discouraged from airing them. Why? Because the person managing 'down' is more likely to be judged 'right' in any conflict with a subordinate! But, as the example of the disgruntled airline staffer shows, poorly managed workplace conflict can produce resentful employees who can go the whole hog and sabotage things.

Management writers James Kouzes and Barry Posner, in their book, *The Leadership Challenge,* proffer a solution to this inability to manage conflict with subordinates that dogs the process of managing 'down', saying "In a credible organization, conflicts are resolved based on principles, not position; on problems, not personalities." Their words hint that managers who are in conflict with subordinates must disavow the use of power as a *first* tool for settling disputes. Interestingly, the writer of Job, in his discussion of how Job (a successful businessman and employer of labor) managed conflicts with his own staff, corroborates that line of thinking, saying,

> "If I have denied justice to my menservants and maidservants when they had a grievance against me, what will I do when God confronts me? What will I answer when called to account? Did not

he who made me in the womb make them? Did not the same one form us both within our mothers?" (Job 31:13–15, NIV)

"*If I have denied justice to my manservants and maidservants [employees] when they had a grievance against me . . .* " To today's average person, Job, the greatest businessman in his day, is like Amazon's Jeff Bezos—a very wealthy and powerful man. The only difference is that while the latter is hamstrung and constrained on every side by a raft of laws, Job was regulated only conscience and convention. In effect, in his day, Job could have gotten away with blue murder! But, in this illuminating passage, Job makes an astonishing claim; he asserts that, though he was boss, his employees were not only allowed to bring their complaints against him to him, he also never rejected—out of hand—their grievances! Thus, we learn from Job the 'big boss man' that, when people manage 'down' . . .

Conflict Between Boss and Subordinate Comes With the Territory!

"If I have denied justice to my [employees . . . when they brought a complaint against me to me]." Job was righteous to the point that God spoke glowingly of him to Satan (Job 1:8)—and yet he still had employees with grievances! That is, no matter how well run an organization is, and no matter how upstanding the conduct of its bosses, you will still have aggrieved employees and conflict.

Effective Leaders Resolve Conflict By First Drawing Strength from Principles, Not Position

"If I have denied justice to my maidservant . . . when they had a grievance against me . . . Did not he who made me in the womb make them?" Though Job was boss, he hardly ever borrowed strength from his position when dealing with complaints from aggrieved staff. He didn't feel affronted when people with less power than he brought their grievances against him to him. Why? Because he was guided by the principle that the same God who created him was also the Creator of his 'lowly' subordinates! Next time you are involved in a workplace dispute, take a deep breath and make sure you're dealing with the facts of the matter and not using the power of your position to your advantage. I know this is new thinking for many of us positional leaders, but it can decrease some of the resentment that disgruntled employees feel and the subtle acts of sabotage they engage in. As you do this, always keep in mind the words of management teacher Stephen Covey "When people with formal power and positional authority refuse to use their power except as a last resort . . . their moral authority increases because it is obvious that they have subordinated their ego and position power and use reasoning and persuasion instead." Job only used his position power as a last resort. Go thou and do the likewise!

In the final analysis, the abuse of power that often dogs the process of managing 'down' begins when leaders borrow strength from their positions and use their powers as a *first* resort to settle workplace disputes. That kind of behavior builds huge resentment in associates and subordinates, and may even lead to sabotage. Which is why MIT professor Edgar Schein, in his book, *Organizational Culture And Leadership*, said that " . . . a good time to observe an organization very closely is when acts of insubordination take place . . . No better opportunity exists for leaders to send signals about their own assumptions about human nature and relationships than when they themselves are challenged." While times of conflict can be threatening to order and authority, Professor Schein's words help us see that they can also be an opportunity to " . . . send signals about human nature . . . "—times to first draw strength from principles and not position. Like I said before, the major pitfall of managing 'down' is this tendency to abuse positional power—to borrow strength from position and use it as a first resort to resolve conflict with subordinates. The best leaders fight off that temptation and use principles as the first resort in managing conflict with subordinates. In this way, they avoid the insidious phenomenon in poorly run organizations where, the higher up the person is, the more likely she is to be 'right' in any dispute!

SECTION 4

Managing Yourself

PREAMBLE: WHAT DOES IT MEAN TO MANAGE YOURSELF?

'You can't be successful with others if you haven't paid the price of success with yourself.' —STEPHEN COVEY

FOR MOST PEOPLE, THE answer to the question "What factor is most crucial to success at work?" is "My professional competence and personal smarts."—a top-of-mind answer that falls squarely in the ballpark of personal management. Probably the most poignant picture of the importance of managing yourself is the airline industry's instruction to passengers just before takeoff. The firm voice of the cabin crew reminds adult passengers that, in the event of an emergency, they must first put on their own oxygen masks before attempting to help accompanying children! The reason? It is only an adult who is able to breathe that can help a child in distress! The moral of that instruction is clear: you can't manage your relationships with others until you first manage yourself. But, and this is important, not only do people who can't manage themselves find it difficult to manage others, they also become burdens to others. I mean, if you can't manage yourself, then your boss (or some other person) is going to have to spend time trying to manage you—a real drain on her own time. No wonder leadership expert John Maxwell said that "Nothing will make a better impression on your leader than your ability to manage yourself. If your leader must continually expend energy managing you, then you will be perceived as a drain on time and energy." This is why I consider managing yourself to be the most important of the four "relationships" that must be managed if a person is to experience career success. Managing yourself involves managing the things under your control—your time, talent and training—in ways that help you accomplish things ostensibly outside your control—work targets set by your 'employer' (users, audiences or markets). Therefore, this section will deal with the 2 major themes of personal management—personal effectiveness and personal development.

Paul the apostle—Christianity's greatest evangelist—is undoubtedly one of the most productive men to have walked the face of this planet. In a career spanning roughly four decades, he planted multiple churches across the Roman empire, wrote two-thirds of the New Testament, and enunciated thoughts that still influence much of Western thinking today. Surely, such a person must know a thing or two about the links between managing oneself and career success. Unsurprisingly, his life and teachings form the backbone of the lessons in this section.

Chapter 18

Personal Effectiveness 101

MAKING CAREER PROGRESS

Like I highlighted in the preamble to this section, managing yourself is all about managing the things under your control—your time, talent, and training—in ways that help you achieve things that are ostensibly outside your control (work targets, etc.). This means that managing yourself is all about effectiveness, about alignment, and about using the things under your control in ways that help you accomplish your goals. Paul the apostle, while giving some career advice to Timothy his protégé, focuses on time, talent, training, and work targets as the keys to making career progress. Although Paul gave that advice to Timothy, a minister of the gospel, the principles enunciated by Paul apply to us all today. Listen to Paul's advice in his First Letter to Timothy . . .

> "Until I come, devote yourself to the public reading of Scripture, to preaching and teaching. Do not neglect your gift, which was given you through prophecy when the body of elders laid their hands on you. Be diligent in these matters [Practice these things], give yourself wholly to them, so that everyone may see your progress." (1Tim 4:13–15, NIV)

Much reflection on these words has helped me see the following truths,

Section 4 | Managing Yourself

Career Progress Cannot be Hidden!

"*... so that everyone may see your progress.*" Whatever your definition of progress, one thing is clear; progress cannot be hidden. When you make progress in your career or vocation, everyone will know. Therefore, the question isn't 'What is progress?' but rather 'How can I make progress?'

Career Progress Comes When You Close the Gap Between What's Important to You and How You Spend Your Time

"*Until I come, devote yourself to ... Do not neglect ... give yourself wholly to them ... so that everyone may see your progress.*" Notice carefully that these highlighted phrases are all concerned with the use of time. In effect, Paul is saying that 'time management' is key to making career progress. If you must make progress in any endeavor, then you must become more strategic—devoting the lion-share of your time to the things which contribute the most to your goals. Why? Because progress always comes when you close the gap between what's important to you and how you spend your time. Management writer Peter Drucker was correct after all "Intelligence, imagination and knowledge are essential resources, but only effectiveness converts them into results." Timothy, a preacher, needed to be effective, to devote a major chunk of his time (and, by division, his effort) to certain mission-critical activities—public reading of Scriptures, and preaching and teaching—if he wanted to taste the grapes of career success. So also must you devote the lion-share of your own time to activities mission-critical to success at whatever it is that you do. If you work for an organization, then I must add a caveat to what I've been saying ...

Career Progress Comes When You Close the Gap Between What's Required of You and How You Spend Your Time

The key to success in organizational careers is to become proficient at whatever is required by your employer. That last sentence is the root of the popular workplace proverb "Find out how they keep score, and score!" If you work in sales, your bosses will require that you sell a lot of stuff. Therefore career progress comes easiest when you spend your best time on activities crucial to what's important to your bosses—selling. In simple terms, find out what your boss or company requires of you, and spend your best time learning to do it, and actually doing it.

Career Progress Comes When You Do Work that Utilizes Your Strengths

"... *Do not neglect your gift* .... so that everyone may see your progress." Progress comes when you're effective, and effectiveness comes easiest when you work from your areas of strength. People who do work that doesn't utilize their natural strengths, or that only marginally utilizes their core strengths, will find it difficult to experience success. Why? Because results come easiest when you're "in the zone"—in your area of natural giftedness. Some might ask "Why did Paul want Timothy to spend most of his time and energy on the area of his giftedness?" The answer is . . .

Improvement and Performance are Always Related to Natural Ability

Most of us think improvement comes when we shore up our weaknesses, or when we deal with the areas where we naturally perform poorly. But if your performance is naturally weak in a certain area, then a great deal of effort poured into that area can only bring you up to average. Leadership expert John Maxwell, puts it beautifully, saying "You cannot grow to your maximum potential if you continuously work outside your strength zone. Improvement is always related to ability. The greater your natural ability, the greater your potential for improvement." It is only as you spend time and resources on your areas of giftedness that you can begin to make the quantum leap from good to great. Come to think of it, no matter how much time and effort I put into soccer practice, I cannot hope to outperform Cristiano Ronaldo and Lionel Messi. Why? Because those two superlative soccer players are intrinsically more gifted in that area than me! Certainly, if your weakness is a character weakness, then you need to do something about it. But if not, identify and go with your strengths. I often drive home the point about working from your strengths with this parable . . .

The Parable of the Two Coins

One day a poor old woman discovered 2 coins in a cupboard in a dark and neglected area of her tiny house. Overjoyed, she rushed to the goldsmith to have the grimy coins polished. The latter confirmed her find: both coins were valuable; one coin was copper and the other gold. The goldsmith also told her that it would cost $10 to polish each coin. The old woman was in a quandary; she had exactly $10 as her life savings. What to do? Which coin was she to polish first? The answer is a no-brainer. She should polish the gold coin because it is intrinsically more valuable! This parable shows that, because you have limited resources, you get more bang for your buck when you concentrate your best time and resources on your 'gold coin'—on areas of natural strength. For those who work in organizations, the principle is still the same: build on strengths, your boss's strengths, the strengths of your colleagues and the strengths of your organization. And just in case you lead others, always keep in mind this fact: your primary duty is to place your associates in areas where they are naturally gifted. That said, let's return to Paul's advice to Timothy . . .

Career Progress Takes Time. There's No Such Thing as an Overnight Success

"*Continue in them . . .* so that everyone may see your progress." To see progress, you will need to persevere ("continue") and stay with these disciplines day after day. I will delve deeper into the role of time (and chance) in career success in the "Last Word" part of this book.

Career Progress Comes When You Develop the Right Habits

" . . . *Continue in them,* so that your progress may be seen by all" Career success, as we've seen, is certainly not overnight success. To make progress, you will need to repeat the same set of actions over and over again for long periods of time. Since habits are tools for mindlessly repeating actions over and over again, you will need to develop the specific set of habits needed for success in your particular vocation. *Because habits take time to form, the development of habits critical to success is a rate limiting step in a person's journey to career success.* Timothy, a speaker, needed to develop the habits of study and refection critical to making progress in the ministry. You may need to first discover what habits are necessary for success in your vocation and then develop them. Progress comes to the person who has made progress in developing the right habits!

Progress Comes Easiest When You Can Work Without External Supervision

" . . . *Until I come* . . . " Paul the apostle wasn't going to be around to supervise Timothy. Timothy needed to, by himself, learn to do the things Paul instructed him to do. Timothy needed to be a self-starter. Until you can put yourself through your paces without external 'snoopervision', you wouldn't see much progress. Indeed, the ability to work independently and without supervision is the hallmark of a master—the person most likely to experience workplace success. Regardless, progress, according to Paul the apostle, is easy to bring about because it is simply taking action on a generic set of principles of personal management—time management, developing the right habits etc. And, it is to another of those principles that we now turn our attention . . .

GETTING RESULTS

"Productivity puts people at the head of the class. The ability to obtain results is the separating line for success: it is also the qualifying line for leadership."
—John Maxwell

What does it take to be one of the leaders in your vocation? Or, for that matter, what is required to achieve a modicum of success in any field at all? As I read John Maxwell's excellent book, *The 5 Levels of Leadership*, I came to see an answer from the above quote "The ability to obtain results is the separating line for success . . . " After all is said and done, career progress—promotion, recognition, and public acclaim—comes to the person who delivers the goods, the person who consistently gets results. The question becomes, how does one get results? Again, Paul the apostle, using imagery from athletics and boxing, shows us just how to keep the results coming, saying . . .

> "Do you not know that in a race all the runners run, but only one gets the prize? Run in such a way as to get the prize. Everyone who

Section 4 | Managing Yourself

competes in the games goes into strict training. They do it to get a crown that will not last, but we do it to get a crown that will last forever. Therefore I do not run like someone running aimlessly; I do not fight like a boxer beating the air. No, I strike a blow to my body and make it my slave . . . " (1Cor 9:24–27, NIV)

This intriguing passage is a metaphor for winning in the workplace, showing us that if you want to win prizes at work, you must . . .

Change Your Perspective, and Begin to Think Like a Champion Athlete

"*Run in such a way as to get the prize . . .* " Getting results begins with understanding that winning a race doesn't begin on race day and continues with recognizing that there is only one champion in every race. Unlike today's Olympics which has prizes for the top three performers, there were no prizes for second-best athletes in the games of the Roman Empire of Paul's day ("Do you not know that in a race all the runners run, *but only one gets the prize . . .* ") The highly competitive nature of those games meant that people who wanted to become prize winners had to . . . .

Engage in Constant Practice

"Everyone who competes . . . *goes into strict training.*" George Leonard, in his book, *Mastery*, said that "The master of any game is generally a master of practice." To become a master of the game, you must first find out the things you must constantly practice. The champions of soccer and the champions of baseball are both masters of their respective games, but their practice routines differ. For example, the trial lawyer who wants to master her art must engage in higher than normal levels of case study and spend copious amounts of time practicing public speaking. This kind of constant practice demands that you . . .

Hold Yourself to Higher Standards of Performance

"Everyone who competes . . . goes into strict training." High performance requires high commitment. To see a champion athlete like sprinter Usain Bolt defeat all his rivals at the Olympics is one thing; to see the gruelling training regimen he puts himself through daily is another thing. The stricter the training, the higher the standards to which you hold yourself. No matter what vocation you pursue, to become more productive than others, you must first hold yourself to higher standards than everyone else. One way to hold yourself to a higher standard is to always go the extra mile, as this story of Joseph reveals . . .

> "Please *go to Shechem* and see if it is well with your brothers and the flock . . . So . . . [Joseph] went to Shechem . . . And a [certain man] found him . . . wandering in the fields . . . and asked him . . . what are you seeking? So he said, I am seeking my brothers . . . And the man said . . . I heard them say, Let us go to Dothan. *So Joseph went after his brothers and found them in Dothan.*" (Emphases mine) (Gen 37:14–17, NIV)

Joseph Goes the Extra Mile!

Joseph's orders were to go to Shechem and see how his brothers were faring, but, on reaching Shechem, he couldn't find his brothers. What to do? He began to look for a way to get his task done. His willingness to go the extra mile paid off; he found a way to locate his brothers—finding them in Dothan sixty miles from Shechem! Don't fall into the habit of making excuses for why the job can't be done, rather, train yourself to do more than is required.

Set Tangible Goals and then Strive to Reach them

"*Therefore, I do not run like a man running aimlessly . . .* " Have an aim, target or goal you want to accomplish. Rate yourself by the goals you accomplish and not by the effort you expend. Accept responsibility for your results and don't blame anyone else for poor outcomes. Every Olympic-level athlete races against a clock; he has a time limit to complete his race. Never make excuses. Do all that is within your power to reach your goals. Crucially also, take yourself out of situations in which you're unproductive. In other words, in addition to a "Things to do list," you should also have a "Things to stop doing list." As you do this, keep in mind the words of management teacher Stephen Covey "Effectiveness . . . doesnot depend on how much effort we expend, but on whether the effort we expend is on the right [things]."

Always Keep it in Mind that You're Your Own Worst Enemy!

"No, I beat my body and make it my slave.." Before the boxer can throw a blow that knocks out his opponent, he must first "beat" himself and make his body subject to him. In other words, the boxer's real enemy is not his opponent; it is his own body! Former seven-time Tour de France champion, Lance Armstrong, drives the point home, saying "There's a point in every race when a rider encounters his real opponent and understands that it's himself." The more you can discipline yourself to do what's necessary, the greater your chances of success.

Make Yourself Accountable to Others

There are no champions without coaches. The athletes who compete in the Olympics all have coaches. Humble yourself. Every once in a while, make sure you have trusted persons on your team who can help review your actions, and provide you clear and unbiased feedback. Another way to make yourself accountable is to make your goals public. Leadership expert John Maxwell puts it beautifully, saying "Few things prompt a person to follow through like accountability. One of the ways you can do that is to make your goals public. When you tell others about what you intend to do, it puts pressure on you to keep working at it." After all is said and done, getting results is a very personal thing—the epitome of managing yourself. The leaders who get results time after time are those who have made the necessary personal decisions in the areas of self-discipline, work ethics, skill, and priorities. What are the standards of behavior to which you hold yourself? Are they higher than the standards the leaders in your field of endeavor set for themselves? If they aren't, you will continue to be an underdog. If they are, you've taken the first step to becoming one of the leaders in that field. To whom are you accountable for the results you get? Remember, even champion athletes like Lionel Messi and Cristiano Ronaldo have coaches.

While the last two lessons have been advice from one of the most successful men to walk the face of planet Earth, the next lesson isn't advice, it's practice—the things Paul did that made him so successful . . .

GETTING RESULTS (2)

"Individual differences in performance in a wide variety of talent domains can be largely attributed to the number of hours devoted to the direct acquisition of the necessary knowledge and skills."—DEAN KEITH SIMONTON

Everyone knows that Paul the apostle was intellectually productive. I mean, with his being responsible for almost two-thirds of the New Testament, the sheer volume and erudition of his teachings are open for all to see. But, was Paul also productive in the material sense, in the sense of economic resources generated from the work of his own hands? The writer of Acts helps us answer that intriguing question, saying,

> "I have not coveted any man's silver, gold or clothing. You know that these hands of mine have supplied my needs and those of my companions. In everything I showed you that by this kind of hard work, we must help the weak, remembering the words of the Lord Jesus, "It is more blessed to give than to receive." " (Acts 20:33–35, NIV)

These words help us see a much neglected truth . . .

Paul was Also Financially Productive!

"*You know that these hands of mine have supplied my needs and those of my companions . . .* " There it is in black and white: if the hallmark of productivity is surplus, then Paul's work generated a surplus—meeting, not only his own material needs, but also the needs of seven of his traveling companions (Acts 20:4–5), and the weak and needy! The question becomes, how did Paul generate such a surplus? As usual, the answers lie hidden in the words of the writer of Acts . . .

Productivity Requires a Certain Kind of Hard Work!

"I showed you that by *this kind* of hard work . . . " These words say it all: productivity requires a certain kind of hard work. Interestingly, as I studied the book of Galatians, I came to better understand the kind of hard work that made Paul so productive. Listen to the writer of Galatians (who, by the way, happens to be Paul) . . .

> "For you have heard of my former conduct in Judaism . . . And I advanced in Judaism beyond many of my own contemporaries in my own nation, being more exceeding zealous for the traditions of my fathers." (Gal 1:13–14, NIV)

Passion Puts You at the Head of the Class!

"I advanced in Judaism beyond many of my own contemporaries . . . *being more exceeding zealous . . .* " Not only does this intriguing passage show us that Paul was outstripping and outproducing his peers long before he came to know Christ, it also gives us the reason—zeal, enthusiasm, passion—for Paul's unusual productivity. In short, Paul was productive because he was passionate about his work. When you're passionate about the work you do then, like Paul, you'll leave many of your peers behind. So what edge does enthusiasm for the work you do give you? Or, how does passion affect your work habits? The writer of Second Corinthians (who, again, happens to be Paul), proffers an answer, saying . . .

> "Now concerning the ministering to the saints, it is superfluous for me to write to you, for I know your readiness, of which I boast about you to the people of Macedonia, saying that Achaia was ready since last year. And your zeal has stirred up most of them." (2Cor 9:1–2, NIV)

Passion Inspires Preparation

"*Achaia was ready since last year. And your zeal has provoked many.*" The Church in Achaia was full of zeal (passion and enthusiasm) for the work of ministering to poor Christians. And how did that zeal show up? It showed up as preparation ("Achaia was *ready a year ago.*"). Imagine that you are ready for your engagement or work one year before you need to perform the task. You certainly will be more productive, and might even just outproduce your peers! This means that Paul's passion showed up in his preparation, in how he spent his time. He spent more time at his work because he was passionate about it. Passion, because it prepares, puts a person over and makes her more productive than her peers. Preparation takes something from today's scarce resources (time, sleep, money etc.) and uses it to meet an upcoming challenge. And it can do all this without external supervision.

Psychologist Dean Keith Simonton was correct after all "Individual differences in performance in a wide variety of talent domains can be largely attributed to the number of hours devoted to the direct acquisition of the necessary knowledge and skills." Passion for a task makes it easier for you to put more time into it—and since skill and productivity correlate with the amount of time you put into a task, passion improves productivity and skill. Do work for which you are passionate!

Having seen the link between passion and preparation, it's fitting to close this chapter by answering the very practical question . . .

WHAT IS PREPARATION, AND HOW DO YOU KNOW THAT YOU'RE PREPARED?

In the period just before World War 2 (1933-1939), as Germany under Adolf Hitler spent huge sums of money rebuilding her army, Winston Churchill tried—in vain—to warn his fellow Britons that Hitler was preparing for war. By the time war broke out in 1939, an ill-prepared British Expeditionary Force was routed by a better prepared German Army. Preparation—at least in the beginning—was the reason Germany had great success on the battlefield. The question becomes: What is preparation, and how do I know (like Winston Churchill) that you're prepared or preparing? Interestingly, the words of Joel the prophet provide answers to that weighty question . . . .

> "Proclaim this among the nations: Prepare for war! Rouse the warriors! Let all the fighting men draw near and attack. Beat your plowshares into swords and your pruning hooks into spears. Let the weakling say, 'I am strong!' " (Joel 3:9-10, NIV)

Preparation is Action Today to Help You Cope With an Expected or Upcoming Event

"*Prepare for war . . .* " The war was coming up in the future, but the preparation was to begin now. Preparation is time sensitive. It always begins with acknowledgement—an acceptance that a particular event can occur in the future. It continues with action—practical steps that you take today to cope with the action you foresee.

Section 4 | Managing Yourself

Preparation Requires—and Reallocates—Resources

"Prepare . . . Beat your plowshares into swords and your pruning hooks into spears . . . " Preparing for an upcoming event not only requires resources, it can also reallocate available resources. To meet the threat of war, the leaders of Israel had to shift resources away from peacetime agriculture (plowshares and pruning hooks) to weapons (swords and spears). The one sure sign that you are preparing for an upcoming event is the reallocation of currently available resources in ways that can help you cope with the events you foresee.

Preparation Forces You to Prioritize

Since available resources are always finite, to prepare is to make trade-offs, to prioritize, or choose a one line of action over another. The leaders of Israel who were warned of war by Joel the prophet had to prioritize—to cut back on agricultural spending in order to invest in weapons of war. These words of Joel the prophet make knowing whether someone or some organization is prepared or preparing for an upcoming event more objective and easier to measure. How? By simply applying . . .

- The "Resource Test": Measure the amount and proportion of resources being spent on a particular project. The greater the proportion of available resources spent on a project, the more prepared that person is. Hitler spent unusual proportions of Germany's GDP on rearming his military—proof positive that he was preparing for war! To check your preparation, simply measure the amount of time and material resources you are putting into a project. The earlier you start, and the greater the amount of resources you use, the more prepared you are.

- The "Best People Test": After all is said and done, people are an organization's greatest resource, and groups that prepare for an upcoming event often show that they're giving it priority by staffing it with their best people. Therefore, where leaders deploy their best hands is a dead giveaway about what they're preparing to do.

Chapter 19

Personal Effectiveness 102

MANAGING YOUR EMOTIONS

As a lifelong student of leadership, performance—why one person or organization does better than another—has always fascinated me. Undoubtedly, there are as many reasons for excellent performance as there are researchers of performance, but the firelighter for me came when I read the following words in Psychologist Daniel Goleman's bestselling book, *Emotional Intelligence* "What seems to set apart those at the very top of competitive pursuits from others of roughly equal ability is the degree to which, beginning early in life, they can pursue an arduous practice routine for years and years." In simple terms, Dr. Goleman is saying that people who reach the apex of competitive vocations are those most committed to the tedium of practice. But, here's the rub, engaging in consistent practice means you must first overcome a natural aversion to doing that which is tedious. Therefore, career excellence requires leaders to first succeed at self-management, to delay gratification and to persist in doing that which is painful and tedious—in effect, to first succeed at managing their own emotions. Interestingly, the writer of Genesis, in his account of the last words of the patriach Jacob, corroborates this line of thinking, saying,

> """Reuben, you are my firstborn, My might and the beginning of my strength, The excellency of dignity and the excellency of power. Unstable as water, you shall not excel, Because you went up

to your father's bed; then you defiled it—He went up to my couch." (Gen 49:3-4, NKJV)

These weighty words mean that . . .

Managing Your Emotions is a Key to Career Excelence

Notice carefully that the writer of Genesis did *not* say "Unstable as water, you shall not *prosper*." Neither did he say "Unstable as water, you shall not *succeed*." He actually said "Unstable as water, you shall not *excel*." Since, to excel is to surpass others, these words reveal a much overlooked truth: Reuben's natural birth advantages as firstborn weren't enough to make him the best! To be the best, he had to add the ability to manage his emotions to his birth advantages. Excellence, therefore, is an inside job. Certainly, people who don't properly manage their emotions can succeed, prosper and get along just fine but, and this is crucial, they hardly can excel—be head-and-shoulders above others or become the best at what they do! Why? Because excellence takes more than talent, aptitude or even the advantages of birth; it also requires that leaders manage their impulses, emotions and proclivities—the things that make them want to stop practicing, studying, learning or paying the price.

The best way to know what emotional management is, is to know what it is not. . . to see what happens when it is lacking. From this depressing story of Reuben, we see that people who are emotionally incompetent . . .

Reflect External Conditions

"Unstable as water, you shall not excel." To help you better understand the concept of emotional incompetence, the writer of Genesis paints a picture of a large body of water (e.g., the Mediterranean Sea). On "good" days, the Mediterranean is only slightly affected by the winds which blow over her. At such times, she is a great place to go sailing and fishing. On "bad" days, gale force winds generate huge storms that can destroy ships and endanger sailors' lives. An emotionally unstable person is like the Mediterranean—unstable, undependable and constantly mirroring his environment. When things are rosy, all seems well; but, when the inevitable challenges of life come, the person breaks down and is unable to continue practicing, preparing or doing the things that make for excellence. This kind of person is held hostage by "feelings" and only produces when he "feels" like doing so. Paradoxically, people who are emotionally incompetent also . . .

Reflect Internal Conditions

"Unstable as water, you shall not excel . . . *Because you went up to your father's couch . . .* "" Reuben, by sleeping with his father's wife (which is what is referred to in this passage), revealed an egregious lack of self control that ultimately unfitted him for leadership. Daniel Goleman puts it beautifully, saying "Every strong emotion has its roots in an impulse to action: managing those impulses is basic to emotional intelligence." Certainly, all leaders feel the pull of untoward emotions. I mean, who hasn't felt the urge to give up and call it quits when things aren't going our way? Or, for that matter, who hasn't felt the urge to to worry and stop doing the right things? But the best leaders—the ones who outstrip others—subordinate their impulses and urges to principles. No matter how bad I "feel" about things today, I know that I must study and prepare. No matter the negative results today brings, the best leaders continue to do the important things everyday.

After all is said and done, emotionally less-competent persons are like "mirrors" that simply reflect their internal and external environments. Like thermometers, when pressed or harassed externally or internally, they largely allow those pressures determine their responses. In contrast, effective self-management makes you like a thermostat—able to influence the temperature and conditions of your environment. Because the road to excellence runs through a major stop called self-management, it's not surprising that people with great self-management and less talent tend to go farther than those with great talent and less self-management.

Having seen *what* managing your emotions can do for your career, the question becomes "*Why* is managing your emotions so decisive for excellence in the workplace?" The writer of Proverbs proffers an answer, saying,

> "Above all else, guard your heart, for everything you do flows from it." (Prov 4:23, NIV)

The phrase "*Above all else,*" is a dead giveaway—revealing the most important thing among a plethora of competing things. In this case, the most important thing is to "*guard your heart.*" The question becomes "What exactly does the term "heart," mean?" Again, the answer lies in the words of the writer of Proverbs . . .

"Each heart knows its own bitterness, and no one else can share it's joy." (Prov 14:20, NIV)

The "Heart" is the Center of the Emotions

"*Each heart knows its own bitterness. . . . and . . . joy.*" Bitterness and joy are emotions known and felt only in a person's 'heart'. Therefore, the heart is symbolically the center of emotion. In effect, the writer of Proverbs is saying that "Above all else, guard your [emotions], for everything you do flows from it." Guarding your emotions is crucial to everything you do because . . .

Your Emotions Set the Pace for Your Actions

" . . . guard your heart [emotions], *for everything you do flows from it.*" 'Doings' flow from feelings. Where there is a strong or long-held emotion, as sure as night follows day, there will soon be corresponding action. A long held emotion of anger and hate will sooner or later reveal itself as conflict. Why? Because emotions are the seed and actions are the fruit! To control actions, you must swim upstream and deal with the underlying emotions. The writer of First Peter drives the point home, saying,

> "Therefore prepare your minds for action; be self-controlled, hope for the grace . . . " (1Pet 1:13, NIV)

Taking Charge of Your Emotions Prepares Your Mind for Action

Psychologist Daniel Goleman, in his best-selling book, *Emotional Intelligence,* popularized the concept of EQ (emotional intelligence) and showed us just how important our emotions are. Before Dr. Goleman's book, most people were majorly acquainted with the intelligence quotient (IQ)—a measure of academic intelligence—as the main determinant of success. But, long before Dr. Goleman's book, the writer of First Peter had stressed the importance of EQ. By saying "Prepare your minds for action . . . [by being] . . . self controlled," he shows us that taking charge of your emotions (e.g., by exercising self control) is what prepares your mind for action. In effect, people whose emotional lives are out of control cannot fully tap into the potential of their rational, thinking minds. EQ trumps IQ. Stanford psychologist Walter Mischel, proved this conclusively in his now-famous "Marshmallow experiment" in 1972. A little child was offered a choice between an immediate treat (a marshmallow) and 2 small rewards (another marshmallow or two small pretzels) if only he could wait. During the waiting period, the researcher left the room for about 15 minutes. On returning, some of the children had "chosen" to eat the marshmallow, while others were able to delay gratification in order to receive the 2 small rewards. Years later, follow-up studies showed that the children who were able to delay gratification (manage their emotions) tended to have better life outcomes (as measured by SAT scores, educational attainment etc.). Although the results of that experiment have since been challenged by other researchers, the general takeaway is this: taking charge of your emotions prepares your mind for action.

Until now, you can be forgiven if you think that my ability to manage my emotions has consequences only in my own life. The truth is that a leader's emotions have very public consequences. Come to think of it, a group with a leader whose feelings are out of control is not just going to have a leader who suffers personally, it's also going to have plenty of followers who suffer. The writer of Hosea makes this clear, saying,

> "They are all adulterers, burning like an oven whose fire the baker need not stir . . . On the day of the festival of our king, the princes become inflamed with wine . . . Their hearts are like an oven; they approach him with intrigue. Their passion smolders all night; in the morning it blazes like a flaming fire. All of them are hot as an oven; they devour their rulers. All their kings fall, and none of them calls on me." (Hos 7:4–7, NIV)

The Emotions Leaders Openly Display Soon Become those Displayed by Followers

"They are all adulterers, burning like an oven . . . All of them are hot as an oven . . . " With these words, the writer of Hosea helps us see that everyone in Israel was inflamed with passion and, like archetypal adulterers, unable to control themselves. But, by going onto say "On the day of the festival of our king, the princes [leaders] become inflamed with wine," he shows just why everyone seemed unable to manage themselves. It was because their leaders were unable to manage themselves! In other words, emotions are contagious, and the emotions openly and continuously displayed by the leaders of a group soon become those displayed by people in that group.

If, as we've seen, emotions play a major role in career excellence, the question becomes "How can you manage your emotions?" The answer is, "Three ways"—role-playing, re-framing, and redirecting . . .

Role-Playing (Planning to be Angry!)

"Anyone can become angry — that is easy. But to be angry with the right person, to the right degree, at the right time, for the right purpose, and in the right way — that is not easy."—ARISTOTLE

Anger is the 'ultimate' emotion—expressing extreme displeasure with someone or something—that is associated with "losing one's cool." Therefore, it is fitting that we use anger to model how people can manage their emotions. That anger can be destructive is not news, that it can be managed might be news to some, and that God manages his own anger is probably news to all. The Psalmist, by showing how God manages his anger, wittingly shows us how most emotions can be managed . . .

> "He unleashed his hot anger, his wrath, indignation and hostility—
> a band of destroying angels. He prepared a path for his anger . . . "
> (Ps 78:49–50, NIV)

As I reflected on this passage, I came to see that . . .

Anger Can Be Destructive

When God unleashed his hot anger, some things got destroyed because he simultaneously unleashed a band of destroying angels. This shows how your anger can quickly get out of hand except you engage in . .

Role-playing: Preparing to be Angry Before the Fact!

" . . . *He prepared a path for his anger* . . . " These illuminating words show just how God manages to be not unduly destructive while still expressing his anger. It is because he has *prepared* a path for his anger. In other words, he first accepts that certain situations and persons can make him angry, then he goes on to lay out the exact responses he will make when he is angered. In simple terms, his anger runs along a prepared path that is bounded on both sides. He knows which exact actions he would take—and which actions are off-limits—when he does get angry. Come to think of it, every time God is angry, he simply does what he has said he would do in the Scripture beforehand. For you to properly manage your anger, you must first agree that people and situations will indeed make you angry, and then you must decide beforehand what it is that you will do when you do become angry. This means that you . . .

1. Accept that certain situations will make you angry.
2. Decide what you would do and how indeed you would react when you do become angry (At this stage you can write out what you would do when angered and sift the actions that are unacceptable to you, e.g., you would not hit anyone or make a nasty retort, etc.)
3. Determine exactly how long your anger will last. Anger unchecked graduates into fury and wrath—the more destructive cousins of anger. Write out how long you would stay angry.

Planning to be angry, which is what role-playing is all about, means preparing yourself to be angry. It means using your imagination to simulate the conditions that make you angry. For example, if coming home and meeting the house in disarray is your red flag, then use your imagination to place yourself coming home to a disarranged house. See yourself get safely angry without being abusive. Constantly role-play this scene over and over again in your mind, so that when you do come up against the real thing, you are ready to act according to script. More importantly, do some 'after action reviews'—look back on your performance and see where you didn't act according to script. This kind of role-playing leaves nothing to chance; helping you do only those things you have written beforehand.

Re-framing (Reinterpreting the Facts of the Matter)

> "Finally, people can cultivate positive emotions by learning to change the stories they tell themselves about the events in their lives. Often, people in conflict cast themselves in the role of victim, blaming others or external circumstances for their problems. Becoming aware of the difference between the facts in a given

situation and the way we interpret those facts can be powerful in itself."- Tony Schwartz

Have you ever had an experience where you heard what a person said to or about you and didn't feel offended, only to have the same event reinterpreted by a friend in a way that made you lose your cool? If you have, then welcome to the club! Psychologist Angela Duckworth, in her bestselling book, *Grit: The Power of Passion and Perseverance*, said that,

> " . . . that the same objective event —losing a job, getting into an argument with a coworker, forgetting to call a friend—can lead to very different subjective interpretations. And it is those interpretations —rather than the objective events themselves—that can give rise to our feelings and our behavior."

Dr. Duckworth wittingly lets us in on an open secret: most of our emotions and feelings are entirely subjective—the result of how we interpret or 'frame' the events that happen to us. The writer of Lamentations, drives this point home, saying,

> "Mine eye affecteth mine heart because of all the daughters of my city." (Lam 3:51, KJV)

Your Interpretation of the Event—Not Just the Event Itself— Determines How You Feel

By saying "*Mine eye* [how I see the matter] *affecteth mine heart* [emotions]," the writer of Lamentations shows us that what we see, or more accurately, how we see—the 'spin' we put on things, the meanings we ascribe to events, and our interpretation of issues—influences how we feel. In this sense, it is not the objective experience that determines our feelings, but the subjective experience (our explanations or the explanations of significant others about what happened). This immediately opens a door to managing our emotions and feelings. For example, most people find waiting for a partner at a bus station frustrating, especially if the partner delays or doesn't show up. The objective event—my partner stood me up—is certainly enough to make anyone angry. But, what if you looked at the situation like this: my partner must have been held up somewhere or delayed by some other person, and I do hope she's alright. Re-framing the event in this manner turns your frustration into a solicitousness that worries about her welfare. The same objective event, interpreted in a different subjective way, produced care and concern, rather than frustration. Consistently practised, this method—while not denying the reality of the event—puts you in the driver's seat and helps you better manage your emotions and relationships.

Re-framing is like "re-viewing" the facts of the matter, and taking . . .

1. The long view: ask yourself "How will I see this matter one year from now?"
2. The reverse view: ask yourself "How does the person on the other side of the table see this matter, and in what ways might her views be correct?"
3. The wide view: ask yourself "After all is said and done, in what ways can I learn and grow from this matter?"

Notice carefully that "re-viewing" is at the heart of re-framing, and that the former works best by asking questions that throw new light on the matter. Journalist and business author Tony Schwartz, in an illuminating article, *Manage Your Energy, Not Your Time*, in the Harvard Business Review, puts it beautifully, saying,

> "The most effective way people can change a story is to view it through any of three new lenses, which are all alternatives to seeing the world from the victim perspective. With the reverse lens, for example, people ask themselves, "What would the other person in this conflict say and in what ways might that be true?" With the long lens they ask, "How will I most likely view this situation in six months?" With the wide lens they ask themselves, "Regardless of the outcome of this issue, how can I grow and learn from it?" Each of these lenses can help people intentionally cultivate more positive emotions."

Re-directing (Venting or Safely Expressing Your Emotions)

What does it take to manage destructive emotions like anger and resentment without blowing up? Do we, as some advise, repress or even deny them? The writer of Proverbs gives us an unusual solution to this problem, saying,

> "A fool gives full vent to his anger, but a wise man keeps himself under control." (Prov 29:11, NIV)

SECTION 4 | MANAGING YOURSELF

This illuminating passage shows us the real nature of self-control . . .

Self-Control is Not Denial or Repression

How does a wise man manage his emotions and " . . . keep himself under control?" Easy. By simply never " . . . [giving] *full* vent to his anger." The key word in the last sentence is "full." People who have their emotions under control have the same issues as everyone else, but—and this is where they are different—they safely ventilate their own emotions. They never let things come to a head or "blow up" in destructive ways. The picture painted in this passage is taken from Physics: our emotions are like a head of steam or gas confined in a small space with only a small opening or vent through which the gas can escape (much like those old steam kettles that whistle when the water in them has boiled and generated a head of steam to pass through their small vents). It bears repeating: managing your emotions isn't denying or repressing feelings, it is acknowledging and safely expressing them. Safely expressing emotions—the hallmark of well-managed emotions—means that you . . .

Never Allow the Pressure Build Up to a Full Head of Steam

Remember that, using imagery from Physics, the writer of Proverbs compares our emotions to a gas confined in a space with only a small vent or aperture for escape. Therefore, the key to managing destructive emotions is to never let the pressure build up, but to safely ventilate or 'let off steam'. You do this by . . .

Confronting ASAP

Bottled up emotions can result in dangerous 'blow outs'. Deal with contentious issues as soon as possible. Deal with irritating and annoying issues, issues that get "under your skin" quickly and separately. For example, if you have an anger problem, as much as lies in your power, never let issues accumulate or build up before taking action or doing something positive about them. The more you delay action and confrontation, the more likely you'll fly off the handle when you do eventually come to deal with them.

Practicing 'Avoidance'

Another way to avoid "blow outs"—situations where you give full vent to, and lose control of, your feelings—is to practice avoidance. As much as possible, extricate yourself from the influence and reach of chronic provocateurs—people and situations that 'get under your skin', irritate, and provoke you.

Staying Cool!

In their excellent book, *Primal Leadership,* Daniel Goleman, Richard Boyatzis and Anne McKee said that "The original sense of the hipster term 'cool' referred to the capacity of African - American jazz musicians who could control their rage at the racism of the times, even as they channeled their anger into an extraordinary expression of deep feeling." Career excellence demands that same capacity for 'staying cool'. Indeed, it's noteworthy that some of the Psalms of King David were written after he'd suffered traumatic experiences (Psalms 3, 7 & 52.). Writing may have been therapeutic—helping him re-direct his feelings into more constructive endeavors. In this light, one way to manage turbulent emotions is to channel them into creative pursuits. Take up a hobby like writing, poetry or even sport, so that whenever you 'feel the pressure,' you can channel it into something creative and positive.

Like I said before, managing yourself is founded on the 2 great themes of personal effectiveness and personal development. At the core of the former are the subjects of managing your time, emotions and effort. In this chapter, we have looked at managing your emotions, and in Chapter 18—where we drew lessons from the life of Paul the apostle—we looked at managing your time. We now turn our attention to managing your effort (work), a thing which leads us directly to . . .

THE 80/20 RULE

"All actions are not created equal. Some actions have more impact than others . . ."—SEAN COVEY

The 80/20 Principle in Action:

"Everyday language is a good illustration. Sir Isaac Pitman, who invented shorthand, discovered that just 700 common words make up two-thirds of our conversation. Including the derivatives of these words, Pitman found that these words account for 80 per cent of common speech. In this case, fewer than 1 per cent of words (the New Oxford Shorter Oxford English Dictionary lists over half a million words) are used 80 per cent of the time. We could call this an 80/1 principle." - Richard Koch

The writer of Ecclesiastes explains just why, when it comes to productivity and performance, less is always more, saying,

"As dead flies give perfume a bad smell, so a little folly outweighs wisdom and honor." (Eccl 10:1, NIV)

This amazing Scripture has helped me see that,

A Minority of Actions Often Has a Disproportionate Impact on Results

Perfumery is an expensive, sophisticated and profitable business. I mean, just check out how much a small bottle of designer perfume costs! But, with all the expertise and effort that goes into making perfume, a single dead fly falling into the bottle can ruin all the perfumer's work. This means that the perfumer should pay greater attention to the part of the perfume-making process that is vulnerable to contamination by flies. Why? Because that 'small' part exerts a disproportionate impact on results. The moral of these words of the writer of Ecclesiastes? No matter the line of business you are engaged in, not every activity is equally important. Some activities are more important than others, and . . .

Foolishness in a Few Mission-critical Areas Outweighs Wisdom in Many Other Areas

Certainly, all areas of your work have an impact on the results you obtain but, and this is important, a few areas have disproportionately greater effects than others. Effectiveness demands that you locate this small number of areas and give them more attention. These intriguing words of the writer of Ecclesiastes reveal the biblical foundation of the Pareto Principle or the 80/20 Rule—a rule of thumb which states that eighty percent of the results we obtain in life and work can be traced to just twenty percent of our efforts. The effect of this rule is that, when it comes to increasing your personal productivity, less is always more. The key to making maximum impact is to first identify those 20 percent of activities that produce eighty percent of your results, and then concentrate on doing them well. Management writer Peter Drucker hammers the point home, saying "Work on only those things that make a great deal of difference if you succeed."

To help you locate the 20 percent of actions responsible for 80 percent of your results, leadership teacher John Maxwell requires that you ask yourself these 3 questions...

1. What is required of me? (What I must do).
2. What gives me the greatest return? (What I should do).
3. What is most rewarding to me? (What I love to do)

Early in your career, #1 should fill your plate as you're required to do lots of things. But as you progress in your career, #2 and #3—what you should do and what you love to do—should dominate if you're to remain productive. In other words, the 80/20 Rule becomes more important the higher up the career ladder you've climbed. Many of my colleagues marvel at my productivity, but the reason for my productivity is that I put the 80/20 Rule into practice in my life. How do I mean? I spend the lion-share of my time and resources on the three areas that are absolutely mission-critical to getting results for a writer (I call them my 3Cs).

- C.reating resources for leaders (writing).
- C.ommunicating those resources (consulting, speaking & writing).
- C.onnecting with people (relationships & intentional networking).

Take some time to write out the actions that contribute the most to your work. Are you concentrating your best resources on these areas?

Wrap Around

Managing your emotions and managing your effort (the 80/20 Rule) are two dimensions of personal management that are crucial to workplace success. The former helps you harness your natural gifts and strengths in ways that can help you achieve your potential, while the latter, like a compass needle that always points to true north, points out areas of work where you can be most productive. Together, managing your emotions and the 80/20 Rule are like a boxer's right and left hands—equally necessary to deliver the one-two punches needed to win a bout.

Chapter 20

Principles of Personal Development

USING THE POWER OF "ROUTINE" TO BUILD PROFESSIONAL CAPACITY

"Most people don't see me do this every day. They only see the 10 seconds I run on TV." —Usain Bolt (speaking about his practice routine)

Sometime ago on BBC Television, I watched champion sprinter Usain Bolt go through his gruelling daily practice routine in a location far away from the prying eyes of the public. Bathed in sweat and exhausted at the end of the practice session, the champion went on to say "Most people don't see me do this every day. They only see the 10 seconds I run on TV." For me, the key words in that sentence is "every day." While it's not news that you need to develop yourself to become better at what you do, not everyone knows that improvement comes easiest when you practice every day. In other words, routine—what author Darren Hardy, in his book, *The Compound Effect*, refers to as " . . . something you do every day without fail, so that eventually, like brushing your teeth or putting on your seatbelt, you do it without conscious thought,"—is at the heart of personal development. All this calls to mind the words of the writer of Deuteronomy,

> "And of Asher he [Moses] said: "Asher is most blessed of sons; Let him be favored by his brothers, And let him dip his foot in oil. Your sandals shall be iron and bronze; *As your days, so shall your strength be.*" (Emphasis mine) (Deut 33:24–25, NKJV)

Capacity is Built by Routine—by Doing the Same things Over and Over Again

By saying, " . . . As your *days* are, so shall your strength be," the writer of Deuteronomy helps us see that it is what we do *daily* (how we spend our days) that builds strength, capacity and expertise. In essence, a person's future state is really only the sum of his many "todays." Like a champion weightlifter builds capacity by consistently lifting weights, so a workplace champion builds capacity by consistently engaging in a select group of activities. There's no magic to building capacity because capacity isn't built in a day; it is built daily! Further reflection on the words of the writer of 'Deuteronomy' has also helped me see that because a "day" is really only a small part of a person's life, his words must also mean that,

Genuine Routines are Characterized by Size, Consistency and Feedback

Size: the best routines are activities that require relatively small inputs to be effective. Better small and regular, than large and random. Novelist Anthony Trollope drives the point home, saying "Nothing surely is so potent as a law that may not be disobeyed. It has the force of the water drop that hollows the stone. A small daily task, if it be really daily, will beat the labours of a spasmodic Hercules." In other words, it is eating the proverbial apple a day, not seven apples in one day, that keeps the doctor away.

Consistency: the best routines require that you do them repeatedly, regularly and for extended periods of time before you see any improvement. Personal development expert Sean Covey, in his coauthored book, *The Four Disciplines of Execution*, puts it this way: "This consistency is critical. Without it [you] will never be able to establish a sustained rhythm of performance. Missing even a single week causes you to lose valuable momentum, and this loss of momentum impacts your results."

Feedback Provision: the best routines are made up of activities that provide feedback to enable you make course corrections and improve performance. In other words, the actions you engage in should have some direct and measureable link to the results you get.

How you use today—and every other day—is predictive of your future but, and this is crucial, how you use today is entirely up to you. In that sense, personal development is "personal"—no one, not even your spouse, can do your push-ups for you. Personal development requires that you take a 'daily' approach to life—first finding out what practices can help you become better at serving your audiences, and then doing them every day. Take another look at your calendar: is there anything you did today that you've been doing for the last 30 days? If your answer is "Yes," then as sure as night follows day, you're going to develop strength in that area. If your answer is "No," then you're not going to become proficient at that task. Personal development requires that you set professional goals. Why? Because goals drive action. For example, I decided to write 70 lessons on biblical personal finance this year (2021)—meaning that I had to read one book on that subject monthly. My goal drove my repeated actions, and my repeated actions increased my capacity. And, it is to the effect of repeated actions that we next turn our attention . . .

THE FORCE OF HABIT

"Habits are cobwebs at first, and cables at last."—Old Chinese proverb

World War 2 was humankind's single bloodiest conflict. That horrible war led to the death of about fifty-five million persons, with most of the war-dead made up of choice young men of the belligerent nations. Although death and destruction are the most vivid signs of war, another little-appreciated sign is the widespread loss, restriction, or denial of the normal freedom to choose an occupation. Come to think of it, in wartime, able-bodied young men are often press-ganged or conscripted into the armed forces, with no one being eligible for release until the war ends. The writer of Ecclesiastes, using imagery drawn from war, paints a picture of the power of habits, saying,

> "No man has power over the wind to contain it; so no one has power over the day of his death. As no one is discharged in time of war, so wickedness will not release those who practice it." (Eccl 8:8, NIV)

His words mean that . . .

Section 4 | Managing Yourself

Habits are like Governments in Time of War—Restricting Peoples' Freedoms

"As no one is discharged in time of war, so wickedness will not release those who practice [*habitually engage in*] it." Just like wartime governments strip citizens of their right to freely choose their occupations and make military service compulsory for all able-bodied young men, so too with 'wickedness'. The latter will not release people who practice it—i.e., *people who have formed the habit of practicing wickedness*. In effect, habits once formed, are like governments in time of war, stripping you of your freewill and "forcing" you to do whatever you've formed the habit of doing. The question becomes, why are habits so powerful? The answers come thick and fast as one takes into account the words of the writer of Jeremiah,

> "Can the Ethiopian change his skin or the leopard his spots? Then also can you do good who are accustomed and taught [even trained] to do evil." (Jer 13:23, AMP)

These insightful words throw more light on the power of habits, showing us that,

Habits are as Powerful as the Genetic Forces Which Determine Racial Identity!

"Can the Ethiopian change his skin [color] . . .?" The answer to that question is an emphatic "No." An Ethiopian (black African) cannot change his skin color, because that defining characteristic is genetically determined and therefore outside his control. But, and this is where things get interesting, by going on to say "Then also can you do good who are accustomed to [have formed a habit of] . . . .doing evil," the writer of Jeremiah drives the point home—habits are as powerful as the genetic forces which determine racial identity! Why? Because forming a habit means that you give up control—much like a genetic factor is outside your control. Forewarned, they say, is forearmed. People who want to break old habits need to know what they're up against: habits are powerful because they assume "control" and lock you into specific patterns of behavior from which it is difficult to come out—the reason anyone who has formed the habit of doing evil cannot simultaneously do good. The old Chinese proverb is correct after all "Habits are cobwebs at first, and cables at last."

Principles of Personal Development

Habits Tend to Occur in Mutually Exclusive Pairs or 'Twins'

"... Then may you also do *good* who ... [have formed a habit of] ... doing *evil*." Good and evil are the classic complementary set of "twins." People who have formed a habit of doing evil cannot also, simultaneously, alongside with, or at the same time, do good. That is, habit formation involves trade-offs—doing one thing precludes the doing of another 'opposite', complementary, or mutually exclusive thing. In effect, habits form more easily when trade-offs can occur, and trade-offs occur when activities are mutually exclusive (where more of one thing necessitates less of another). To help you better understand this truth, just take a look at what psychologists refer to as "handedness"—the natural tendency to use one hand more often than the other. The more you use your right hand, the greater your habit of using that hand and, you guessed right, the less you can use your left hand.

Habits are Barriers to Change, and the Best Way to Develop a New Habit is to Weaken the Old 'Complementing' One

"Can the Ethiopian *change* his skin [color] ... ?" The reason the person accustomed to doing evil couldn't simply changeover and begin doing good was because, you guessed right again, he had formed a habit of doing evil. Therefore, habits are powerful barriers to change. If you want to begin doing something, you need to first check whether you've already formed a mutually exclusive habit. If the latter is present, then it will act as a latent barrier to the change you want to make. Therefore, the best way to develop a habit that's "opposite" or "complementary" to one you've already formed is to first break or weaken the old habit. If you have a habit of doing "evil" and want to begin doing "good," you need to first break or weaken the habit of doing "evil." But, and this is crucial, conventional thinking leaves the habit of doing "evil" unaddressed while simultaneously attempting to begin doing "good"—a key reason many new year resolutions are broken by the end of January! All of this leads us to the words of the writer of Proverbs ...

> "Train up a child in the way that he should go; and when he is old, he will not depart from it." (Prov 22:6, NKJV)

These words show us that another reason habits are so powerful is because,

Section 4 | Managing Yourself

A Habit is an Automatic and Mindless Behavior

" . . . when he is old [mature], *he will not depart from it.*" Down the line, sometime in the future when the child has been perfectly trained, he will not depart from the way he started out on. Why? Because he has formed a habit! In simple terms, habit formation is a learning process which allows for the development of automatic and mindless behavior down the line. The key phrase that differentiates habit formation from other types of learning is "the development of automatic and mindless behavior." If it's a habit, you can do it without consciously thinking about it. While the habit formation process begins with making conscious decisions and choices, it ends when those choices begin to be made nonconsciously.

Habits are Formed and Firmed by Practice

"*Train* up a child . . . when he is [mature] he will not depart from it." The word, "Train," is the root word for trainer, one who does more than just teach; someone who also shows another how a task is done. Habits are more easily formed and firmed by first seeing the task accomplished in another's life (or in your mind's eye) and then putting into practice what is seen.

Habits Often Occur in Mutually Exclusive Pairs

"Train up a child *in the way that he should go* . . . " When you train a child to walk "in the way that he should go," you automatically are training him to *not* walk in the way that he should *not* go. Learning to go one way often means that you forego movement in another opposite or mutually exclusive way. This, like we saw from the words of the writer of Jeremiah, seems to paint a picture of complementary pairs; forming a habit in just one aspect of a pair automatically precludes you from forming a habit in its complementary pair.

Habits Take Time to Form

"Train up a child in the way that he should go, and *when he is old* [mature], he will not depart from it." Did you notice the time lapse between beginning to learn a new habit and its formation? The time required is from childhood to old age (maturity). This means that habit formation takes time and new habits aren't developed overnight. Indeed, the more complex the habit you want to form, the longer the time you have to put in.

Habits are formed at the Intersection of Knowledge, Desire (Openness) and Practice

"Train up a child in the way that he should go, and when he is old, he will not depart from it." The term 'training' talks about practice—about what you consciously and repeatedly do. The term 'child', is symbolic of openness to, and desire for, new experiences, while " . . . the way that he should go," speaks of knowledge. Taken together, these words help us see that habits form easiest at the intersection of practice, desire and knowledge. Psychologists have definitively disproved the old saw that says "You can't teach an old dog new tricks." Indeed, old dogs can, and do, learn new tricks. The key to learning new habits doesn't lie in chronological or biological age, it lies in openness and willingness to learn new things—what psychologists refer to as neoteny, the ability to retain the childlike qualities of curiosity and openness to new experiences. Your openness and desire make you willing to learn and put into practice new information.

HOW THE RIGHT HABITS CAN MAKE YOU A MASTER IN THE WORKPLACE

"The master of any game is also the master of practice."—GEORGE LEONARD

Sometime ago as I read Thomas Friedman's bestselling book, *The Lexus and the Olive Tree*, I came across these intriguing words,

> "Michael Jordan is indeed the winner who took it all. But there are twelve players on an NBA team. Sitting on the same bench with Jordan in his final season—sitting in fact just eleven places away from him—was someone else whose shooting skills were only marginally less effective than his, someone whose jump shot was only slightly less consistent . . . But he was still a great basketball player . . . His name was Joe Klein . . . and his salary was . . . $272,250 a year—or roughly $79,727,750 less than Jordan's total. Same game, same league, same bench!"

SECTION 4 | MANAGING YOURSELF

Joe Klein and Michael Jordan may have sat close to each other, but the humongous difference in thei salaries is, to say the least, scary. In fact, Joe Klein isn't even recognized or acclaimed by the public (at least, not on the scale of the man they call 'Air Jordan'). The question becomes, why is Michael Jordan so widely acclaimed? With phrases like " . . . someone . . . whose shooting skills were only marginally less effective," and, " . . . someone whose jump shot was only slightly less consistent," Thomas Friedman gives the game away. A major reason for this disturbing inequality is that Michael Jordan was a master, an expert at the game of basketball! Look around you and see: the masters at any game or vocation tend to receive the lion-share of the available attention, recognition, and remuneration. Which is why, at this point, the question on your mind should be: how does a person become a master? The Psalmist shows us the way, saying,

> "Gird Your sword upon Your thigh, O mighty One . . . And in Your majesty ride prosperously . . . and your right hand shall reach you awesome things. Your arrows are sharp in the heart of the king's enemies . . . " (Ps 45:3–5, NKJV)

This beautiful messianic passage points at Jesus Christ, but it also reveals keys to mastery that are available to everyone. It shows us that . . .

Mastery is the Ability to Hit the Target and Deliver the Goods

"Your arrows are sharp in the heart of the king's enemies . . . " Bullseye! The Mighty One was a first class soldier who could accomplish an extremely difficult task—hit the enemy's heart with a single shot from his bow even while riding furiously on horseback! Mastery, expertise—call it what you want—is the ability to deliver the goods, to get the job done as and when it should be done. So how did this 'Mighty One' become a master at his vocation? The Psalmist lets us in on the answer, saying " . . . *and your right hand shall reach you awesome things . . .* [which is why] . . . Your arrows are sharp in the heart of the King's enemies . . . " This means that,

The Master of Any Game is also the Master of Practice!

The right hand, for most people, is the preferred hand at birth. But the real reason the right hand is stronger and more skillful than the left hand isn't just because it's the preferred hand; it's because it is the one more often used in daily life. In simple terms, the reason your right hand is more skillful than your left hand is because you practice with or use it more often. Practice is the key to mastery. Before the arrows of the mighty One could be "sharp in the heart of the King's enemies," his "right hand [practice] taught Him awesome things." Interestingly, Michael Jordan not only out-earned every player on the NBA, he also out-practiced them all. Author and aikido expert George Leonard was correct after all "The master at any game is also the master of practice."

Practice is the Seemingly Endless Repetition of Routine Tasks

"Your right hand shall teach You awesome things . . . " Practice is a great teacher, but only if you're willing to endlessly repeat the same lesson over and over again. It is this inherent tedium associated with routine that discourages many from beginning or continuing the journey of mastery. Research has revealed that the masters in any field or vocation have to put in at least 10,000 hours or 10-years of practice—the so called 10,000-hour Rule. "So, what roles," you might ask, " do habits play in the development of mastery?" The answer lies hidden in Paul's professional advice to Timothy his protégé . . .

> "Till I come, give attention to reading, to exhortation, to doctrine. Do not neglect the gift that is in you, which was given to you by prophecy with the laying on of the hands of the eldership. Meditate on these things; give yourself entirely to them, that your progress may be evident to all. Take heed to yourself and to the doctrine. *Continue in them*, for in doing this you will save both yourself and those who hear you." (Emphasis mine) (1Tim 4:13–16, NKJV)

Habits Help You Repeat a Task

Recall that these words were penned by Paul the apostle as professional advice to show Timothy his protégé the multiple steps to making career progress. Those steps included, closing the gap between what's important to you and how you use your time, the ability to work without supervision, etc (see Chapter 18). The problem is that, not only must Timothy carry out these steps, he must also "*Continue* in them," or regularly and repeatedly put them into practice if he hoped to make progress. The truth is that habits are the keys to continuously repeating the steps that can make you a master. Why? Because they allow you automatically repeat the task. Daniel Goleman drives the point home, saying "What seems to set apart those at the very top of competitive pursuits from others of roughly equal ability is the degree to which, beginning early in life, they can pursue an arduous practice routine for years and years." Pursuing "an arduous practice routine for years and years," is easier if you first develop a habit.

The principles of productivity—the 80/20 Rule, habits etc—enunciated thus far are principles which demand that you actively *do something*. We now turn our attention to a productivity principle that demands that you *do nothing* . . .

THE FALLOW GROUND PRINCIPLE: HOW REST AND RECREATION CAN INCREASE YOUR PRODUCTIVITY

"We live in a world that celebrates work and activity, ignores renewal and recovery, and fails to recognize that both are necessary for sustained high performance."—Tony Schwartz and Jim Loehr

We live in the "24/7/365 Age," an age where everyone works round the clock—twenty-four hours a day, seven days a week, and three hundred and sixty days a year. But, and this is crucial, even machines (and we also live in the age of machines) cannot produce optimally if they are run round the clock—they must have specific periods for refitting and maintenance. In other words, long-term and sustainable productivity requires regular periods of rest—of downtimes when nothing is done. Management writer David Burkus, in his book, *Under New Management,* drives the point home, saying "The best way to stay productive all the time is to spend a good portion of the time being deliberately unproductive." I believe the phrase "*being deliberately unproductive*," refers to regular and scheduled periods of rest. In other words, the times when you deliberately do no work are crucial to your long-term productivity. The writer of Proverbs, with word pictures from an agrarian age, corroborates this line of thinking, saying,

> "Much food is in the fallow ground of the poor, And for lack of justice there's waste." (Prov 13:23, NKJV)

Principles of Personal Development

The Productivity of an Asset Increases When You Regularly Rest it

"Much food [increase] is in the *fallow ground* . . . " There it is in black and white: "*much* food," not just "food," is in the " *fallow* ground," not merely in the ground now under cultivation. Fallow ground, according to Gardeningknowhow.com, is simply,

> " . . . ground or soil which has been left unplanted for a period of time. In other words, fallow land is land left to rest and regenerate. A field, or several fields, are taken out of crop rotation for a specific period of time, usually one to five years, depending on crop. Fallowing soil is a method of sustainable land management that has been used by farmers for centuries in regions of the Mediterranean, North Africa, Asia and other places."

Rest and Recreation is a Cost-free Way to Increase Productivity

By going on to say "Much food is in the fallow ground of *the poor*," and, since the poor are by definition people with little or no resources, the writer of Proverbs drives the point home: rest and recreation increase productivity without your needing to invest money or know-how! Most teaching on personal development tends to slight or downplay the importance of rest, recreation, and renewal, but these wise words of the writer of Proverbs show us that taking some time to rest—yourself and your tools—doesn't cost; it pays! In plain terms, rest and recreation are just as crucial to personal effectiveness as routine, practice, forming the right habits, etc. The question becomes, how do I know that I am taking enough rest and putting the Fallow Ground Principle to work in my life? The Psalmist proffers an answer, saying,

> "Unless the Lord builds the house, They labor in vain who build it; Unless the Lord guards the city, The watchman stays awake in vain. It is vain for you to rise up early, To sit up late, To eat the bread of sorrows; For so He gives his beloved sleep." (Ps 127:1-2, NKJV)

Section 4 | Managing Yourself

The Fallow Ground Principle Takes a Daily Approach to Rest and Recreation

"It is vain for you to rise up early, To sit up late . . . " These words ram the point home: rest and recreation from work is something you do *daily*. This goes against the yearly perspective—taking a month-long holiday after a year of hectic work. This biblical approach requires that you ensure that you rest daily, not put off rest until the yearly holiday.

Arriving Early, and Closing Late is a Telltale Sign of an Unbalanced Life

"It is vain for you to rise up early, To sit up late. To eat the bread of sorrows [sickness] . . . " Did you notice that the people who "eat the bread of sorrows" are the ones whose work-lives are unbalanced? By using the word "vain" to describe this group of persons, the Psalmist helps us see that rising up early and closing late is inefficient. Which brings me to a crucial point . . .

A Healthy Work-life Balance is Proof of a Genuine Vision

"Except the Lord build the house, the builders labor in vain . . . [rising] up early, and [staying] up late . . . " When God is the builder—the architect—then the human builder has a healthy work-life balance. One sign that you are outside God's plan is when your life is out of balance—rising up early and sleeping late; having little or no time for family, friends, recreation etc. If you have to burn the candle at both ends and sacrifice your health for success, your dream is way too costly!

Newly Birthed Visions Can Produce a Temporary Work-life Imbalance

Having said all that, I must quickly add the following caveat: just like caring for a new born baby "unbalances" a mother's life and causes her to abandon all else in favor of caring for her child, so too with a new vision, project or initiative. Those projects often cause us to lead temporarily unbalanced lives. But, and this is crucial, a genuine vision rights itself over time, while a false one continues to cause huge imbalances in people's lives. Take some time to evaluate how much time you put into your work? Does your work still (after all these years) cause you to rise up early and close late? If it does, then it's either you've strayed from an originally genuine vision or you're pursuing one whose provenance is suspect.

Last Word

Untangling the Roles of Chance,
Time, and Skill in Career Success

"The consequences of our efforts, both good and bad, reflect an element within our control—skill—and an element outside our control—luck. In this sense, luck is residual: it's what's left over after you'we've subtracted skill from an outcome."—MICHAEL MAUBOUSSIN

IMAGINE THAT I PLAY some games against the World Champion Ludo player. You wouldn't be too surprised if I defeated him a few times would you? Why? Because Ludo is a game where winning is largely determined by chance—by the throw of dice. Imagine again, that I play a few games against the World Chess Champion. Certainly, you'd be astonished if I—a rank amateur—even wins one game. Why? Because chess is a game where winning is almost wholly determined by skill. These two 'extreme' examples highlight the roles of chance and skill in career success. They help us see that when it comes to activities on the extreme right of the chance-skill continuum (skill-intensive activities), chance plays little part in success. With activities on the extreme left (chance-intensive activities), chance plays a greater role. In the middle of that continuum, chance and skill have mixed actions in determining who wins. The writer of Ecclesiastes, using imagery from athletics, war, and the workplace, sheds more light on the roles chance, skill, and time play in career success, saying,

> "I have seen something else under the sun: The race is not to the swift or the battle to the strong, nor does food come to the wise or wealth to the brilliant or favor to the learned; but time and chance happen to them all." (Eccl 9:11, NIV)

Last Word

These intriguing words mean that,

The More Complex the Career, the Greater the Role Chance Plays— and the Lesser the Role Skill Plays—in Determining Success

"The *race* . . . the *battle* . . . favor to the *learned* . . ." Did you notice that complexity increases as we move from winning the race through emerging victorious in battle to the obtaining of favor by the learned. In other words, while there are set rules for running a race, the rules for deciding who gets favored or how wealth comes to the brilliant are less definite. I mean, the rules for participating in and winning the 100-meters in the Olympics are pretty straight forward. In contrast, the rules for who gets to be the most successful in medical practice or politics are a little less clear. Drawing from my example on Ludo and Chess, it means that the influence of chance will increase (and that of skill decrease) as we move from the "race," to how favor is obtained by the learned. Why? Easy. Because as complexity increases, the role of chance increases and the role of skill diminishes. Investor Michael Mauboussin, in his bestselling book, *The Success Equation: Untangling Skill and Luck in Business, Sports and Investing*, drives the point home, saying,

> "This analysis of skill and luck will focus on business, sports, and investing because these are the areas I know best. Naturally, these realms are quite different. Sports are the easiest activities to analyze because the rules are relatively stable over time and there is lots of data. Other social processes, including business, have fewer rules and boundaries than sports and therefore tend to be more complex."

Before we go ahead to take a detailed look at the words of the writer of Ecclesiastes (who is also known as the Preacher), it behooves us to define the word "chance" . . .

Chance Events are Events Over Which You Have No Control

" . . . time and *chance* happen to them all." The word "chance" means an event or occurrence over which one has no control. Management writer Jim Collins, in his co-authored book, *Great By Choice*, drives the point home,

> "We defined a [chance] event as one that meets three tests: (1) some significant aspect of the event occurs largely or entirely

independent of the actions of the key actors in the enterprise, (2) the event has a potentially significant consequence (good or bad), and (3) the event has some element of unpredictability."

That said, we can now return to analyzing the intriguing words of the Preacher...

There is an Element of Chance—of the Circumstantial—in Career Success

"... time and chance *happen to them all.*" There it is in black and white: chance plays a role (small or big) in every case of workplace success! To put it bluntly, there is an element of chance, of the circumstantial, of good fortune, and of providence in every case of career success. Writer Michael Mauboussin was correct after all "The consequences of our efforts, both good and bad, reflect an element within our control—skill—and an element outside of our control—luck."

Chance Alone Doesn't Determine Career Success

Saying that chance influences results is not the same thing as saying that chance determines results. How do I mean? By saying "... time and chance happen *to them all,*" the Preacher helps us see that chance (random good or bad fortune) happens to everyone in the race. In other words, chance doesn't play favorites or give special favors and advantages to anyone. Chance is an equal opportunity employer. It bears repeating; if chance "happens" to *everyone* who enters the race and to *everyone* who fights the battle, then it cannot be the decider of who wins *in the long run*. People who depend on chance, "luck," or fortune may be favored today but, and this is crucial, they will also sooner or later fall into its disfavor. This leads directly to the next point...

The Longer the Career, the Less the Influence of Chance

"... the race is not to the swift... but time *and* chance happen to them all." Notice carefully that it is time *and* chance that influences who wins the race—not merely chance alone. So how does time influence the outcome of a race? Here's one way: chance plays a greater role in shorter races than in longer ones. Come to think of it, making a slight mistake in the 100-meter race will most likely see you lose because there's so little time to adjust and recover. In contrast, making the same error in a marathon isn't so decisive because you have more time to recover. Indeed, this was the reason British long-distance runner Mo Farah could fall in a race, pick himself up, and still go on to win the same race! In contrast, no one has ever fallen in a 100-meters race and gone on to win the gold medal! What does this mean for career success? It means that leaders can significantly reduce the influence of chance events by persevering, by having longer careers, and by staying with their jobs for longer durations. Statistician and investor Nassim Nicholas Taleb, in his book, *Fooled By Randomness,* corroborates this point, saying " . . . the properties of ergodicity, namely, that time will eliminate the annoying effects of randomness." His words describe a technical property—ergodicity—which, simply put, is that " . . . time [if you stay in the game] will eliminate the annoying effects of randomness [chance]." In other words, if you're reasonably competent and have been fruitlessly attempting an endeavor, keep at it, because time will eliminate the unfortunate effects of chance. Over time, the influence of chance on the results of a race decreases. And the corollary is also true; over time, the influence of skill on results increases.

The Paradox of Skill—Chance Becomes Even More Important as People Become More Skillful

" . . . The race is not to the swift, nor the battle to the strong . . . " That the race is not to the swift doesn't mean that the race is to the slow! Skill plays a role in determining who wins the race but, and this is important, the more skill the race requires then, paradoxically, the greater the effects of chance. As the skill-level of the athletes who compete in the Olympic 100-meters race has dramatically increased, the effects of chance events have also increased dramatically. One small mistake or misjudgment might just be the difference between winning and losing. Michael Mauboussin refers to this as the Paradox of Skill—increasing levels of skill make chance events even more decisive.

Career Success is Determined by a Mixture of Skill and Chance

"The race is not to the swift nor the battle to the strong . . . but time and chance happen to them all." Like I said before, just because " . . . the race is not to the swift," doesn't mean that the race is to the slow. Although "time and chance," can certainly influence outcomes, it's highly unlikely that an unprepared and slow athlete can win a competitive race, or an untrained soldier can come out victorious in battle. Some folks think that skill is the only determinant of career success, while others suppose that chance trumps everything, but the words of the Preacher take a hammer to those two schools of thought. His words offer a more nuanced view of the roles of chance and skill in workplace success.

An unstated assumption underlying all we've been able to infer so far from the words of the Preacher is this: the chance events which occur are not game changers—events (good or bad)—that can make or mar a person's career. Which brings us to.the subject of . . .

SYMMETRIIC CAREERS VS. ASYMMETRIC CAREERS

Symmetric Career: no single chance event—good or bad—is able to overly influence a person's career trajectory.

Asymmetric Career: one or just a few chance events—good or bad—can make or mar a person's career.

All careers are not the same. Success in some careers is more hugely influenced by chance than others. Nothing reveals this truth better than the sordid history of military coups in my country Nigeria. Soldiers involved in coups are often misled by the tantalizing upside—success and residence in the presidential mansion—when they should be more guided by the grim downside—failure and death by firing squad! For a soldier involved in coups (a 'coupist'), a 'bad" chance event can be disastrous, because that event can lead to failure and death by firing squad—something from which there is no recovery. I refer to careers (like those of the aforementioned coupists) where one or just a few chance events can make or mar your career prospects as "Asymmetric" careers, and those in which no single chance event can make or mar it as "Symmetric" careers.

From the definitions above, it's easy to see that, because chance plays a greater role in asymmetric careers, huge inequalities or disparities in results (winner-take-all markets) can develop. Harvard psychologist Nancy Etcoff, in her book, *Survival of the Prettiest: the Science of Beauty*, illustrates the point, saying,

> " . . . modeling is a winner-take-all market . . . [where] the potential rewards are huge and the difference between making it and a near miss is the difference between great fortune and total obscurity . . . there are a small number people at the top competing for the big prizes. There are only about a dozen supermodels in the world. In such a market, tiny advantages can mean all the difference, and the difference is meaningful, earning millions versus earning almost nothing. Modeling is a high-paying profession only for the top few."

" . . . *tiny advantages can mean all the difference* . . . " Those "tiny advantages," or difference-makers may just be a few chance events. In effect, modeling is an asymmetric career. *This means that persons in asymmetric careers must, in addition to mastering the technical aspects of their careers, also learn to 'manage' chance events*—the topic to which we now turn our attention . . .

Managing Asymmetric Careers

The Preacher continues his discussion of the impact of chance on the fortunes of humankind by showing us just how to manage the chance events that characterize asymmetric careers, saying,

> "Cast your bread upon the waters, For you will find it after many days. Give a portion to seven, and also to eight, For you do not know what evil will be on the earth. If the clouds are full of rain, They empty themselves upon the earth; And if a tree falls to the south or the north, In the place where the tree falls, there it shall lie." (Eccl 11:1–3, NIV)

These intriguing words reveal the telltale signs of asymmetric careers . . .

Extreme Outcomes—Financial Disaster and Windfall Income—are Likely to Occur

"... For you do not know what evil [disaster] will be on the earth. If the clouds are full of rain, They empty themselves upon the earth ... " Here, we see the Preacher describe a certain type of endeavor that's characterized by the extremes of financial disaster ("evil") and windfall wealth ("clouds . . . full of rain"). Financial Disaster can wipe you out; while windfall wealth can make you incredibly rich. Naturally, the people who experience windfall wealth just once are, as it were 'made for life'; while those who taste disaster just once are ruined—a classic winner-take-all dynamic. Notice carefully that there is little or no middle ground; it's an all-or-nothing situation, and people who fail experience the opposite of those who succeed. Whenever the penalty for *not* reaching the top—or for missing reaching the top by a whisker—is the very opposite of reaching the top, you're dealing with a winner-take-all system. Using a sports metaphor, in a winner-take-all system, there are no draws, only winners and losers.

Relatively Huge Capital Outlays

"Cast your *bread* [not your seed] upon the waters . . . " Notice that this endeavor requires the investment of "bread," not "seed." "So, what," you might ask, "is the difference between bread and seed?" The answer in brief is this: 'seed', in the Scripture, is symbolic of resources set aside for investment, while 'bread' symbolizes resources set aside for consumption (Isaiah 55:10); with the one being of greater magnitude than the other. This means that asymmetric ventures require relatively larger amounts of capital or, if you like, relatively greater investments of money, effort, and commitment. Which is why the 'coupist' has to make a huge capital outlay—risk his very life—in the course of pursuing his 'career'!

Prolonged Payback Periods and Greater Levels of Uncertainty

" . . . for you will find it *after many days*." Although the capital outlays required are huge ('bread', not 'seed'), the time period within which you can expect to earn a return on your investment are unusually long ("after many days"). Anyone with elementary training in finance knows that the longer the payback period, the riskier the investment becomes. That is, asymmetric careers are *inherently* riskier than symmetric ones because, not only do they require greater upfront investment and commitment, they also typically don't produce fruit on time.

Extreme outcomes, huge upfront investments, and prolonged payback periods are a deadly combo—the telltale signs of a risk-intensive enterprise, of a winner-take-all system with extremely good pay for a few winners and comparatively horrible pay for plenty of "losers." Notwithstanding, the Preacher, in the same passage, shows us how to succeed in asymmetric endeavors, saying " . . . Give a portion to seven, and also to eight, For [because] you do not what evil shall be upon the earth." His words mean that you can protect yourself from the downsides of asymmetric careers by,

Never Putting All Your Eggs in One Basket

Notice carefully that this verse doesn't say "Give a portion to *one*," rather it says, "Give a portion to *seven*, and also to *eight, for* [because] *you don't know what evil shall be upon the earth.*" In other words, a key to protecting yourself from 'evil' (the downside of asymmetric careers) is to hedge your bets. Simply put, never put all your eggs in one basket and never invest more than you can afford to lose! The best way to handle winner-take-all endeavors is to begin by deliberately protecting yourself from their huge career-ending downsides. The Preacher is really saying that If you have money invested in one project whose failure can wipe you out, then you have invested too much money in that project. Invest only what you can afford to lose. Michael Mauboussin puts it beautifully, saying "One common and conspicuous error in dealing with complex systems is betting too much on a particular outcome."

It bears repeating: most leaders see only the huge gains that occur in asymmetric careers, but the words of the Preacher show that they're better served by looking majorly at the huge losses that can also occur. Like I said before, the words of the Preacher also mean that people who succeed in asymmetric careers must develop 2 different types of skill—technical skill at the things they do, and skill at managing chance.

Examples of asymmetric careers/ endeavors include,

- Real estate & property.
- Government contractors.
- Investors in the stock market.

- Professions/ Endeavors with one or just a few influential buyers.
- Professions/Endeavors requiring relatively huge capital outlays.

If asymmetric careers are associated with chance events that can make or mar your career then, symmetric careers are the opposite—no single chance event can make or mar your career. And, it's to the latter that we now turn our attention . . .

Managing Symmetric Careers

> "In the morning sow your *seed* , And in the evening do not withhold your hand; For you do not know which will prosper, Either this or that, Or whether both alike will be good." (Eccl 11:6, NIV)

Recall that the Preacher began his treatise on the effects of time and chance on career success with the words "Cast your *bread* upon the waters . . . . " Here, we see him take a different tack and say "In the morning sow your *seed*. . . . " Since, as we've seen, "bread" is symbolically different from "seed," the Preacher must be describing another kind of endeavor—one that doesn't demand huge investment outlays and isn't prone to winner-take-all dynamics. He is describing 'symmetric careers'. His words mean that . . .

Symmetric Careers are Characterized by Slow and Steady Growth and Accumulation

In symmetric careers, no single event has the power to overly impact results. These careers are like planting a crop—one harvest builds upon another; and you certainly don't expect windfall wealth. If you're in a business where your income today is related to your income yesterday and to the effort you put in, then you're engaged in a business that carries symmetric risk. Symmetric careers are managed by . . .

Patience and Persistence

"In the *morning* sow your seed, And at *evening* do not withhold your hand . . . " To win in a business or profession with symmetric risk, you must stay in the game, and you must be patient and persistent—willing to remain at the task all day (figuratively speaking, from *morning* until *evening*). If one endeavor fails, pick yourself up and start another one. You must do everything to remain in the game. Here the saying "Failure is never final" applies (it doesn't necessarily apply in asymmetric careers where one failure can wipe you out).

Making Plenty of Small Bets

"... *for you do not know which would prosper, whether this or that, or whether both will prosper.*" When faced with multiple events with equal or near-equal probabilities of success or failure, the Preacher advises that you sow plenty of seeds daily. In other words, you can increase your chances of success by simply increasing the absolute number of bets you make. Invest in plenty of projects and write plenty of proposals—things which increase your probability of success.

Having seen the effects of chance on career success, and because the Preacher said "*time* and chance happens to them all," we now turn our attention to the effects of time on workplace success . . .

WHAT ROLE DOES TIME PLAY IN CAREER SUCCESS?

"The opportunity of a lifetime must be taken within the lifetime of the opportunity."—LEONARD RAVENHILL

"There is a tide in the affairs of men which, taken at the flood, leads on to fortune. Omitted, all the voyage of their lives is bound in shallows and miseries."—WILLIAM SHAKESPEARE

The first effect of time on career success, as we've already seen, is that time (the long-run) can mitigate the effects of chance. Quick, stop and think, if you've suffered any negative chance events, staying in the game is one way to experience the positive chance events that can reverse your fortunes. In that case, time works *against* or cancels out chance. But there are times when time works *with* chance to influence career success. Statistician Nassim Nicholas Taleb, in his book, *Fooled by Randomness*, makes this point clear, saying "[M]ost successes are caused by very few "windows of opportunity," failing to grab one can be deadly for one's career. Take your luck!" These "*windows of opportunity*" can be described as positive chance events with short lifespans—classic intertwinings of time and chance—that, when grasped, in the words of Shakespeare "lead on to fortune." And, when they slip out of your grasp, they cause, again in the words of Shakespeare "all the voyage of [our] lives [to be] bound in shallows and miseries." The writer of Jeremiah, in his account of the defeat of the army of Pharaoh king of Egypt, throws more light on the matter, saying,

> "Why have your warriors fled in terror? They cannot stand because the LORD has driven them away. They stumble and fall over each other and say among themselves, 'Come, let's go back to our homeland where we were born. Let's get away from the sword of the enemy!' " (Jer 46:15-16, NLT)

Pharaoh's elite army was taking a beating on the battlefield, so much so that his troops began to desert! The question became "Why have your warriors fled in terror?" The writer of Jeremiah, leaving nothing to the imagination, delivers an earthshaking answer, saying,

> "There they will say, 'Pharaoh, the king of Egypt, is a loudmouth who missed his opportunity!'" (Jer 46:17, NLT)

Opportunity—the Coming Together of Time and Chance—is the 'X' Factor in Career Success

The elite army of Egypt, valiant, highly trained, and well-resourced, was routed on the battlefield. The reason? "Pharaoh, the king of Egypt.. [had] . . . *missed his opportunity.*" These words help us see that Pharaoh was defeated because he was unable to exploit the good fortune that came his way. Missing an opportunity meant that all of the work of preparation couldn't be brought to bear on the situation. In effect, opportunity is the X factor—what some variously refer to as fortune, providence, the ducks lining up, etc—that decides who wins the race or gets the prize. As Pharaoh's experience reveals, opportunity is of especial importance in win-lose or winner-take-all situations as the following case study shows . . .

The Ducks Line Up for Hitler at Dunkirk!

The words of the writer of Jeremiah call to mind World War 2, Adolf Hitler, and the British Expeditionary Force. The latter, after taking a beating from

Hitler's forces, was trapped around Dunkirk, a port city located on the coast of France. Everyone expected Hitler to destroy the expeditionary force, but inexplicably Hitler issued a halt order to his armored troops—allowing over three hundred thousand British soldiers to escape via that port back to Britain. Most of the soldiers who escaped were to form the bulk of an Allied Expeditionary Force which landed in France aboutt four years later—and put Hitler's troops to flight! Many commentators believe that Hitler began to lose World War 2 when he missed the opportunity to destroy the British Expeditionary Force at Dunkirk. Like Pharaoh King of Egypt, Hitler was defeated because he "missed his opportunity." Writer Leonard Ravenhill was correct after all "The opportunity of a lifetime must be taken within the lifetime of the opportunity."

Notwithstanding, when it comes to unraveling the role of time on career success, the intriguing phrase " . . . time and chance happen to them all," can still give birth to one more 'child'! That "child" is this: the greater the knowledge to be mastered, the longer the time it takes to achieve career success.

HOW LONG DOES IT TAKE TO BECOME A MASTER OF THE GAME?

Sometime ago, Italian Maurizio Sarri, coach of English Premiership clubside, Chelsea, led his team to win the Europa Cup. It was Mr. Sarri's first career championship win ever and he was a full sixty years old! That incident brought to the fore questions that had previously been on my backburner, questions which Dean Keith Simonton—world-leading researcher on the subject of performance and genius—in an article he contributed in the book, *The Road to Excellence,* also asked,

> "What factors govem the age at which a creative individual's career takes off? Why do some creators bloom early and others late? We cannot begin to answer this question until we recognize that creative potential is not born from nothing. It takes a considerable amount of preparation - knowledge acquisition and skill practice - before the foundation has been laid for constructing a creative career."

"*What factors govem the age at which a creative individual's career takes off? Why do some creators bloom early and others late?*"" In simple terms, Professor Simonton is attempting to answer the question; what role does time play in career success? He ends up positing that, in creative careers, the age with which a person becomes successful is determined by his ability to acquire the knowledge required to master his profession. Interestingly enough, the writer of Galatians (who, by the way, happens to be Paul the apostle), in an autobiographical treatment of his own amazing career, shows us just how long it can take to become a master of the game...

> "I want you to know, brothers and sisters, that the gospel I preached is not of human origin. I did not receive it from any man, nor was I taught it; rather, I received it by revelation from Jesus Christ... But when God, who set me apart from my mother's womb and called me by his grace, was pleased to reveal his Son in me so that I might preach him among the Gentiles, my immediate response was not to consult any human being... Then after three years, I went up to Jerusalem to get acquainted with Cephas and stayed with him fifteen days. I saw none of the other apostles—only James, the Lord's brother. I assure you before God that what I am writing you is no lie. Then I went to Syria and Cilicia. I was personally unknown to the churches of Judea that are in Christ... Then after fourteen years, I went up again to Jerusalem,..As for those who were held in high esteem —whatever they were makes no difference to me; God does not show favoritism—they added nothing to my message." (Gal 1:11-2:1-6, NIV)

Reflection on this passage has helped me see that,

It Took All of Seventeen Years for Paul to Master his Trade!

"*... Then after three years... Then after* [another interval of] *fourteen years, I went up again to Jerusalem... As for those who were held in high esteem —whatever they were makes no difference to me... they added nothing to my message.*" No doubt about it, Paul was a master of the game who wrote two-thirds of the New Testament. But, only in this passage, do we see that it took him all of seventeen years to become a master—to reach the point where he could say that the leaders of the Church at Jerusalem (who, by the way, came to the Faith before him) couldn't add or subtract from his message. This tells us that...

Last Word

The Age at Which a Creative Career Takes off is Determined by the Volume and Difficulty of the Knowledge Which Must be Mastered

As a doctor of law trained under Gamaliel in the famous Temple School at Jerusalem, Paul brought a tremendous amount of learning to the table, yet it still took him all of seventeen years to become a master of the subject of salvation by righteousness according to faith. Research has shown that it takes roughly ten years or ten thousand hours of practice (the famous 10-year/10,000-hour rule) to master a vocation. So why did it take Paul a whole seventeen years to master his field? The answer, as usual, lies hidden in the words of the writer of Galatians . . .

> "I want you to know, brothers and sisters, that the gospel I preached is not of human origin. I did not receive it from any man, nor was I taught it; rather, I received it by revelation from Jesus Christ." (Gal 1:11–12, NIV)

The Age at Which a Creative Career Takes off is Determined by the State of the Art

"I did not receive it from any man, nor was I taught it . . . " There it is in black and white: Paul's timeline to mastery was lengthened because he was a pioneer who had no one to teach him much of what he had to learn (he learned by revelation from Jesus). Just like blazing a trail is much harder than going down a beaten path, so attempting to master an emerging field is a lot harder than mastering an established one. In simple terms, the time needed to master a field is longer when you have no one to teach or coach you. But the state of the art, like a two-edged sword, cuts both ways—since emerging fields have smaller amounts of knowledge, they can be mastered in shorter time periods. Which is why many new fields tend to have "masters" who are relatively young.

Wrap Around

Career success in the minds of many is determined by one, and only one, factor—individual skill. But the words of the Preacher offer a more nuanced view that broadens our perspectives and helps us see that workplace progress actually rides on the back of three interconnected factors—skill, chance and time. The less complex the career, the greater the influence of skill (and the lesser the influence of chance) on career success and vice versa. In contrast, time's effects on workplace success are basically twofold—its work *with* or *against* chance, and its effect on skill acquisition. In its work *against* chance, time mitigates and dampens the effect of negative chance events (bad luck, bad fortune, etc), while its work *with* positive chance events creates game changing windows of opportunity. Time's second way of influencing career success is straight forward and pretty old-fashioned—as in the duration or time needed to master the skills necessary for workplace success. However you look at it, the words " . . . time and chance happens to them all," drive home our final takeaway: no career is exempt from the effects of time and chance!

Bibliography

Arthur, Michael B., and Kram, Kathy E. "Reciprocity at Work: the Separate, Yet Inseparable Possibilities for Individual and Organizational Development." In *Handbook of Career Theory*, edited by Michael B. Arthur, Douglas T. Hall, and Barbara S. Lawrence, 292–312. New York: Cambridge University Press, 2010.

Berger, Jonah. *Contagious: Why Things Catch On.* New York: Simon and Schuster, 2016

Bock, Lazlo. *Work Rules! Insights from Inside Google That Will Transform How You Live and Lead.* New York: Twelve, 2015.

Bolton, Robert. *People Skills: How to Assert Yourself, Listen to Others and Resolve Conflicts.* New York: Simon and Schuster, 1988.

Brass, Galaskiewicz, et al. "Taking Stock of Networks and Organizations: A Multilevel Perspective." In *The Academy of Management Journal* 47(6) 795-817.

Burkus, David. *Under New Management: How Leading Organizations Are Upending Business As Usual.* Boston: Houghton Mifflin Harcourt, 2016.

Burt, Ronald S. *Structural Holes: The Social Structure of Competition.* Cambridge, MA: Harvard University Press, 1992.

Cannella, Finkelstein, et al. *Strategic Leadership: Theory and Research on Executives, Top Management Teams, and Boards.* New York: Wiley, 2009.

Charan, Drotter, et al. *The Leadership Pipeline: How to Build the Leadership-Powered Company.* San Francisco: Jossey-Bass, 2001.

Christakis, Nicholas A., and Fowler, James H. *Connected: The Surprising Power of Our Social Networks and How They Shape Our Lives.* New York: Hachette, 2009.

Collins, Jim. *Good to Great: Why Some Companies Make the Leap . . . And Others Don't.* New York: HarperCollins, 2001.

Collins, Jim, and Hansen, Morten T. *Great By Choice: Uncertainty, Chaos, and Luck—Why Some Thrive Despite Them All.* New York: HarperCollins, 2011.

Covey, Stephen R. *Principle-Centered Leadership.* New York: Fireside, 1982.

Covey, Merrill, et al. *First Things First: To Live, To Love, To Leave a Legacy.* New York: Simon and Schuster, 2017.

Cowler, Dan, and Legg, Karen. "Rhetoric in Bureaucratic Careers: Managing the Meaning of Management Success." In *Handbook of Career Theory*, edited by Michael B. Arthur, Douglas T. Hall, and Barbara S. Lawrence, 437-54. New York: Cambridge University Press, 2010.

Cross, Rob, and Prusak, Laurence. "The People Who Make Organizations Go—Or Stop." In *Harvard Business Review*, June 2002.

Bibliography

Crowley, Katherine, and Elster, Kathi. *Working for You Isn't Working for Me: The Ultimate Guide to Managing Your Boss.* New York: Portfolio, 2009.

Dalton, Gene W. "Developmental Views of Careers in Organizations." In *Handbook of Career Theory,* edited by Michael B. Arthur, Douglas T. Hall, and Barbara S. Lawrence, 89–109. New York: Cambridge University Press, 2010.

Derr, Brooklyn C., and Laurent, André. "The Internal and External Career: A Theoretical and Cross-cultural Perspective." In *Handbook of Career Theory,* edited by Michael B. Arthur, Douglas T. Hall, and Barbara S. Lawrence, 454–74. New York: Cambridge University Press, 2010.

Drucker, Peter F. *Management: Tasks, Responsibilities, Practices.* New York: Transaction, 2007.

———. *Managing Oneself,* Boston: Harvard Business School Publishing Corporation, 2008.

Duckworth, Angela. *Grit: The Power of Passion and Perseverance.* New York: Scribner, 2016.

Etcoff, Nancy. *Survival of the Prettiest: The Science of Beauty.* New York: Anchor, 1999.

Friedman, Thomas L. *The Lexus and the Olive Tree: Understanding Globalization.* New York: Picador, 2012.

Friedman, Thomas L., and Mandelbaum, Michael. *That Used to Be Us: How America Fell Behind in the World It Invented and How We Can Come Back.* New York: Farrar, Straus and Giroux, 2011.

Fukuyama, Francis. "Social Capital." The Tanner Lectures on Human Values. Delivered at Brasenose College, Oxford. May 12, 14, and 15, 1997.

Goldstein, Martin, et al. *Yes! 50 Scientifically Proven Ways to Be Persuasive.* New York: Free, 2009.

Grant, Adam. *Give and Take: A Revolutionary Approach to Success.* New York: Viking, 2013.

Goleman, Daniel. *Emotional Intelligence: Why It Can Matter More than IQ.* New York: Bloomsbury, 2009.

———. *Social Intelligence: The New Science of Human Relationships.* New York: Bantam, 2006.

Goleman, Boyatzis, et al. *Primal Leadership: Learning to Lead With Emotional Intelligence.* Boston: Harvard Business Press, 2004.

Hambrick, Donald C., and Fukutomi, Gregory D. S. "The Seasons of a CEO's Tenure." In *The Academy of Management Review* 16.4 (1999) 719–42.

Hersey, Blanchard, et al. *Management of Organizational Behavior: Leading Human Resources.* New York: Pearson, 2013.

Hill, Linda A. *Becoming a Manager: Mastery of a New Identity.* Boston: Harvard Business School Press, 1992.

Hofstede, Hofstede, et al. *Cultures and Organizations: Software of the Mind.* New York: McGraw Hill, 2010.

Kadushin, Charles. *Understanding Social Networks: Theories, Concepts, and Findings.* London: Oxford University Press, 2001.

Keller, Gary, and Papasan, Jay. *The One Thing: The Surprisingly Simple Truth Behind Extraordinary Results.* Austin, TX: Hard, 2012.

Kennedy, Paul. *The Rise and Fall of the Great Powers: Economic Change and Military Conflict from 1500 to 2000.* New York: Vintage, 1987.

Koch, Richard. *The 80/20 Principle: The Secret of Achieving More With Less.* London: Nicholas Brealey, 1997.

Bibliography

Kouzes, James M., and Posner, Barry Z. *Credibility: How Leaders Gain and Lose It, Why People Demand It.* San Francisco: Jossey-Bass, 2010.

———. *The Leadership Challenge: How to Make Extraordinary Things Happen in Organizations.* San Francisco: Jossey-Bass, 2017.

Lukes, Steven. *Power: A Radical View.* New York: Palgrave Macmillan, 2005.

Manchester, William. *The Last Lion: Winston Spencer Churchill, Volume 2: Alone, 1932–1940.* New York: Black white Audio, 1988.

Mauboussin, Michael J. *The Success Equation: Untangling Skill and Luck in Business, Sports and Investing.* Boston: Harvard Business Review Press, 2012.

Maxwell, John C. *5 Levels of Leadership.* New York: Center Street, 2014.

———. *Leadership Gold: Lessons I've Learned from a Lifetime of Leadership.* New York: Thomas Nelson, 2008.

McChesney, Covey, et al. *The 4 Disciplines of Execution.* New York: Simon & Schuster, 2013.

Mintzberg, Henry. *The Nature of Managerial Work.* New York: Prentice-Hall, 1973.

———. *Managing.* San Francisco: Berret-Koehler, 2009.

Nicholson, Nigel., and West, Michael. "Transitions, Work Histories and Careers." In *Handbook of Career Theory,* edited by Michael B. Arthur, Douglas T. Hall, and Barbara S. Lawrence, 181–201. New York: Cambridge University Press, 2010.

Oncken, William, and Wass, Donald. "Management Time: Who's Got the Monkey." In *HBR's 10 Must Reads.* Boston: Harvard Business School Publishing, 2007.

Pfeffer, Jeffrey. *Leadership BS: Fixing Workplaces and Careers One Truth at a Time.* New York: HarperCollins, 2015.

———. *Managing With Power: Politics and Influence in Organizations.* Boston: Harvard Business Review Press, 1993.

———. *Power: Why Some People Have It And Others Don't.* New York: HarperCollins, 2010.

Pfeffer, Jeffrey, and Sutton, Robert. I. *Hard Facts, Dangerous, Half-truths and Total Nonsense: Profiting from Evidence-based Management.* Boston: Harvard Business School Press, 2006.

Sanders, Tim. *Love Is the Killer App.* New York: Currency, 2003.

Schawbel, Dan. *Promote Yourself: The New Rules for Career Success.* New York: St. Martins, 2013.

Schein, Edgar H. *Career Dynamics: Matching Individual and Organizational Needs.* Menlo Park, CA: Addison-Wesley, 1978.

———. *Organizational Culture and Leadership.* San Francisco: Jossey-Bass, 2004.

Schwartz, Tony. "Manage Your Energy, Not Your Time." In *HBR's 10 Must Reads On Managing Yourself.* Boston: Harvard Business School Publishing, 2003.

Scott, Richard W., and Davis, Gerald. F. *Organizations and Organizing: Rational, Natural, and Open Systems Perspectives.* New York: Routledge, 2016.

Simonton, Dean Keith. "Creative Expertise: A Life-Span Developmental Perspective." In *The Road to Excellence: the Acquisition of Expert Performance in the Arts and Sciences, Sports, and Games,* edited by K. Anders Ericsson, 227–54. New York: Psychology, 2014.

———. "Historiometric Studies of Genius." In *The Wiley Handbook of Genius,* edited by Dean Keith Simonton, 87–106. West Sussex: Wiley, 2014.

Taleb, Nassim Nicholas. *Fooled By Randomness: The Hidden Role of Chance in Life and in the Markets.* New York: Random House, 2005.

www.ingramcontent.com/pod-product-compliance
Lightning Source LLC
Chambersburg PA
CBHW050841230426
43667CB00012B/2099